Donate Life Hollywood is a national campaign serving as a liaison and an advocate between the organ, eye and tissue donation and transplant community and the entertainment industry. Our goal is to help save and heal lives by supporting authentic and positive stories about donation and transplantation and developing partnerships with actors, producers, directors and writers who encourage people to Donate Life.

Tenaya Wallace
Founder
Donate Life Hollywood
tenayaspeaks@gmail.com

Praise for *Justin Time*

"I've known Joe for a couple decades as he's gone through the kinds of trials that most people couldn't imagine. His story—captured in this beautiful book—is an incredible treasure, a great adventure, and labor of pure love. I couldn't put it down! Read this, and you'll be moved by Joe's life and encouraged in yours.
~ **Dr. John Stahl-Wert, International Bestselling Author of**
The Serving Leader* and *Ten Thousand Horses

"Despite my Florida roots, the people of Pittsburgh are like no other when they welcomed me into their community. Joe Lafferty was one of these folks. He reaches out daily to inspire and offer support."
~ **Dr. Anthony Hamlet, Superintendent,**
Pittsburgh Public Schools

"I met Joe Lafferty the same month I signed two Pennsylvania recruits to play for 'the [_].' Joe's high school(Woodland Hills) teammate Tirrell Greene and Dwayne Johnson. (Freedom High School, Bethlehem). I loved finding great players in my home state. Tirrell started for 3 seasons at center and Dwayne has done well too. Read this book and see Joe lead like Tirrell and be as tough as a 'Rock.' Lafferty's life of overcoming ain't no joke."
~ **Art Kehoe, Coach, 5 Time NCAA National Champion,**
UM Sports Hall of Fame

"*Justin Time* is one life and death battle after another, and Joe keeps winning."
~ **Joshua Colbert, Author, *Male by Birth, Man by Choice***

Justin Time

Justin Time

A memoir of faith and
the fight for life

Jeff Schober (signature)

Joe Lafferty *and* Jeff Schober

Printed in the United States of America

ISBN-13: 978-1-7336208-0-2 (paperback)
ISBN-13: 978-1-7336208-1-9 (ebooks)

First Edition

Cover design: Deana Riddle and Jason Vuori
Interior Design: Adina Cucicov

He Carries Me Through

RAIN HAD STOPPED BEFORE SUNRISE, but it remained a warm, misty morning in June 2012 as I drove across damp asphalt toward the tiny town of Elderton, Pennsylvania, forty-five minutes northeast of Pittsburgh. It was strange to navigate a car again, so I focused on the road, the feel of the steering wheel against my palms. Thanks to the transplant, circulation had improved my vision enough that I could drive again, but only during daylight. It had been nine long years. Now that I was regaining my health, this would be my first stop. I needed to go alone.

I was nervous, more anxious than I had been for any first date or job interview. I kept the radio off, so the only sound was the humming engine with rare interruptions from the GPS tracker.

"In one-quarter mile," the audio instructed me, "turn right onto Cemetery Road."

Directions would lead me there, but I wasn't sure how to find Justin once I arrived. More importantly, what would I say?

A few days earlier, when I had mentioned my anxiety to Justin's mother, Rhonda's sentiment was simple.

"Just talk to him," she said. "He's a great listener."

Her advice had calmed me then. Now that peace had faded; I was jittery again.

Tire tracks were visible through the grass. Driving slowly, foot hovering over the brake, I saw a black onyx grave stone etched with the silhouette of a guitar. Too distant to read any name, I knew this was the spot.

Putting the car in park, I emerged tentatively from the driver's seat, unsteady and humble. Morning sunshine reflected off the inscription, so I stepped forward, shading my eyes as I stooped down to read:

> Precious are the memories of Justin.
> He laughed often and loved much.
> His love will never be forgotten and
> never will his memory fade as
> he now shares his smile with the angels.

"Hey," I said without preamble. "It's an honor."

There was a lump in my throat. I tried to hold back the tears, but they leaked out anyway. We had never met before, but this young man would forever be part of me. His tragedy gave me another chance at life. His sacrifice was the beginning of my resurrection.

The grave was beautifully landscaped, surrounded by a bed of white pebbles and wooden edging. On the ground were weathered crosses and offerings from previous visitors: a miniature flag, a landscaping rock that read "friend," colorful flowers. I was embarrassed that I had nothing to share. I circled to the front of the stone, which read:

Our Son, Brother, and Friend
JUSTIN DALE BOYER
June 23, 1993-February 13, 2010
He Lived—He Loved—He Laughed—He Smiled

I had seen the phrase "live, love, laugh" before. Justin must have read it too during his short life. But here, "smile" was added as the capstone. It seemed appropriate. The word brought forth an image of the young man.

The first time I met his family, they gave me a print of his school portrait. He had a great smile, with bright, dark eyes. Skin was creamy, with typical teenage hair, a straight brown shade that was long in front but didn't spill onto his collar. It reminded me of the Beatles. On the bottom edge of the frame the word "smile" was written.

Smiling can be a foundation. You can't love and laugh all the time, but you can always smile. Sometimes you just have to fake it until the sentiment becomes real. I read the Bible every day, and scripture tells us that if you have faith, faith will be delivered unto you. Justin believed that if you can force a smile, you're on the road to living and laughing. It's a wonderful, joyous sentiment.

His family explained that Justin had been a colorful kid. When a friend was feeling down, Justin wasn't shy about cracking a joke or making a fool of himself simply to elicit a laugh and change the mood. How many teenagers care more about the people around them than they do about themselves?

From the top of the hill, morning fog burned off in the valley below. I stared at his headstone, wishing that I was musical so I could play a song for Justin. He loved the guitar.

Fifty yards away was a stout, squat tree with branches curling down in a mushroom shape. An adult would have to crouch and duck beneath low-hanging leaves to touch the trunk. Despite the sun, the base of the tree was wreathed in shadow. It was a perfect spot. I took a deep breath.

"I guess that's your spot to sit and play guitar, right?" I said out loud. I heard only silence, but I'm certain he agreed. It was a peaceful, quiet morning.

Two years earlier, I had major health struggles. I was only in my thirties, but my body had endured too much, and things were slowly shutting down. By volunteering to be organ donors, Justin and his family had given me a gift. They sent a blessing into the world not knowing how it would affect the future. They believed in goodness and helping others.

Now, before his grave, I wondered why Justin wasn't on this earth any longer but I was. It didn't seem fair. I foolishly wished that I could trade places with him. He had been sixteen and deserved a shot to grow up. But those are decisions that only God gets to make.

Justin is part of me now. As a Christian, I know I'm not responsible for two souls. I don't believe it works that way. But I do believe that I'm responsible for whatever time I have left here. I want to use that time to honor Justin's memory. I want my time to be good so I can contribute positively in the world. I want to love people and spread peace and not take a moment for granted.

But that can be a tough hang. It's not always easy.

To reflect back on my days, I'm amazed. I've had so many once-in-a-lifetime opportunities. I've experienced so many blessings.

I became friends with Dan Marino while I was in high school and he was the best quarterback in football, setting NFL records. I've befriended celebrities like Bucky Dent and spent time with legendary football coaches Chuck Knox and Mike Ditka. I've coached young men, many of whom went on to play in the NFL, like Rob Gronkowski and Ryan Mundy. I have great friends, a wonderful family, and the love of a beautiful woman.

But there have been dark times too. Cancer. Diabetes. I've lost my eye and endured a kidney and pancreas transplant. I even died on a hospital table. Six days passed before I woke, and I have no memory of that missing time. I've cheated death more than once, so I understand hope and value each new day. I'm alive because God carries me through.

I was once asked what I would give to be healthy again. At the time, I felt weak. My answer came quickly, surprising those around me.

"I'd jump off a building and break every bone in my body," I professed.

It would be a fair tradeoff for kidneys that worked perfectly or having 20-20 vision. With broken bones, despite the casts, the pain and the hardships, there is an end in sight. I could rehab and heal and eventually work my way back to normal. That's not a luxury I have.

But I refuse to complain. It's been an incredible life, and there's plenty to come. This is my story so far.

CHAPTER 1

In the Deep End

AFTER FINISHING THIRD GRADE, LIKE any eight-year-old, I was excited to begin summer. During the winter of 1980 and into the spring of 1981, I had begun swimming competitively and had quickly gotten good at racing.

At the start of summer, I looked forward to two months of freedom, splashing in the pool and playing with my friends through a wonderful realm of childhood. My home swimming club, just a short walk from my house, was hosting the championships that year. I knew it would be the highlight of the season. As June turned toward July, it was all I could think about.

I grew up in Forest Hills, a suburb on the eastern side of Pittsburgh. Pittsburgh is known as a blue-collar town, famous for its industry and full of people who find simple pleasure in sports and family. It's ethnically diverse. My family embraced many of those working class values.

My father, Joseph Lafferty Sr., was a 24-year-old Irishman when I was born. He was part-owner of a gas station, and later became a Teamster who worked for thirty-six years in the circulation department of the Pittsburgh Post-Gazette before retiring in 2011.

Linda Persichetti, my mother, was the same age as my dad. She is a proud Italian who worked as a Pittsburgh school teacher. While I was in high school, she earned a master's degree in library information systems and became a computer teacher.

Our family was close-knit. I have one sister, Tara, who is fourteen months older than I am. Also living in our house was my grandfather, Jim Lafferty. He was a stern man who married for the first time at age 36. My grandmother had died before I was born and Grandpa had survived a heart attack. Since the time he had been alone, my parents took care of him. He had lived with us all my life.

Like most boys, I was active. My father had gotten me involved with an outdoor group called Indian Guides. It's like fathers and sons boy scouts based on the history of the Native Americans, trying to teach kids respect for the land and living life outdoors. We went camping and canoeing and shot BB guns. I had a group of friends, and we were part of the Genesee Tribe. We believe our fathers came up with this name after a night of drinking. These were good men, and there was always Genesee beer around.

We went on an overnight camping trip in Ohio, where we slept in tents. All the boys clustered into one big tent and the dads occupied another. It was a fun experience, something different, and we boys bubbled with excitement.

Problem was, nobody got any sleep because of me. Once I dozed off, I snored so loudly that I cleared the tent. My dad woke me and for the sake of everyone else, we moved to sleep in our own tent. I fell back to snoring quickly. While I wheezed, he put his hand on the back of my neck and could feel that my glands were swollen. That was the cause of my loud noises. Dad compared the thickness of my neck with an older neighbor boy's who was with us, and my neck was much bigger. He sensed something was wrong.

So we went to the doctor. I had this old, plain-spoken, very loving Jewish doctor named Dr. Schwartz. He must have been in his seventies. He treated me for swollen glands for about a week, but nothing much was helping. Dr. Schwartz pulled Mom aside and said we may need to do a biopsy. He feared something bad. I learned later that he was worried it might be cancer. If so, he told Mom, he was going to retire because he didn't want to see this happen.

After two weeks of antibiotics, I wasn't getting any better. My parents explained that I was going to West Penn Hospital to have a test. They were going to put a little hole in my neck and look at things. No one had any idea what the problem was. After the biopsy, I was transferred to Pittsburgh Children's Hospital.

I remember that July 14 was a blazing hot day. It was also my sister's birthday. In the hospital lobby, there is a six-foot-high Curious George stuffed animal in the corner. Little kids ran up to hug it. It was touching to see.

I was led into a little side room and my parents explained my diagnosis. I had cancer of the lymph notes. It was called non-Hogkin lymphoma. These were big words that I didn't fully understand. That day I was given a seventy-percent chance of survival.

If you're betting money, seven out of ten are great odds. A gambler would take those odds every day. But if you're talking about the life of your child, that is a horrible probability. Imagine being at a dinner with nine relatives, and someone walks in with a gun and says three of you aren't leaving. Those are terrible chances. Even if I gave the same scenario to a parent with ninety-nine other kids in a room, and said three of them aren't leaving, that's three percent, not thirty. No parent would accept those terms.

But my parents didn't have any choice. They were smart, and turned into expert salespeople. They sold me that seven out of ten were great odds. If you said that to an adult, it would almost sound stupid, but I was a child and they made it very obvious. They had a great way of putting things, and they sold me that day.

Even at that young age, I was well versed in life and death. Just the year before, I had lost two grandparents and a great grandparent. My mom's mom died after a nine-year battle with cancer. A week later, her mom died. Earlier that year, my grandfather who lived with us passed away. So I understood about death. For a while I thought we lived part-time in a funeral home.

Non-Hogkin lymphoma. A scary disease for anyone, especially an eight-year old. But my family made sure I didn't get hung up on the fear.

What my father told me in the hospital lobby that day shaped me for life. Chemo, he explained, was going to make me sick. No one likes getting sick, but that would be my reality. He said I could go on swimming and playing tennis in the afternoon and run around and have as much activity as I can during summer when I wasn't sick. Sure, I'd be down for a few days, but after the sickness wore off, I could get back up, go out, and have fun. The other option he pitched was that I could lay on the couch for two years through the cycle of treatments. He looked me square in the eye.

"So what do you want to do?" he asked.

That's a no-brainer for an eight-year-old. I wasted no time in my reply. If I didn't feel well, I promised to lie down. When I wasn't sick, I planned to be at the pool or playing on the tennis team because that's what I loved to do. From that day on, it became the mantra.

My parents are amazing people. They strived to be sure all of us had a sense of normalcy. There was no pity. They didn't treat me any differently because I was sick. If I got in an argument with my sister, they didn't take my side because I was the kid with cancer. I was still responsible for chores. I was a good kid, but if I did something wrong, I was punished. If I didn't clean up after myself, I was reprimanded. The only exception was if I was lying on the couch after a chemo treatment.

The Bible says, "He that spareth the rod hateth his child." I needed to be reined in from time to time. My dad did the heavy lifting on discipline. He was authoritarian, but fair with his punishment and measured with his praise.

I don't want anyone to think my parents were heartless dragons. They didn't say, hey, it's only cancer. Just get over it. Our house was very loving. They didn't want to worry me. They empowered me to get better. Listen to the doctors and nurses, I was told. And they were adults and authority figures, so I followed what they said.

It seems laughable now, but when I was told I had cancer, all I cared about was getting back to my swim team. That's how passionate I was. It was the middle of summer swim season, and I was having a great year, pretty much first place at every meet. My birthday is late—September 2—so I got to swim in the eight-and-under age group. Everyone in my grade was already in the nine-and-ten group.

The winter swim season had been good for my confidence. I was swimming better than many of the older kids. I had set the pool record for 25-meter freestyle, and participated in the mixed relay, a race that involves someone from every age group. I was the best backstroker in that relay.

Shortly after my first chemo treatment, I got my head shaved. I didn't want my golden locks falling out. My barber, Denny

Pasquzzi, came to the hospital and gave me a military crew cut. Denny had been cutting my hair since I was two, and remains a family friend. I justified the new look because I had swim championships coming up.

My home pool, Forest Hills, hosted that year. It was a big deal. The day before, I watched them erect the winner's platform where kids stand to take pictures. Everything about it was exciting. Our team was strong from top to bottom, and I believed we had a "home field advantage."

On the day of the meet, twelve teams and their parents packed the deck. I was swimming the fifth event. As swimmers approached the blocks, kids' names were broadcast and supporters cheered. When Mr. Spahr, the announcer, said my name for lane four, the eruption was louder than it had been for other kids. This was more than just home fans cheering. It amped me up.

Standing behind me was Debbie Spahr, the announcer's daughter, who I had met in first grade. I had fallen in love with her the day I met her. She was my elementary school crush, and she was cheering for me, yelling "come on, Joey!" She was an athlete herself, intense with a competitive streak. (Debbie and I later became lab partners in tenth grade, and with it came the realization that I never had a shot. She thought of me as a brother, and was kind enough to let me down easy. Being her friend was the best consolation prize. By senior year, she was our homecoming queen in a class of five-hundred-thirty-five... so I can pick a winner.)

In the lane next to me was Matt Brady. He was my rival in summer, although we swam together during the winter season. Matt was a great guy. In fact, my only loss in the prior months had been to him, and I was hoping to flip that scenario here.

"Swimmers, take your mark," Mr. Spahr boomed, then fired the starter pistol.

I stretched far, lunging into the water. It was just a 25-meter sprint. Stroking and kicking fast, I could see Matt right next to me, a little bit ahead. I knew it would be close. I wanted to win, so pushed even harder. We almost hit the wall at the same time, but he touched me out. Matt took first place and I was second. My time was 16.08 seconds, the fastest I had ever swum. I had broken my own personal best. Although I didn't win, I was content, knowing I had given everything I could. Matt was just a beast. He was better than me, and I was happy for him. Years later, he went on to swim for the University of Pittsburgh on full scholarship and was All Big East nine times.

When it came time to stand on the podium, they announced my name for second place. The deck erupted. People stood and cheered. It dawned on me how loud it was.

I hadn't wanted everyone to know I had cancer, but they all did. My story had spread. Thirteen days earlier I had taken chemo. Later I recognized that this was one of the crowning achievements of my childhood. This moment reinforced what my parents had taught me: that you can have cancer but still do interesting and exciting things. Cancer doesn't have to take over your life.

After mine, Matt's name was announced as the winner. It was anticlimactic, and I always felt like I stole my friend's moment. But he was such a generous guy. As I looked up at him on the top step, he reached down, grasped my hand, and raised it up with his. We both waved to the cheering crowd.

Sports can bring out the best of people, even eight-year-olds.

The most important thing in my adult life is being a Christian and honoring God. As a kid, however, it was sports that kept a stranglehold on me. Games and competition were such a big part of growing up in Pittsburgh. The stereotype surrounding the Steel City is that ethnic men work at the factory for five days, drink beer on weekends, and are passionate about the Steelers, Pirates, and Penguins. Truth is, it's not only men. Pittsburgh women can be rabid Steelers' fans as well. They know football and love the game. Count my mom among those women. She once bought her best friend a Steelers' jersey as a Christmas present, knowing her friend already owned jerseys—but not the one Mom had chosen for her.

Local travel agencies played off the Steelers' popularity. They offered weekend packages for away games that included airfare, hotel accommodations, and game tickets. Because of the time invested and the emotional drain caused by my treatments, Dad thought a weekend getaway would be a great gift for Mom. The Steelers were playing the Saints, so she could fly to New Orleans, spend Friday night and Saturday in the Big Easy with her friend Ellen, see the game Sunday and then be home before bed.

Mom was reluctant. It would be the first time she was away since my diagnosis. We assured her that everyone would be fine. An English pastor once said, "the bow that is always bent will break," but Mom needed convincing. She had provided strength to our family and served as our backbone. Everyone knew she deserved a couple days away. Besides, we implored her, what could go wrong?

She left on Friday, and when I woke Saturday morning, I didn't feel right. Dad made breakfast, but I threw it up. He had me lie on the couch. As afternoon progressed, I suffered severe pain in my stomach and back. I'd never felt pain like that before, and after what I'd been through so far, I was accustomed to pain. We didn't know what was wrong. Dad thought maybe I had a cold or the flu, brought on by my weakened immune system due to chemother-apy. As darkness fell, Dad put me in his bed so he could keep an eye on me overnight. Soon things turned worse. After throwing up everything in my stomach, I began to dry heave, spitting out bile.

Dad phoned Mom in New Orleans, then loaded Tara and I into the car and we headed for the Pittsburgh Children's Hospital Emergency Room around 2 a.m. It was busy that night, or maybe the hospital was short staffed. I spent hours in the waiting room. It wasn't until sunrise when I was led back to have a battery of blood tests, followed by more waiting. My sister remembers attending CCD class that morning, so it was just Dad and me at the hospital. He tried to remain composed, but I sensed his frustration from the long delay.

On Sunday afternoon, nearing 1 p.m., I laid in a narrow room by myself. I wanted the nurses to turn on the overhead TV so I could watch the Steelers game. As silly as it sounds, I hoped to catch a glimpse of Mom in the crowd. But the TV and lights remained off. Doctors had ordered me to rest.

As I laid there, I heard my dad's voice from the room across the hall. He was on the phone, but his tone sounded different. My bed was near the door, so I leaned over and tugged the handle to eavesdrop. It was wrong and disrespectful—I knew that—but I was curious. I shifted slowly so he didn't hear the paper sheet crinkle beneath me as I moved. His words terrified me. Even now, more than thirty-five years later, I don't ever remember being as afraid as I was at that moment.

My dad was crying. I had never heard him cry.

"I don't know what to tell him, Lin," he spoke in low tones, addressing my mother. "I don't know how to tell him like you would."

I eased the door shut again. Pain was excruciating, and now it felt like added daggers stabbing at my brain. The only thing that would made Dad cry, I realized, was if I was about to die.

So this was it. I was going to die, and Dad didn't know how to tell me. He needed my mom there to break the news.

I was nine years old, convinced I would soon leave this earth, but a strange aura of peace settled over me. I resigned myself. I had fought the good fight and when I died, it would be okay. After what I'd been through, I was acutely aware that death could happen, that for me it was a very real possibility. So this was my time. This was the way it had to be.

A few minutes later, my dad came back into the room. Since the phone call to Mom, he had composed himself. There was no evidence of his tears, no hint he had been crying.

"Okay, they found a bed for you upstairs," he said evenly. "You've got something called pancreatitis."

"Am I going to be okay?" I asked.

"They're going to pump your stomach and you won't eat anything for a while," he explained. "They'll feed you through a tube because your insides are inflamed and infected."

I was impressed with his acting. Here was his only son, about to pass on, and he was calming talking about feeding tubes. Dad could demand an Oscar for this performance.

Well, I knew what was going on and wanted to cut through the unspoken truth. I took a breath and asked the next question, steeling myself for the hard facts.

"Dad, am I going to die?"

His face split into a warm, reassuring smile. "Of course not, Joey."

I didn't understand, but I knew then that I would be okay, because Dad was a straight shooter. He'd never lie to me about what was going on, despite the challenges we faced. I must have misread the situation. It was only later, as I got older, that I realized why he had been crying. Mom was the primary caregiver who dealt with hard medical decisions. Dad had been busy caring for Tara, carting her to dance lessons, making sure her childhood was as normal as possible. She was an active kid too, and so much of Mom's time had been filled with my sickness that he had taken up the slack everywhere else. I had been attached to Mom, and without her there, Dad didn't have the confidence or experience to deal with unexpected health issues.

Mom never made it to the Steelers game that day. She flew home early, and I spent fifteen days in the hospital eating nothing but ice chips. They were forbidden, but sometimes Dad would sneak me some. My stomach was pumped with gallons of fluids. Mom slept in the chair next to me, summoning nurses to change the sheets whenever I wet the bed. The two of them giggled at my tan lines, fading evidence from an active summer. Laughing was a way for Mom to mask the pain of watching her son struggle. My treatment was hardest on Mom.

There were many nights when a chemo session ran long or blood work got delayed. Our family always ate well, but I know that Dad and Tara grabbed take out from a drive-thru while Mom stayed behind with me. Food, in fact, was one of the ways my parents motivated me through tough times.

The day before a chemo treatment, Mom would take me to the store and let me pick out a special treat in advance of the nausea and vomiting that were to follow. Once those passed, the food was waiting for me. I chose Mancini's bread or a Hostess pie, things I didn't normally eat. Mom would also prepare delicious homemade pasta. Even with lingering effects, I couldn't wait to dive into such goodies.

My parents were motivating me to get past the treatments and feel better. Having a mini celebration seems simple, but it's really visionary. They were empowering me to get better.

When I'd go in to the short stay unit for a chemo treatment, other children would be crying, throwing up before the needle hit their arm. I never understood that. Early on, I became accustomed to being injected with needles. It's never fun, but I went to a quiet place in my head, training myself to not think about it.

Part of it was my upbringing. My parents taught me to respect older people and those in authority. I was instructed to listen to my teachers, pay attention to doctors and nurses and follow the rules, because that's what you should do. Everyone insisted that if you tense up, you make it worse than it is. I remembered that.

Of course getting jabbed with needles hurts. I've taken them in my arm and back and neck and hip for bone marrow extractions. I've had four of those. It's very painful. I had regular spinal taps to be sure the cancer didn't spread there. I laid on my side, uncomfortable while fluid was drawn.

I give credit to God. He makes me strong. People sometimes assume that I can withstand more pain than others because of everything I've gone through. They think needles don't hurt me, that my nerve endings are somehow dulled. That's not clear thinking. I don't know of any study that would show my body is more or less sensitive than yours. It's very cut and dried with me. Pain is pain.

When the needle hits, it hurts. But rather than shout about it and make it worse, I choose to relax and stay calm. I'm willing to listen to the experts and remain disciplined.

Across a year and a half of my childhood, I just kept taking chemotherapy. Yeah, I was a kid, but I knew it was always too early to give up.

CHAPTER 2

Whirlwind

SHORTLY AFTER MY DIAGNOSIS, I had brushes with the media spotlight. Three times, I appeared on a show called "Pittsburgh's Talking" as part of a segment featuring young people who suffered from medical issues. In one visit, I sat on a couch and answered questions with a boy who had been born without the lower half of his body. His name was Kenny, and he walked on his hands and moved around on a skateboard. Kenny later became famous as a regular on *The Jerry Springer Show*. He was a neat kid, but his segment alongside his father was bland. He and his parents were not great interview subjects. I was told that because of my personality, my spot played better to the audience.

Maybe that's why I was approached by KDKA, a CBS-affiliate TV station, in the fall of 1981. The call letters KDKA are famous because it was the first radio station in America, and remains one of the the rare broadcast networks east of the Mississippi River that start with K rather than W. Every year, KDKA-TV ran a Christmas telethon, featuring three or four children undergoing health challenges. The producers wanted to film me and highlight my story.

Money raised from the telethon was donated to Pittsburgh Children's Hospital. We were fortunate to live nearby—it was a twenty minute car ride from our house to the hospital. This was a world-class facility, and some families traveled long distances to receive treatment there. The telethon solicited money offset such expenses. I was eager to do anything to help.

So a camera crew followed me around for several days, taking footage everywhere I went. They filmed me at home, having dinner, doing all the things I would normally do. They filmed me at school, reading a book report to my class, eating with friends in the lunchroom, playing basketball and kickball. They even filmed me taking chemotherapy. The camera framed my arm in close-up while the needle was inserted, and in the background, a voice groaned "ouch!" My friends made fun of me, thinking I was whining, but it wasn't me that complained. It was my mom. She always cringed, nearly crying each time I had to have a needle inserted. She still does that today.

Over several November days, I was filmed for nearly nine total hours, and that footage was edited down to a final product that lasted thirty minutes. The camera crew didn't make us redo anything. I learned how time consuming it is to produce something for TV.

Today you'd call it a reality show, but we didn't use the phrase back then. The experience was fun and I loved doing it, but it also lent an air of falsehood to my life. It was unnerving to have someone stick a camera in my face for so long. I began to understand that I wasn't the same person when I was being observed all the time. Who I was changed when I was in frame.

The only true reality is when someone is observed without knowing it. But I played along, displaying my bravery to the world.

∞

The late 1970s and early 80s were a difficult time in Pittsburgh with a transitioning economy and steel mills shutting down. Politics reared its head. Around this time, a court order decreed that a merger needed to happen between the Churchill Area School District and several other schools. People were moving out of Braddock, a nearby town, because the tax base was eroding. Because of that, the judge deemed the schools weren't fit for children. The plan was to bus students across different municipalities and shift kids into nicer schools. The problem was that some kids were transported far from home and into poorer schools. Unfortunately, the issue became racial, split along color lines.

My mother was politically active back then. She was a council member for the Borough of Forest Hills and became president of a group called "S.O.S.," short for "Save our Schools." She spoke against the shift as a public figure, as a mother, and as a teacher. If schools were too bad for black kids to attend, what was the point of shipping white kids there? Why not bring the black kids to our schools? These changes affected me. Years later, I became friends with people all over the sprawling district, both black and white, and it became a large part of who I am. But at the time, little about this shift made sense. I was supposed to attend Forest Hills Middle School, which was close to my house. In fact, from my front yard, I could see a corner of the building. Instead, new laws required that I be bussed across town. It didn't seem like the best idea for anyone, so my parents pulled me from public school and sent me to St. Philomena's in the Squirrel Hill neighborhood. They wanted to try a Catholic school for a year or two to see how everything would shake out.

Changing schools is traumatic for a kid. It's hard to leave behind the familiarity and comfort of a routine. I knew I would miss my public school friends, although everyone said I would keep them and add new friends to the mix. One way to do this was by joining the football team.

As I neared fifth grade, I had lost interest in swimming. I wanted to do something in the fall, and St. Philomena's had a football team. That excited me because I had grown curious about the sport. I found myself on Cloud Nine anticipating our opening practice. I was so excited that driving to the field that first day felt like it took forever.

I wore shorts and a colored jersey when I got out of the car at Magee Field. The other kids had jerseys too, but it was a rainbow of colors. No one matched. The field seemed shorter too. Grass didn't span 120 yards. This created a unique set of challenges. As a team drove toward the end zone, referees had to stop the game and move the ball back fifteen yards. If a runner broke away, the refs had to make a judgement about whether the ball carrier would have been tackled before reaching the end zone.

I noticed right away that I was one of the bigger kids at practice. Most of the other boys were younger. I introduced myself to the coach, Steve Orlando, and told him my name was Joe.

"I thought your name was Josh," he said.

"No, it's Joe," I assured him. "I'm from Forest Hills."

"You're the one," he nodded. "Put your spikes on, stretch and talk to the guys."

We began jogging and warming up, while a coach for the older boys on the grade seven and eight varsity team came by, spitting gross puddles of maroon tobacco onto the hard ground. I noticed him staring at me as he crossed the field.

"Who's that kid?" the varsity coach wondered. When Orlando told him, he was met with a head shake. "The kid from Forest Hills has red hair. This kid is blonde. That ain't him."

I learned they had been looking forward to the arrival of Josh Hogan, a fellow fifth-grader from Forest Hills. He ended up being the tallest kid on the team, and the coaches had heard about him in advance. A big kid at a small school was worth waiting for.

That autumn was my introduction to football and I quickly grew to love it. With such a small roster—Josh's arrival gave us thirteen boys—everyone played both ways and contributed on special teams. I was a guard on offense and defense. This was where I learned how to hit.

Our drills were intense. One guy ran the ball while three others tried to tackle him. We sprinted up hills for conditioning. Coach Orlando whipped us into shape and made us tough, even though we looked like the Bad News Bears. We didn't have matching uniforms and we stored our footballs and kicking tees in old tattered laundry bags.

We never knew we were any good until we started playing other teams. Quarters lasted eight minutes. We went undefeated that year, even beating St. Peter's, a school whose sports programs were funded by the Rooney family, owners of the Pittsburgh Steelers. They had fancy uniforms and brand new footballs and were skeptical of our record when they noticed how small our roster was. We shut them out that day.

St. Philomena's was great for another reason. The parish was rich in Italians and Irish families. It fit me perfectly because that was my ethnic makeup. The football team was made up of Irish kids like me, Kevin McSwigan, Dennis Hanley, Pat Knipp, Danny Murphy, Marty Devine. There were also Italians like Todd Orlando, the coach's son, and Eugene and Rocco DePasquale. Two of the kids from that roster went on to play Division 1 college football, another played Quad A football, which in Pennsylvania is the division with the biggest schools, and another played Quad A baseball. Todd later played linebacker at Wisconsin despite being only six feet tall. He was a great guy who went on to be a defensive coordinator at several colleges, including UConn and the University of Texas. And we didn't just excel at football. Eugene is the auditor general of Pennsylvania. It was an impressive group.

With a limited roster, we were all given the opportunity to play. I had responsibility for anything that happened on the field. And once again, I listened to adults. Coaches taught us if you run hard and train well and stretch, you'll be a stronger player. I took that as chapter and verse.

This experience ignited my hunger for everything about football. I would continue to play through middle school, high school, and into college. I later went on to coach and work in professional sports. So much happened in my life around this time. Amid the whirlwind of illness, shifting schools, and changing social factors, football helped ground me and provide something to look forward to.

While I underwent chemotherapy, I visited doctors regularly. I never went more than two weeks without seeing a pediatric oncologist. Sometimes appointments were more frequent, like once a week.

I dealt with Dr. Michael Wollman, a Jewish doctor originally from Brooklyn. I say that he was Jewish with all the love and respect in my heart, because he was very matter-of-fact. Like my parents, he didn't pull any punches. He could be hilarious, but also knew when to be serious and caring. Part of the reason I felt strong was because he told me what to do. I was convinced he wouldn't con me or tell me something that wasn't true. He promised that I'd get through cancer treatments and be okay. So I believed him.

At an appointment during the late stages of my treatment, after we dispensed with the update, Dr. Wollman asked my mom and me a pointed question.

"Are you interested in working with the Leukemia Society?" he wondered.

I frowned, confused. I didn't have leukemia.

Non-Hogkin lymphoma, he explained, was a cousin of leukemia. The Leukemia Society had phoned his office looking for a child approaching the end of chemotherapy. They wanted an outgoing kid to participate in some of their events. They needed someone who was responding well to treatment. Their last few ad campaigns had been grim, showing sickly children, bald but covered by hats. It was clear that cancer was a hard thing for a young person to endure. They hoped to shift directions: find a kid with a personality and highlight a success story.

"Joe, you're a success story," Dr. Wollman said proudly.

This made me feel good. There was a finish line. Without using the words, the doctor was telling me that he didn't believe I would stumble along the way.

"Absolutely," I replied, nodding to mom. "I'd love to help raise money to fight cancer."

We were given the name and phone number of George Omiros, the Executive Director of the Leukemia and Lymphoma Society of Western Pennsylvania and West Virginia. We set up an appointment, and within a few days, mom drove me to their office downtown.

I was excited. They had already asked what my favorite foods were, so there were cookies and milk laid out when I arrived. From the moment I walked in, they treated me like a star. After introductions and getting comfortable, George ushered me into his office. He requested that mom wait outside. George wanted to hear my words without interruption.

We sat across the desk from each other and he asked a series of questions. How did your cancer start? How do you feel now? What was the secret to getting through tough days? He took notes during our chat. I didn't realize it then, but we were developing what I would later refer to as my "stump speech." When I was called on to speak in public, these responses would form the basis of my presentation.

"If you were standing in a room full of donors," George wondered, "what would you want to say to them?"

I thought for a moment. "I know the money that's donated today won't have helped me," I reflected. "But the generosity of donors like you in years past probably saved my life."

"Perfect," George beamed.

We honed the lines and, over time, worked the presentation into five good minutes. Eventually, I could stand in front of any crowd and talk with authority. The speech was general enough that it could be adapted to almost any situation. Going through cancer wasn't easy for anyone, I explained. One of the main pillars of the speech came when I talked about surviving the odds. In my mind, it was a speech of thanks.

Studies show that people's number one phobia is speaking in public. Number two is dying. I'd eventually be able to make that comparison.

People can get butterflies before giving a presentation, but I started young. After doing it once, it became easy for me to get up in front of a crowd. Now, as an adult, I sometimes challenge myself, and wonder if could I present to strangers for five minutes in some unfamiliar setting. Most often, I think I could.

The first speech I gave was a big one. It was at the Foge Fazio Leukemia Golf Open, and I was being given the Courage Award. It was May, 1984, at the Pittsburgh Field Club in Fox Chapel. Picture a regal old banquet hall, with dark wood paneling. The room seated 450. I was only eleven years old.

Foge Fazio coached the Pitt Panthers. He was a hometown guy. Everyone knew who he was, because the Panthers were a good football team. The golf tournament began on a Monday, and the night before was the kickoff dinner. Husbands in suits and ties brought their wives, clad in cocktail dresses. It was swanky, and I was excited.

My sister and I were the only kids in the room, and I was The Kid. I remember being nervous when I surveyed the adults. There were so many important people there. It was a who's who of future football stars: Dan Marino, Chris Doleman, Bill Fralic, Craig "Ironhead" Heyward, and Keith Hamilton.

Each dinner table featured a celebrity. At our table was Mike Wagner, a safety for the Pittsburgh Steelers. What a down-to-earth guy. He sat next to me and we talked the whole time. He was twelve or thirteen years older than I was, and treated me like a little brother. That's when I learned that players in the NFL are regular guys.

After the meal, I stood and adjusted the microphone before delivering my stump speech. I spoke clearly and confidently, the way George and I had practiced. The five minutes passed quickly. When I finished, I received a standing ovation. People were grabbing me, shaking my hand, patting me on the back. It had gone better than I expected. I felt very special, and more importantly, I felt like I was doing good for other kids battling cancer.

∞

Following the dinner, I was invited to a Pitt football practice with my dad. It was the last spring practice and everyone was in a great mood. At the facility, I was given a t-shirt that read "Tough 20." I had no idea what it meant, but later learned there were 20 spring practices. Players who attended all 20 were rewarded with a limited edition t-shirt.

At the end of practice, Coach Fazio called the team together. After speaking to his players, he signaled toward Dad to send me over.

I hurried to the huddle and Fazio rested his hands on my shoulders. I was surrounded by 120 guys in uniforms. They were big, burly, and sweaty.

"Hey everybody, this is Joey," Fazio said. "He's going to be our mascot this year." He recounted the health struggles I had gone through and how I had won the Courage Award at his golf tournament. Players began clapping and cheering. I was then instructed to call the team. A hairy stack of hands thrust toward the middle, and I yelled "P-I-T-T!" They repeated the letters, followed by an explosion of noise as they shouted "Pitt! Pitt! Pitt!" Afterward, many players came up and patted my back, saying "good job, buddy."

During the fall of 1984, I became a ball boy for the Pitt Panthers. I attended all the home games, and even went to training camp in Edinboro. I loved every minute of it, making fast friends with the rest of the staff. Decades later, their names still roll off my tongue.

The equipment manager was Tommy Connors, but his nickname was "Boo." He succeeded his father, who continued to show up at every practice. The head student trainer was Joe Wall, whose voice was damaged due to throat cancer. Speaking in raspy tones, he identified with me immediately, and relied on me to help out.

I'd get to the stadium before the team. My job was to assemble clean socks, jocks, and pants into a roll so they would be ready when players arrived. Jerseys were already hung in the stalls. I helped Joe Wall do whatever was needed. Sometimes I'd run errands. Eventually, other boys showed up. I had expected to throw balls onto the field during the games, but coaches' sons were given that job. Sometimes, a recruit's little brother was told he could do that for a Saturday. It was a way to woo a promising prospect. I understood and didn't mind.

Many of the players befriended me. Craig "Ironhead" Heyward was a freshman that fall. Chris Doleman approached me too, and he was very kind. At the first practice, Bob Buczkowski came up to me. He was a defensive end who, by 1986, would be drafted in the first round by the Los Angeles Raiders. He went on to play for the Arizona Cardinals and Cleveland Browns. His Wikipedia page identifies him as "one of the biggest busts in NFL Draft History." Twenty-one years later, he was arrested for a series of crimes. But all that was still to come. On this hot summer day, he was a college kid who asked where I was from. When I said Forest Hills, he smiled and nodded.

"I'm from Monroeville," he said, referring to the next town.

Bob's best friend on the team was Dennis Atiyeh. Dennis was raised in Scranton, one of several children from a big Syrian family. His brother George wrestled in the 1984 Olympics. Dennis was a hellraiser. At nineteen, he was arrested after drinking too much, getting into a fight, and pushing a female cop through a window. Like Bob, he got in trouble with the law as an adult too.

But I never saw that side of either of them. I only knew their good parts. Bob and Dennis became my buddies right off the bat. They would pick me up at home, take me to the movies, and we'd share ice cream afterwards. They didn't have to do any of that. They were legitimately nice guys around me. Dennis had married in college and had a baby son named Adam. He and his wife were struggling college kids, so my mom bought them gifts. Ironically, she thought Dennis was a saint. Around this time, I participated in a fashion show for the Leukemia Society and was told by the organizers that I could keep the clothes. Instead, I requested baby clothes so I could pass them on to Adam. It felt pretty special to be twelve years old and hang out with the Pitt Panthers.

Not everyone embraced me. Some players treated me differently. Some didn't want me around because they worried they had to watch their mouth. There wasn't one specific group that kept me at arm's length. It cut across race or position. I learned quickly who to stay away from, and settled into the role so I didn't offend anyone.

More than anything, I spent the season appreciating the unique experience that had been granted to me. I was beginning to realize that having cancer had led me down a special path, so different from anyone else that I knew.

A Mother's Love
—Linda Lafferty

AS A TWENTY-THREE-YEAR-OLD first time mother, Linda Lafferty sat her daughter atop the dining room table, watching to be sure the baby didn't crawl toward the edge. Little Tara, seven months old, looked adorable in her tiny red dress. She smiled and cooed while Linda beamed with admiration.

"I was so in love with her," Linda recalled. "She was such a good baby, and she was gorgeous. I couldn't believe that she was mine."

Linda turned to her own mother, Antoinette Persichetti, who was visiting.

"I don't know what I'd do if something ever happened to Tara," she said.

Linda's mother gasped. The older woman maintained a deep Christian faith, although she rarely preached to others and did not attend regular church services.

"Don't you say that," she scolded. "This little girl is on loan to you from God. You're taking care of her. But Linda, if God wants to take her back, he can!"

The moment was sobering. Linda was forced to acknowledge that so much of life was beyond her control. The conversation came to mind a decade later when Joe contracted non-Hogkin lymphoma.

"After he was diagnosed, I came home and cried," Linda said. "I cried and cried and cried and cried. But it was very important that Joey didn't see me cry, and he never did. Once I got all the crying out, I made a deal with God."

Doctors had promised the family that the survival rate of non-Hogkin lymphoma was seventy percent. If you're going to get a cancer, they were told, this is the one to get. They prescribed an eighteen-month cycle of chemotherapy. Knowing there was a rigid protocol brought comfort to Linda. Nevertheless, this was her beloved son. What parent would be comfortable with a thirty-percent chance of death?

"I said to God, if you want him, you take him now!" Linda recalled, voice tinged with fire. "But don't you dare let him suffer through eighteen months of chemotherapy and then take him! I'm willing to give him to you now!" She paused and nodded. "When God didn't take him early, I thought, this is good."

Linda has led an active life. Growing up in Edgewood, a neighborhood outside of Pittsburgh, she met her future husband when they were both sixteen and her dog impregnated the Lafferty family dog who lived several houses away. Linda grew up to work in Pittsburgh City schools as a computer teacher and school librarian. During eastern Pittsburgh's district consolidations in the 1980s, she became a political activist, forming "Save Our Schools"—S.O.S.—and serving two years on the Forest Hills Borough Council.

Now retired, she volunteers with the national program "Blessings in a Backpack," which fights childhood hunger by providing healthy snacks for children to bring home on weekends. The time between school lunches on Friday and school breakfasts on Monday is sixty-five hours—too long a span for kids to go without a good meal. Since 2011, Linda has averaged ten hours each week coordinating food distribution in Wilkinsburg.

In 1981-1982, the cycle of Joe's chemotherapy became predictable. He underwent treatment on Friday, then came home and began throwing up at six o'clock Saturday morning. Through bouts of vomiting, he laid on the living room couch watching cartoons. By 2 p.m., the sickness would pass.

When Joe called, "Mom, can I have my Doritos and Coke now?" Linda knew he had made it through another cycle.

"Joey was always very different from a typical nine-year-old," she said. "He was bright and wise beyond his years. One day after we left the hospital, I was driving down Fifth Avenue in Pittsburgh. He stared at the car next to us."

"Mom, that guy's got a lot of dough," Joe said.

Linda watched on the road. "How do you know he's got money?" Then she glanced sidelong to see loaves of Italian bread protruding from grocery bags in the backseat.

"That's how Joey was," Linda explained. "He joked and never complained. Honestly, he could have laid on the couch for eighteen months and not done anything, and I would have let him. But that wasn't what he wanted. That first Halloween after he was diagnosed, Rubik's Cube was very popular. So I got a cardboard box, cut out holes for his head and arms, and decorated his costume. He went to two or three houses to collect candy, then came home. It was all he could handle because he was so tired, but he still wanted to do it."

Once, Linda tried to sympathize with her son as he prepared for yet another medical procedure.

"I'm so sorry, honey," she said. "I know how you feel."

"No you don't," Joe replied.

Linda paused, then realized that she had chosen her words poorly. Her son was right. Although she had coordinated his health plan and provided daily support, she had never undergone the challenges he faced. To assume otherwise was not fair.

"He was always an enigma to doctors and nurses," she recalled. "Even when he was little, he asked questions about chemotherapy. He wanted to know everything that was going into his body and what its effect would be."

The medications had short-term effects, including hair loss, nausea, hives. Long-term effects included developing diabetes and even an increased risk for different forms of cancer. Linda was by his side through all Joe endured.

"Attitude is important, and he had such a positive attitude," she said. "We believed that after eighteen months, the journey would be over and Joey would be cured."

Joe faced new obstacles along the way, including pancreatitis, and later, becoming an insulin-dependent diabetic.

"There were plenty of times when Joey could have complained, but he didn't," Linda reflected. "He never turned mean or hateful. He's never worn his troubles on his sleeve, and he could have, many times over. I sometimes forget he's been through so much. How can he have endured everything and still be a good, wholesome person?"

Linda shook her head, searching for the proper words.

"Joey says I made him strong, but that's not the way it was. The reality is he kept me strong."

CHAPTER 3

Flash

AS I APPROACHED THE AWKWARD teen years, my love
for football grew. After two years at St. Philomena's, I moved back
to the public school, attending Edgewood Middle School while
participating in the Churchill Area Midget League. The best kids
on that team were in ninth grade, but I was only in seventh. I was
five feet, seven inches tall and weighed 120 pounds. Thanks to my
size, I got on the field. I'd catch the ball as a tight end then get laid
out. I played limited snaps on the defensive line too, serving as a
tackling dummy. Bumps and bruises didn't bother me. I had fun
going to practice every day.

The best thing about football at that age was reading my name
in the local newspaper, which printed yardage and tackling stats
as they recapped midget games. It gave me a sense of pride to
open the pages and see myself in black and white. But make no

mistake—I was never a star. I've been a small cog in the machine of every team that I've played on.

My ninth grade coach, Ron Suvak, moved me from defensive end to quarterback. I'm still not sure why. He must have seen me throwing footballs in the gym. Mr. Suvak had been my eighth grade history teacher, and he promised me the spring before that I was going to be under center for his team in the fall. I had never played quarterback, so I laughed, thinking he was kidding.

Mr. Suvak's son, Ron Jr., was a year older than me. My sister cheered for the ninth grade team, so I had attended those games and watched Mr. Suvak grab his son by the face mask and yell at him when he did something wrong on the field. I thought he only did that because Ron was family, but I quickly learned that's how he treated all his quarterbacks. I was next in line.

But he wasn't really mean. Once you knew Mr. Suvak, it was clear how much he loved kids. He was sarcastic and funny, especially in the classroom. He used to ask his students bonus questions every Monday, and we had until Friday to research the answers. There was no internet in the 1980s, so I'd visit the library during lunch, or skim the encyclopedia set at home. What does "e pluribus unum" mean? Why is the Washington Monument two different colors? Where was Sigmund Freud born? They were trivia questions that forced us to learn about history.

On the football field, I was limited in talent. Mr. Suvak dubbed me "Flash." It wasn't for my quick feet, which weren't that quick, but because I was a fast thinker. The nickname stuck through high school. Even today, some friends call me "Flash."

The east side of Pittsburgh was changing, and many socio-economic issues factored into the neighborhood shifts. There were two district mergers in the years before I entered high school. I've already mentioned how Braddock combined with Churchill.

Following that, in 1982, Turtle Creek and Swissville were also assimilated into Churchill to make a spanning district that united parts of twelve municipalities. A contest was held among the students to come up with a name for the new school district. Thad Wilson, a young man I played football with, suggested "Woodland Hills." Kids voted, and that was selected the winner. For naming the new district, Thad was awarded a savings bond. (He was always a smart kid. After high school, Thad attended Harvard.)

So in ninth grade, I attended Swissvale High School, knowing the following year I'd end up at Woodland Hills High School, which included grades ten through twelve. The most significant event in ninth grade was that I met two guys who became my best friends during high school.

Wayne Anderson was a 240-pound fullback, and Chris Uram was a right guard who was built straight up and down, like a rectangle. They had wrestled together in eighth grade, so they knew each other before I met them. We quickly became the three amigos.

Chris lived in Swissvale. On the end of his street were train tracks, and beyond that was Rankin, where Wayne lived. They walked home from practice together. It was an odd sight to see Wayne, a black kid, alongside Chris, who was white, especially when there were other black kids walking home in groups and Wayne could have easily joined them.

Wayne was among the most popular kids in our class. He had been a lineman in seventh grade, but he begged the coach to let him carry the ball. Built low to the ground, Wayne was agile and fast. Because he was a little knock-kneed, coach realized that running side to side wasn't his forte. Wayne was best in a straight line. We got to be friends in practice, when I spent hours handing balls off to him. He had great feet and was a punishing, powerful runner. People used to call him "Little Ironhead" after University of

Pittsburgh star Craig "Ironhead" Heyward. I had known Ironhead from my days as a ballboy, and I believe that Wayne was faster. So we christened him with a better nickname: Wayne the Train.

Although we never had any of the same classes, Chris, Wayne and I would hang out together. After an early season game we went to a pizza shop, and that was the start of it. In days before cell phones, I would sometimes arrive home and Wayne and Chris would be in my family's kitchen with mom serving them dinner. My friends had just showed up and waited. It was the greatest thing ever.

Chris was tough too. He was five feet, eleven inches tall, 215 pounds, but he looks even bigger. He had great feet. As an offensive lineman, he knew how to run a trap. He'd pull and flatten his opponent quickly, opening holes for Wayne or whoever else ran the ball.

Our freshman games were held on Thursday nights, and the Swissvale varsity team played on Friday. Had the coach decided to elevate Wayne to varsity, he would have started. He was that good. They could have used Chris and me as backups as well. But no freshman were promoted because the school was closing, and it was thought that seniors should savor their final year. Coaches knew some of the juniors were going to get lost in the wash with the merger at Woodland Hills, so they should play out the final season. As a result, we had Wayne the whole year, and it was great.

By the time high school began, I had been cancer free for three years. I was as healthy as any kid my age. I played football in the fall and volleyball in the spring, so I had moved on from being sick. Like all kids, I was a little self-centered, so I didn't think much about it, believing that I had been cured. My work with the Leukemia Society made me feel special for having conquered it. Near the end of my freshman year, however, my health began to change.

My parents purchased insurance policies for my sister and me. A salesman came to our house, and part of the required health test involved a urine sample. It was supposed to be routine, but sugar was discovered in my urine and I was instructed to see a doctor. I was still younger than eighteen, so my primary care physician was my pediatric oncologist. They did blood work, and I was sent to an endocrinologist, who diagnosed me as an insulin-dependent diabetic.

The signs had been there. I wasn't a junk food eater, but I used to wake up each night to use the bathroom. My mouth would be so dry that I would take a 32-ounce souvenir cup from my room, fill it with water, and guzzle it down before heading back to bed. I'd get up to pee three or four times a night. I didn't think anything of it.

That spring I had to visit the hospital to learn about insulin. A nurse taught me how to give myself a shot. She showed me how to swab skin with alcohol, draw insulin out of a vial and click it with my fingers to remove any bubbles. She didn't know my history as a cancer survivor, so she expected me to be more squeamish, but I had been on the receiving end of so many shots over the years.

"No problem," I told her. "I can do this."

The nurse soon realized that I had some experience. Different needles have different gauges. The lower the number, the bigger the gauge, and bigger gauges hurt more. The insulin syringe was thin so I knew it wouldn't hurt much. I pinched up the skin on my thigh and put the needle in my leg. It's a tiny prick unless you get too close to a nerve ending. Over the years, I not only got used to it, but I became callous to syringe pain.

I quickly learned to re-orient myself and become very aware of my food intake. I got into a rhythm and routine. Once school began again in the fall, I munched snacks at my locker between classes. A few times, my blood sugar dipped low during class, so I asked to see the nurse. She would give me orange juice, and once she sent me to lunch early. Taking a shot became my new normal. In fact, I did it every day for the next twenty-three years, from 1987 until my kidney and pancreas transplant in 2010.

Because I was in the hospital, I was absent for the final three days of freshman year. I missed saying goodbye as Swissvale High School closed.

Doctors told me that as a diabetic, I could do anything but join the military. This broke my heart, because that had been one of my dreams. I loved sports, but knew I wasn't good enough to play professionally. The military, however, had been on my radar.

I had seen the movie *Taps* with Tom Cruise, Sean Penn, and Timothy Hutton. The story is set at Bunker Hill Military Academy, but it was filmed at Valley Forge near Philadelphia. Years earlier, my family had driven by there and I had seen the building up close. I even asked my mom if I could attend Valley Forge for high school.

"We'll see," she murmured. "Maybe next year."

I don't know what it would have cost, but I had just beaten cancer, so I see now there was no way mom was going to let me out of her sight. She probably looked at it as a passing fancy, but I don't think it was. I like authority, even today. I can be a good soldier and have no problem taking orders. In fact, much of my life has been based on the belief that if I do what others ask of me, I'll be fine. At fourteen years old, it was hard to accept that joining the military was no longer an option.

Everyone around Eastern Pittsburgh in those days knows the story of the mergers. A racial element hovered in the background, almost like the movie *Remember the Titans*. Even though that story is set in the early 1970s, our community experienced the same issues fifteen years later.

Churchill High School added a huge addition before being rechristened as Woodland Hills. Suddenly, there was a new era. Churchill had already been infused with African American kids from Braddock. There was a balance of white and black kids from Swissvale, but Turtle Creek had been predominantly white. Now, everyone was poured in together: blacks, whites, rich, poor. Living through that experience shaped my beliefs and allowed me to befriend and accept people of all colors, religions, and economic backgrounds.

There was so much internal chaos that first year at Woodland Hills. It was an interesting time. All the rooms had been renumbered from when it was Churchill High School, so even kids who had taken classes in the building got lost as they wandered the halls that autumn day in 1987.

By our graduation year, 1990, my class would be the first group to complete all three years in the new school. I joke that we were "the founding fathers." That is a big honor, but the downside was that we were the bottom rung of the social scale for two years in a row: we were ninth graders in a four year high school, then became sophomores in a three year high school.

During the inaugural season at Woodland Hills, everybody wanted to play football. More than 160 kids showed up for practice the first day. By the first game, 130 of us survived. There were only numbers for 99 jerseys, so the kids who didn't dress for a game wore their alternate color jerseys and warmed up with the team, then sat on the bleachers behind the bench wearing their helmets as a show of support.

Woodland Hills' coach, George Novak, was wise enough to recognize that kids learn best by playing. In addition to varsity and junior varsity, he formed a tenth-grade team. I was the starting quarterback on that squad. In our eight-game schedule, we played JV teams from smaller schools. I also served as a backup quarterback on the JV team, and was the third string quarterback—the guy in a cap who holds a clipboard on the sidelines—on the varsity squad. Three days every week I wore a game uniform.

I quarterbacked the varsity scout team, and got punished most of the year. Our defensive coaches taught their lineman to finish blocks and play through the whistle, so I had to pick myself up every time I handed off the ball. It got to the point where I'd bootleg one way or the other just to try to avoid being knocked down. A funny thing happened, though. The seniors respected me because I got up every time after they hit me. They didn't want to see a sophomore lying prone. As I walked through the halls during the school day, older guys would nod and say, "What's up, Laff?"

I grew so much as a player that year. The experience raised my football IQ and made me tougher. I didn't know it was fun while I was doing it, but looking back, it was a blast.

The varsity blew out some teams, so I got to play a couple snaps near the end of a game. What a high. The team won the conference and lost before the championship. Not bad for a first-year program in an area obsessed with football.

Throughout much of high school, I had a strategically scheduled study hall that allowed me to volunteer in the Woodland Hills Athletic Office. I completed odd jobs, making sure basketballs were inflated, filing papers, or inventorying sports equipment. When the secretary went to lunch, I answered phones. My dad was a union steward who coordinated route managers at the Pittsburgh Post-Gazette, so growing up, there were two phone lines in our home. I had been taught phone etiquette at an early age. Those manners helped me thrive in an office setting.

It wasn't unusual for college programs to contact Coach Novak. If they called and he wasn't available, I took a message. One day, I answered the phone to a deep, booming voice.

"Is Coach Novak in? This is Lou Holtz from Notre Dame."

Momentarily starstruck, I quickly recovered.

"He's not in now, sir, but it's a pleasure to hear from you. If you leave your number, I'll be sure he gets the message."

"Son, he better have my number."

"Absolutely, Coach," I told him as I scrawled his name on a pad. "I'll make sure Coach Novak gets this." I hung up and felt my pulse quicken. I had just spoken to the coach of one of the most high-profile college programs in the nation.

When Novak returned, his eyes narrowed strangely when I described the call. I assumed he was put off by my enthusiasm. He shook his head and disappeared into his office, closing the door.

At practice later that afternoon, our offensive line coach approached me. Dan Price was a Vietnam veteran with salt and pepper hair, beard and a mustache. He was tough as nails, and reminded me of Pitt's legendary O-line coach Joe Moore, whom I had met when I was a ballboy. Both were gruff. Neither man had any designs on becoming a coordinator or talking to the press. They simply wanted to coach the offensive line. Another common trait was that their players adored them.

Price was six feet, two inches tall, 170 pounds. Students weren't allowed to use tobacco products, but he and other coaches liked to smoke. Some even sent players for laps around the field so they could squeeze in a cigarette.

"I heard you talked to Lou Holtz today," Price growled.

"Yes sir."

He grinned with mischief. "That was me."

I hadn't recognized Price's deep voice on the phone. Later, when I saw Holtz interviewed on ESPN, it was obvious that I hadn't spoken with him. He had a high voice and a lisp. (Years later, I met Holtz during a trip to Notre Dame.) Danny Price just wanted to mess with Coach Novak. He did that regularly. He used to tuck women's panties into Novak's briefcase when no one was looking.

Little pranks like that made it fun to work in the Athletic Office, and I continued in that role throughout high school.

One winter day during my senior year, I was wearing a Notre Dame sweatshirt that my aunt had given me for Christmas. It was cold and the sweatshirt was warm, but I wasn't a huge Notre Dame fan. In the late 80s and early 90s, I really liked the Miami Hurricanes. Guys at "The U" played with attitude and the roster was stacked with talent.

A bald man with a commanding presence entered the office. It was clear he was a college coach; he looked the part. He asked to speak with Coach Novak.

"I'll track him down, sir," I told him. "My name is Joe. Is there anything I can get you while you wait?"

He noticed my sweatshirt, asking if I was a fan of the Fighting Irish.

"They're all right," I admitted. "But I prefer Miami."

He nodded, then pulled back his jacket sleeve to reveal a Hurricanes championship watch from the Cotton Bowl.

"Whoa," I gasped. The man introduced himself as Art Kehoe, a former Miami player who now recruited for the school.

"I'm here scouting a student," he said. "Can you guess who I'm looking at?"

"Must be Tirrell Greene," I answered. Greene was a six-foot, three-inch tall, 305-pound teammate, a defensive lineman who was fast off the ball. As a fellow senior, we knew he was getting Division I offers.

"That's right," Kehoe said. "We want him to come to Miami and play offensive line. Is he a friend of yours?"

"Yes sir. We've known each other for years."

Tirrell went on to become a three-year starter on Miami's offensive line and was named an All-American in 1994. He learned the center position and made all the calls. He played on a team with Warren Sapp, Ray Lewis, Dwayne "The Rock" Johnson and Rohan Marley, son of reggae singer Bob Marley. Unfortunately, Terrell separated his shoulder in the Senior Bowl. He did turn pro, playing in NFL Europe for two years and having a brief stint with the Steelers.

Meeting Art Kehoe was important, because we remain friends today. In 1997, when I moved to Miami to work for the Orange Bowl, I found him and reintroduced myself. Like Joe Moore and Danny Price, he was another offensive line coach who was beloved by his players. He spent 31 years both as a player and coach for the Hurricanes until he was dismissed in January 2016.

Working in the Athletic Office throughout high school set the stage for my career in marketing and sports management. It was great training and opened doors toward my future, sparking my love for working in sports. It got me closer to the business side of football, allowing me to see different aspects and learn what happened behind the scenes. Like so many other things in my life, it was a unique opportunity that shaped the person I became.

I kept playing football, but as high school progressed, I recognized that I was an average player. I would never be a big college star. By my senior year, I had been moved to wide receiver when Coach discovered a younger quarterback who was better than I was. We ran a counter-trey, Washington Redskins-type system, hardly ever throwing the ball. I only caught three passes that year, but one was for a touchdown.

The Woodland Hills class of 1990 had seven players who earned Division 1 scholarships. Besides Tirrell Greene at Miami University, other colleges that accepted my teammates included Pitt, Akron, Harvard, and Kent State. Two kids went to Richmond, which was later downgraded to 1A.

Wayne attended Akron, after coach Gerry Faust came to his house and recruited him. Faust was a character, and Wayne trusted him. There were several other schools who wooed him, but Wayne was set on going to Akron, where coaches moved him to nose guard. He's a few weeks younger than I am, so he didn't turn eighteen until college. Like me, Wayne started four college games as a seventeen-year-old. Everyone in Pittsburgh football circles knew about him. In fact, a hometown kid younger than we are, Jason Taylor, idolized Wayne. Taylor attended Akron and roomed with Wayne his freshman year. Taylor, of course, went on to be an NFL star with the Miami Dolphins and was later inducted into the Pro Football Hall of Fame.

Today, Wayne works at Woodland Hills High School as a behavior specialist. He assists with troubled young people and knows how to restrain a kid if things get physical. Although he never married, he has a young daughter.

Our other friend, Chris, attended Westminster College in western Pennsylvania. He suffered a severe concussion during his freshman year while pulling on a trap as an offensive lineman. He hit a guy and woke up the next day. Recurring headaches affected the rest of his college career. Today he lives in the Pittsburgh suburb of Oakmont, where he restored his home, and works as a pharmaceutical representative. A few years ago he married a girl from our high school class.

Sports helped pull the school together through the lingering racial issues. Football helped me grow as a player and a person. Despite the fact I had beaten cancer and was blessed with great friends, part of me felt different, like I was an outsider who never fit in.

During my teenage years, there was a hole inside of me. I loved high school, but something was missing. Wayne and I refused to drink, or smoke cigarettes, or use drugs. Because Wayne was so popular, nobody gave us grief or peer pressure. Surely there were plenty of other kids who didn't do those things. On the surface, appearances looked great.

I was popular and had many girlfriends. I really didn't have any fear around girls. Life is too short. What's the worst thing to happen... a girl tells me no? I cheated death, so I wasn't worried about that. I thought that getting a different girl to like me would fill the hole inside. I didn't really do anything bad, but there was often heartache on my end. It's nothing I'm proud of.

People knew about my childhood illness. That was part of my history. But no one knew how empty I felt. I kept that shielded from everybody. I'm a salesman and always have been. I believe that when you experience something catastrophic as a youth, you're just a little wiser than other people your age. You know the value of life. I know it really well, and appreciate it. So does my sister, from watching my struggles. Maybe because of that, I felt different from everybody. But no one knew.

In years to come, the hole inside me would be filled twice. The first is when I was saved by Jesus Christ, and the second came later, when I fell in love with Jennifer. But I didn't know those blessings lay ahead.

CHAPTER 4

The Kid

IN FEBRUARY 1987, MY SOPHOMORE year of high school,
I got another call from the Leukemia Society. They informed me
that Dan Marino had taken over the annual golf outing that was
previously named for University of Pittsburgh football coach
Serafino Dante "Foge" Fazio. Foge had lost the head coaching job
at Pitt and moved on to become the defensive coordinator at Notre
Dame. Because he was no longer based locally, it made sense to
rebrand the event. Dan, a Pittsburgh native, had previously been
a celebrity attendee. We had met briefly when I was given the
Courage Award in 1984.

In the years since, Marino had established himself as one of the
best quarterbacks in the NFL. I'm biased, but even today, I believe
that he was the best of all time. He had a quick release and was
deadly accurate with his passes. Marino wasn't known as a runner,
but if you break down his skills, he was mobile in the pocket,

moving like a pinball, sliding up or sideways to avoid pressure. He threw for forty-eight touchdowns in 1984. Those numbers have been surpassed, but they're still rare today in a pass-dominated league. Back then, he was years ahead of everyone.

The Leukemia Society wanted to offer me another Courage Award because the event had a new name: The Dan Marino Leukemia Golf Open. I was still doing speeches and events for them, so I was a proven commodity. Of course, I accepted. A press conference was planned at the Hilton Hotel in Pittsburgh. Dan was the star, but we would share the stage.

I wanted to look sharp before I met Marino again. My parents had agreed that I needed a new suit, so after I dressed, Mom complimented me.

"Mom, am I the best looking man in the world?" I teased.

"Of course you are," she said proudly. She was an Italian mother, after all. But when she gushed and turned syrupy, I nudged her further.

"Am I better looking than Dan Marino?"

Her face froze for a long beat. "Joey, he's really good looking!"

On a March afternoon, I traveled downtown. I was led into a room and shook Marino's hand. Before the cameras set up, we sat down to become reacquainted. He asked about me and said that we were going to have fun together.

"Yes, sir," I nodded.

"None of this 'sir' stuff," he said. "Call me Danny."

My head nearly exploded. Dan had an endorsement deal with Zenga suits and had appeared on the cover of GQ magazine. I was a fifteen-year-old high school quarterback, but even if I hadn't played the position, I would have been in awe of him. He always dressed to the nines. When strangers saw him, they would nod and point. Dan Marino owned whatever room he walked into. He had even gotten my mother to admit he was better looking than her own son.

During the second week of May, the Lafferty family traveled again to the Pittsburgh Field Club, just like we had three years earlier. This was common territory for me. The dinner featured a who's who of sports celebrities, including John Elway, Joe Namath, Mario Lemieux, Jim Kelly, Steve Young, Boomer Esiason, Jim Everett, Bernie Kosar, Vinny Testaverde, Mark Duper, and Cris Collinsworth. There were plenty more familiar names.

My mom, dad, and I showed up early. The Marino family had arrived ahead of us, so we all met in an elegant wood-paneled bar room. Danny was accompanied by his parents, Dan Sr. and Veronica; his wife, Claire; and his younger sister, Debbie.

Dan Sr. and my father were members of the same union in the circulation department for the Pittsburgh Post-Gazette. My dad was a route manager and Mr. Marino was a truck driver. When they made eye contact, they recognized each other, but my dad only knew the other man as "Dan." He didn't make the connection that his son was the best quarterback in the NFL. Dan Sr. had not expected to see my dad there.

"Hey, you're Joe," he said with surprise. He had not realized the link either. So our two dads immediately found a common ground and began to chat.

My mom sat down and talked with Dan's mom. They were becoming fast friends when Dan strolled over and leaned down.

"Mrs. Lafferty," he said. "Can I get you something from the bar?" He proceeded to walk back and forth, serving soft drinks to my mom. Dan also brought drinks to his mom, his wife and sister.

That moment stayed with me. It showed me how humble and down to earth he was. I later learned the term "serving leader." I hear that phrase and think of Danny. Here was a legendary quarterback who was taking care of others. Whether under the wide umbrella of a golf tournament or within the narrow confines of a bar, he used his fame to give things back to those around him.

Soon we moved to the dining room as guests and celebrities filtered in. After dinner, I was given a microphone and spoke again about the need to raise money so more children can overcome cancer, as I did. Again, I was given a standing ovation. Yes, I had done this before, but it was still heady stuff for a kid not yet sixteen years old.

The story could have ended there, but I maintained contact with many people from that night. My dad was big on manners, so I sent thank you notes and Christmas cards during the holiday season. It was a way to stay in touch. The following year, I was invited back. Not as a speaker, but as an alum who could help at the golf outing. I had become one of the standard bearers for the Leukemia Society around Pittsburgh.

A week before the Sunday dinner in 1988, I received a phone call from Jim Murphy, a former college football player who lived in Florida and was a golfing buddy of Dan's. We had met the year before, and I had written my phone number in a card I sent him.

"Some of the guys are coming into Pittsburgh a few days early," Murphy said. "We're staying at the Hilton. Do you want to run around with us? Maybe you can be our driver."

"Sure, I'm sixteen," I told him vaguely. I did not have my license yet, but didn't want that inconvenient fact to get in the way of a good time with Danny and his friends.

One of those friends was Michael Talbott, a comedian-turned-actor who played a supporting role on *Miami Vice*, which was the hot show on TV. Danny played football in the city where it was filmed. (There are publicity photos of Dan dressed like Don Johnson in his white suit, leaning against a sports car.) Talbott performed a stand up bit during the post-golf lunch, and he was absolutely hilarious.

Fortunately, I was not asked to drive. Two city of Pittsburgh detectives were detailed to watch the celebrities, ensuring they were protected at all times. I tagged along in the car. On a weekend night, we found ourselves at a gathering in Station Square.

I was five-ten, one hundred ninety five pounds, dressed in khaki pants and a golf shirt. I barely looked sixteen. Even today, I maintain a baby face. I certainly didn't appear old enough to fit in here, but our escorts just said, "Joey, stay beside us." They nodded that I was part of the group, and like that, I was whisked inside. I sipped cranberry juice, surrounded by famous people.

NFL coach Chuck Knox stood nearby, handing out big black cigars. He later lost weight, but at this point, Knox was heavy. I asked him if I could smell one of the cigars. I assume it was Cuban. He held it under my nose and I took a tentative inhale.

"Smells really good," I lied.

"Want to try one?" he asked sarcastically.

I'd never smoked anything, and I didn't take a drink until I was twenty-one. But when he offered it to me, I took the initiative to act like a grown up. I was proud to be part of the adult rituals. Might as well do something bad, I thought.

"Sure," I answered.

After one puff, I realized this might have been a mistake. It tasted awful, burning my throat. Just then, Danny showed up by my side.

"That's a twenty-five dollar cigar," he said. "Those things are valuable. You better smoke that whole thing down past here." He pointed to the label. He was kidding, but I didn't recognize it at the time.

"I will," I assured him. I thought he was mad at me. I told myself all I have to do is finish this cigar and I won't get in trouble.

But every puff was worse than the last. I started to feel sick, yet I pushed through it, putting up a great front.

After the party thinned, a small group left to get a sandwich at a place called Primanti Brothers in Oakland, the neighborhood where Danny had grown up. The place is famous for putting fries and coleslaw right on the sandwich. When we walked in, everyone recognized Dan. We ordered sandwiches, and after I took a bite, I felt like I was swallowing the cigar, even though I had finished smoking it a few hours before. Sitting among Danny, Jim Murphy and Michael Talbott, my taste buds were shot. In fact, I didn't taste food for the next two days.

Eight years later, I met up with Danny again and mentioned the cigar.

"You idiot," he laughed. "I was teaching you a lesson that night. Have you smoked a cigar since?"

"No," I told him. "And I never will."

"Yup. I thought if I could make you throw up during the first one, you'd never do it again. It's a stupid, expensive habit but I keep doing it."

Despite the cigar, that part of my teens was great. The following year, Dan was inducted into the Central Catholic High School Hall of Fame, and his guys called me again, inviting me along to sit at their table. It was another fun night. I was included in these events with adults, but I was just a kid in the group. I was "The Kid," actually.

When I later saw the movie *A Bronx Tale*, I identified with Calogero, Robert DeNiro's son, who was taken under the wing of Sonny. He was the kid who was invited places and allowed to glimpse an adult world that he didn't always understand. But he grew to love his role as a quiet witness. Just like me.

Danny and his crew were good men. None of them ever showed me anything other than guys being silly and having a good time. I remember their laughs and sarcastic banter. They were apart from their wives and girlfriends, but none of them tried to exploit that. I'm sure there were opportunities, but Dan never took advantage of his celebrity. He cared for those around him and tipped well. I didn't realize all that at the time, but I admire it now.

My health issues had opened doors into the lives of famous people. Being around that crew was magical. At that point in my life, it made cancer and diabetes all worth it.

∞

I wasn't always "The Kid." More often than not, I was just a kid, whether it was going to a concert or putting in my time in the classroom.

In February 1990, my senior year in high school, Public Enemy was an established hip hop group. The Syria Mosque in Oakland was a concert venue that seated 3,700 people. Between its construction in 1911 and being torn down in August 1991, it hosted hundreds of concerts and political events, including appearances by several presidents.

My friend Mike Mihaly loved Public Enemy, with Chuck D and Flavor Flav. Like me, he was a white kid from Woodland Hills, but that didn't matter. We listened to hip hop music. Some of the kids we grew up with asked why we liked that genre. In hindsight, we picked great music, because today Public Enemy is in the Rock and Roll Hall of Fame. Their work is acclaimed, politically charged with issues that affect African Americans, social struggles, and media criticism.

My mother was a Pittsburgh school teacher who taught me to love everybody. Color wasn't a dividing line to her or me. It mattered to some kids I grew up with, but by the time Woodland Hills had integrated, I was no longer hanging out with those kids. I think I've lived life the right way, accepting all people.

Mike's dad was a teacher. Back then, teachers used to have two jobs, and Mr. Mihaly worked for Aramark, the concession people. Mike didn't play sports with us, but he was a great kid, voted best dressed in our class. He went on to become a commander in the Navy. In high school, he had always promised that his dad could secure tickets to any event because of his second job.

"Mike, see if he can get us tickets to Public Enemy," I said.

"Two white kids at a Public Enemy concert? I don't think so."

"We'll get my buddies from the football team to go," I assured him. I started naming a crew of guys, and they were all black. One of them was Wayne the Train. With Wayne's size, we felt protected in any venue.

So his dad got us tickets, and Mike and a group of football players—both black and white—served as one another's security. We had great seats, third row center amid a sea of black faces. Sean Gilbert, a defensive lineman from Pitt who later played in the NFL, was part of the muscle hired to guard the performers. He stood with his back to the stage and told people to get off their chairs. The opening acts were Biz Markie, who had a hit the year before with "Just a Friend," followed by Queen Latifah.

We were kids at a concert. The place was going nuts and we thought it was great. When Public Enemy came out, we lost it. They were so good. At one point between songs, Chuck D looked out at the audience and raised a hand to shield his eyes from the glaring stage lights.

"Where are my white brothers and sisters?" he asked.

We started screaming. He looked down and pointed at us.

"Thank you for coming," he said. "Everyone, give it up to them for being here."

The room exploded with applause for us. We felt so special. I get goose bumps just talking about it. It was such a huge moment in my life, to be recognized by Chuck D for attending a hip hop show. That night validated that I belonged. People recognize color differences, but this doesn't have to be a bad thing—it can be used as a message of love. I've read that God wouldn't have painted the lilies in the field if he didn't believe in the importance of color.

A year and a half later, the Syria Mosque was torn down, but not before we attended another hip hop show there. My friends and I saw 3rd Bass, Big Daddy Kane and Digital Underground. Again, there weren't many white people there, but we didn't care. It was a great time.

When I got a Twitter account, I tweeted my memory of attending the Public Enemy concert on February 1, 1990. The tweet somehow made it to Chuck D. He read it and responded. Now Chuck D follows me on social media. The whole experience is just as amazing all these years later.

Meanwhile, in the classroom, I enrolled in an easy-breezy public speaking course during my senior year, confident I would pull an A. On the first day, the teacher, Hugh Coulter, told us we were all required to get up and give an introductory speech. Many of my classmates cringed.

"Does anyone know what an introductory speech is?" he asked.

I raised my hand, eager to answer. I was a bit cocky, confident because I'd given plenty of speeches. Maybe he sensed my arrogance. The teacher wanted to see me in action, so I was pulled to the front of the room and allotted two minutes.

"No problem," I said. I turned to my peers. I knew everybody in the room. "Hi, I'm Joe Lafferty. I'm here to speak about myself."

I met everyone's gaze and began talking. I gave a brief history of my life. After what felt like the appropriate time, I turned back to Mr. Coulter. "How's that? Is that two minutes?" I'd already spoken before crowds of professional athletes and donors, so for me, standing in front of a collection of fellow teenagers was a joke.

Throughout the year, I maintained an A in the course. Some Fridays, the teacher offered to let kids give an impromptu speech for extra credit. We had to pull a topic out of a hat and talk about it. I never needed any extra credit, but I liked doing it, so I volunteered, offering my points to a different kid every time.

Once I drew the subject "Russia." I was no expert on Russia, but I knew the trick is to bridge the topic to something that I could talk about that would connect with my listeners. I knew about Rocky and Ivan Drago. I had read that Raiders quarterback Todd Marinovich worked with a Russian trainer. Off I'd go, and when the time ended, I held everyone's attention without really saying anything about Russia. I could give a speech on anything: physics, thermodynamics. It didn't matter. I have the gift of gab. Addressing an audience is second nature to me.

I was so confident as a speaker that all through high school, I participated in the statewide Junior Achievement contest. Yes, it was nerdy, but I won three years in a row. I competed against the same core group of kids every year. I got to know all the people that ran it. My senior year, the competition was held in Mount Airy, in the Poconos. I decided to go all out and speak about my experience with cancer.

Yes, I pulled the C card to win a contest. The scholarship money helped pay for college.

A few months after graduating from high school, my friend Eddie Balkovec died of the same cancer that I had survived.

Eddie was an only child from Swissvale, a nice kid who played on the baseball team. He wasn't a star. He was good at academics and had a nice sense of humor. We were still in high school when I learned that he had contracted cancer. I heard the news from someone else, then sought him out.

"Why didn't you tell me sooner?" I asked. I was almost angry that he had excluded me from his diagnosis. Everyone knew I had survived, after all. It was a key part of my life. Maybe I could have provided counsel for him.

The back of his head was shaved, and Eddie was given radiation in his lymph nodes. He didn't share much with me about his prognosis.

In mid-September of my freshman year at college, I got a call from Chris's mom, Kate Uram.

"You need to sit down," she warned me.

My initial thought was that something bad had happened to my mom. But Kate wouldn't be the one contacting me if there was a problem. Then my mind flashed to Chris. Was he okay?

"Eddie Balkovec just died," Kate said softly.

He had gone to sleep on the couch watching a baseball game. Word came that he had been sick from chemotherapy, but until then, all indications were that Eddie was beating cancer.

Services were scheduled that weekend, but I planned to travel with my college football team, so I didn't return to Pittsburgh for the funeral. In retrospect, it was a selfish decision, but with my history, I didn't want to look at Mrs. Balkovec or be around all those people. How could a mother endure the loss of her son? I convinced myself that I stayed away because of football, but that wasn't true... I never even took the field that Saturday.

The next time I was home, I visited the Balkovec's house. I talked with his mom and dad, and we cried together. I asked where

Eddie was buried so I could visit his grave. It was the same cemetery where my grandparents are interred. I drove there the next day, and coincidentally, his parents pulled in shortly after me. They hadn't known I would be coming then—they were simply there for a private visit—so it was uncomfortable all over again.

Eddie was just eighteen. His death was tough, and it affected me. My cancer had allowed me to spend time with famous people, to become "The Kid." Eddie barely had time to be a kid.

Why did Eddie die? Why him and not me?

I still don't have a good answer.

"Don't Take Life for Granted"

—Dan Marino

DAN MARINO HAS FOND MEMORIES of fundraising events held in his hometown back when he was the NFL's star quarterback. He grew up in a blue-collar household in the South Oakland neighborhood of Pittsburgh, where his father, Dan Sr., worked at the Pittsburgh Post-Gazette, mostly night shifts, filling coin boxes on street corners around the city. Dan Sr. became active in the Italian-American Sports Hall of Fame, and enlisted his famous son to help raise money for scholarships. That led to further philanthropic causes.

Born in 1961, a teenaged Dan quickly garnered name recognition for his athletic success. He attended Central Catholic High School, where he excelled in both baseball and football, being named a Parade All-American. Drafted by the Kansas City Royals to play baseball, he chose instead to focus on football at the University of Pittsburgh, where he posted three consecutive 11-1 seasons before his senior year. He was selected by the Miami Dolphins near the end of the first round in the 1983 NFL draft. Today that draft remains unique for its distinguished class of quarterbacks. Six were picked in the first round, including John Elway, Jim Kelly, Ken O'Brien, Tony Eason, and Todd Blackledge. Three of them—Elway, first overall; Kelly, fourteenth; and Marino, twenty-seventh—are members of the NFL Hall of Fame.

In the mid-1980s, during his charity work in Pittsburgh, Marino encountered fifteen-year-old Joey Lafferty. By then, Marino was twenty-seven and an established NFL star.

"I got involved with the Leukemia Society through a friend of my dad's," Marino recalled. "We raised some pretty good money, and those were fun times. That's where I got to know Joey. He was one of the kids who worked with us."

Many of Marino's NFL contemporaries attended the golf tournament. Several quarterbacks from that era, including Kelly and Boomer Esiason, hosted their own charity golf tournaments during the offseason; in reciprocation, Marino attended as their guest.

"The golf tournaments were a big party," Marino said. "We were rivals on the field but friends off it. In the summer, it was like going on tour. It was a way to get to know one another outside of football. Guys would come to town a couple days early, and we had a big dinner the night before."

Kids spent the weekend interacting with their sports heroes. Most had stars in their eyes. Because of that, Joe has clear memories of those golf tournaments. Without prompting, he can compile an extensive list of the celebrities he encountered. He felt like a chosen son when Marino asked Joe to address him as "Danny."

"That's how I know if somebody is from Pittsburgh," Marino laughed. "Many people call me Dan, but if you're from Pittsburgh, you call me Danny."

Marino recognized that the golf tournaments were a special opportunity for the young people who battled health issues.

"There were photos taken of Joey with Joe Namath and Terry Bradshaw," Marino remembered. "Guys like Joe Montana and many of the Pittsburgh Steelers came. So it was a great experience for Joey and the other kids we brought in. It allowed them to be part of something."

Marino, according to Joe, went above and beyond the standard celebrity role. Rather than being a sports hero who remained on a pedestal, distant and unapproachable, Marino took an active role, spending time with the kids. Marino grinned when reminded of the time he insisted that young Joe was required to finish fellow Pittsburgh native and coach Chuck Knox's expensive cigar.

"I was just messing with him," Marino said.

He also dragged Joe along when he and his friends wound up at Primanti Brothers, a renowned eatery near Dan's childhood home.

"We'd go there late at night because it's such a great spot," Marino recalled. "They make sandwiches like sausage, egg and cheese with coleslaw and French fries in a bun. The French fries are in the sandwich. It's one of those deals where after a long day, it helps to soak up some of the juice."

Marino retired just before his thirty-eighth birthday after the 1999 season, and was inducted into the NFL Hall of Fame in 2005. He held or still holds dozens of NFL quarterback records. He worked as an analyst for CBS's pregame show from 2002-2013. Now living in Fort Lauderdale, Marino has six children with his wife, Claire. In 2014, he returned to the Miami Dolphins to work as a special advisor.

He takes great pride in the fact that he helped inspire Joe.

"We've stayed in touch here and there over the years," Marino said. "It's hard to believe what Joe has overcome. With what he's been through, you have to love the fact of what he's been able to accomplish in life. It shows you the kind of spirit he has."

As part of Marino's long-standing commitment to philanthropy, he founded the Dan Marino Foundation in 1992 after his son Michael was diagnosed with autism. That organization has raised millions of dollars for people with neurodevelopment disabilities.

"You try to treat people the way you want to be treated," Marino reflected. "That's what life is all about. I tell my kids all the time, you've got to treat everyone right. It doesn't matter who they are or what their circumstances are. You look at the challenges that Joe has been through, and hope that you don't take life for granted, although to a certain extent we probably all do."

CHAPTER 5

Mercy Hurts

IN THE FALL OF 1990, I began studying at Mercyhurst College in Erie, Pennsylvania. Located on the south shore of Lake Erie, the campus was two hours north of home. I majored in marketing and was excited to play H-back on the football team.

Mercyhurst was a non-scholarship Division 2 football program, which meant that we played Division 3 schools. Although there were no athletic scholarships, many of my teammates benefited from an Egan Grant. Mother M. Borgia Egan founded Mercyhurst in 1926. Until the late 1960s, it was an all-girls school. Twenty-plus years after men were first accepted as students, news apparently hadn't reached everyone. When I told people from home where I was attending school, I received a few strange looks.

"It's co-ed now," I explained. "I'm playing football."

Egan grants were a substitute for athletic scholarships. If a kid stopped playing football, his grant mysteriously disappeared.

The size of the grant was based on financial need, but also the level of interest the college had in each player. Playing football got me some money, and I also had a hefty scholarship from Junior Achievement. From my experiences as a public speaker, I knew I wanted to major in business. I liked to talk, and was good at it.

Mercyhurst offered concentrations in sales and public relations. While I was there, they opened a track called sports organizational management. Sports marketing was just beginning as a career path, but there were holes in the curriculum. Athletic trainers were graduating without the skills to manage a budget, so the new degree crossed majors. Marketing students had to take anatomy or biology for background. They needed a general understanding of the human body if they planned to work in athletics. Likewise, trainers had to succeed in basic business courses. Psychology was required because the back end of marketing is knowing how people think.

Mercyhurst is a small Catholic school—2200 or so students—that operated on trimesters. Although I've never liked cold weather, I was drawn to the practical experience of my professors. They weren't pressured to publish papers. Several business teachers ran consulting services or accounting firms. I enjoyed learning about their real life successes and failures.

Because of the school's size, I quickly became known across campus as the kid who didn't drink. I was diabetic, after all. That year I watched fellow students get drunk and be promiscuous. A few guys even hit their girlfriends, then attended church on Sunday. That didn't sit well. I had been raised Catholic, taught that right and wrong were absolutes and most often the easy way was not the proper way. Attending a Catholic college pushed me further from the church when it should have drawn me closer. I allowed the actions of a few to damage my faith.

For nine months of my freshman year, I dated a girl named Chrissy. I was over the moon for her. She was sweet, with dark hair and dark eyes. For a while, everything was great. She nicknamed me "Sweet Hips" because I was agile and liked to dance.

Playing football, however, was less great. We went winless my first year. The offense was designed so H-backs and tight ends split out. If we set on the offensive line, it was a two-point stance. In high school, I had gone inside to block, so I was comfortable and experienced. But doing it from a two-point stance felt awkward. Mostly I played on the "hands team" during kickoffs. Relegated to special teams, I traveled to a few away games, but didn't play often. With our record, there weren't many onside kicks coming toward us.

At Woodland Hills, we had a winning program, so I was unfamiliar with frequent losing. It wasn't fun. One of my teammates, David Kless, was a kid from Cleveland who had attended a small Catholic high school where they hadn't won a game in four seasons. While we started 0-7, and his former school turned things around, going 4-0. He played five straight years without a win. We kept him on suicide watch.

The good times didn't last with Chrissy and I. We ultimately broke up because of something stupid. We had stepped away from each other for a week before she phoned me on a Saturday night and claimed she wanted to get back together. Earlier that afternoon, I had made out with a different girl, and I never told her about it. One of Chrissy's friends knew, so I thought I better come clean. When I finally did, it was a sorry scene.

"You should have told me," she said.

"I know. I was afraid you wouldn't take me back."

She didn't want to date me any longer. As I left, she said softly, "Take care, Sweet Hips." It was heartrending for an eighteen-year-old.

∞

Around this time, I struggled in the relationship with my father. I know he loves me and he often showed affection. He was never afraid to hug or kiss me. While I grew up, he worked on cars in the garage with his friends and attended car shows on weekends. Sometimes, if I mentioned liking a car, he'd bring me home a die-cast metal version of that model. I once told him I hoped to get a Mercedes Gullwing when I grew up.

"You better get a good job," was all he said.

Despite the affection he demonstrates, he is authoritarian. He was never abusive, but as a kid, I retained a healthy fear of him. When he raised his voice, I shuddered. In our church, there was a soundproof room for parents to take children who cried. When we were little, he never took my sister and me there. We were expected to behave and not act out, sitting in the general congregation. For a long time I didn't know how to talk to him.

That year at Mercyhurst, I sometimes wrote letters to my dad telling him what I was going through, frustrations I felt with him or with life in general. I put down in words what I really felt. Sometimes boys hold that back from their dad. It reminded me of the old *M*A*S*H** TV show where the psychologist narrated an episode as a letter to Sigmund Freud. My letters served as an internal monologue, circling back to what I knew my dad would tell me.

I never sent the letters. Years later, I purposely destroyed them. I never even told Dad that I wrote to him. There are times when I don't know how deep he really is. The summer after my first year at college, I not only challenged his authority, but tried to topple it in one fell swoop.

I was home for a short break when Dad and I got into a heated argument about something forgettable. We had such different views about life. In the living room, we began yelling at each other, and I kept inching closer to him, eventually chest-bumping him like an umpire. When he went to push me, I flipped him around and shoved him down on the couch with his arms pinned to his chest. I even drew back to hit him, but instinctively stopped.

I froze, releasing him, then backed away and tore out of the house.

I ran up the road, legs pounding for what seemed like miles, sobbing uncontrollably the entire time. Eventually, the tears subsided, and I walked back to my house, feeling empty and small.

After opening the front door, I found dad sitting in the living room. I was tentative, but he was calm and controlled.

"Please sit down," he said. I did. We stared at each other for what seemed like a long time.

"It doesn't matter what you can do with your body," he told me in measured words. "I'm your father. I'll always be your father. You're my son, and I love you. But you live here, and this is our house. We make the rules, and you need to follow them. It doesn't matter if you can beat me up."

I didn't know how to respond. Maybe he didn't know what else to say. He tried to lighten the mood.

"So you can beat me up. Maybe mom can beat you up. Who knows? Does that change our relationship? Of course not." He kept a straight face.

I knew guys who had been kicked out of their house for less than what I had just done. On his eighteenth birthday, the kid across the street stayed out all night to come home the following morning to two packed suitcases and a father who gave him fifty bucks and sent him away.

"You don't have to go anywhere," my dad said. "I'm not throwing you out. But I am going to insist you follow our rules, because that's how it should be."

And that was it. The matter was resolved. I was never punished, never grounded or ordered to leave. There's no question that ours was—and maybe still is—a complex relationship. We disagree at times, even today. But alongside my mom, Dad made me believe that I would beat cancer, and live the life of a regular kid. I'll always love him for his ability to be reasonable and see the big picture.

I stayed at Mercyhurst for the summer after my freshman year. Despite my failed romance, I really loved college then. But my temper got the best of me, and I was eventually suspended for fighting.

During the summer of 1991, Mercyhurst hosted the Pennsylvania Governor's School for Excellence. This was a state-sponsored summer enrichment program for smart kids, and there were different programs at various colleges across Pennsylvania. The University of Pittsburgh hosted international studies. Wharton hosted a business program. Mercyhurst welcomed young people who studied arts such as sculpting, painting, singing, and dancing. It was a neat mix of kids.

There was also an influx of soon-to-be freshman. I hung out with several football players, guys who had just graduated high school and planned to play that fall, but hadn't taken a snap yet. Even though I was only eighteen, I was a veteran with a year of college experience.

One of my friends, Claire, was studying to be a teacher. She invited me to a dance at the Athletic Center one Thursday evening. It was a Governor's School event. I promised to bring some guys over.

That night, I approached the building with a few freshman. We started to walk in, and a young professor blocked us from the entrance. I later learned that he taught at a different college but was on campus as part of the Governor's school. He was a few years older than me. I'd guess he was 25, but certainly not more than 30.

"Hey, hey, hey," he said. raising a hand to halt us. "I don't think you're allowed in there."

I'm a very literal person, so I noticed that he didn't "think" we were allowed inside.

"No, it's okay," I explained. "Claire invited us."

He sized up the situation, pausing to study us. "I'm in charge," he said. "So I know you're not allowed in there."

"Well, listen, Claire told us to stop by. She's an instructor here."

He shook his head.

"She is," I insisted. "She invited us in. If you think I'm making this up, could you walk inside there and get her? I'm sure she can vouch for us."

He glared at me. "They're high school girls. Just get out of here."

I was a 205-pound, testosterone-filled football player. I wouldn't turn nineteen until September. But with my baby face, I appeared even younger than I was.

"I heard you the first couple times," I told him. "I know they're high school girls inside. I'm not here to see high school girls." I pointed to the guys with me. "These guys are just out of high school. We came to see my friend. But you don't want us here? Fine. We're going."

I turned and began to step away. The young professor had a crowd around him, which is when some people turn bold.

"Yeah, just get the f--- out of here," he spat.

Without blinking, I pivoted, ran at him, and tackled him. We were both on the ground, and I punched his torso a few times. I didn't have a chance to swing at his face before my guys grabbed me and dragged me off him. The whole incident lasted only a few seconds. I'm sure the professor stood up and thought, what just happened?

Campus security arrived and wanted an explanation, so I told them. No one was hurt. I thought the incident was over.

A couple weeks later, my football coach informed me that I needed to report to Dr. Brown, who handled school discipline. This was not good. My roommate had gotten in trouble the previous year, so I had met Dr. Brown as part of that incident.

I entered Dr. Brown's office. He had the heat turned up so it felt like one thousand degrees. He also burned cigarettes in an ashtray, filling the room with smoke. He might have been trying to set the mood for a "good cop" interrogation.

"Joe, Joe, Joe," he lamented, shaking his head. "Tell me what happened."

I told him exactly what had occurred.

"You were walking away?" Brown asked. "So why did you turn and run at him?"

"I don't know," I shrugged. "I felt like I was being disrespected."

Brown stared at me through the haze. "What would you do if you thought I disrespected you?"

I blinked. I knew Dr. Brown; he had earned my respect. "That would be different."

He nodded and shuffled papers. "I don't know what's going to happen. This will have to go before a board."

So during the third week of school, I was sent home for three trimesters. I was banned for that fall, the following spring, and the fall after that. Although we were no longer dating, Chrissy visited my dorm to help me pack. I held fast to the idea we would reconnect in the future.

"You know you'll be okay, right?" she asked.

Her presence served as small consolation, but no, I did not know that. I envisioned dark times ahead.

Mom drove alone to Erie to pick me up. Dad didn't come, which was unusual. It was a quiet car ride home. Back in my parents' house, I was unpacking clothes when Dad stumbled in. He didn't speak, instead heading right to bed. My dad is not a big drinker—he'd sometimes have a beer or two with his buddies when they worked on cars—but that night he had been drinking. It scared me to think that he needed a stiff belt of booze to deal with his prodigal son.

I vowed right away that I was going back to Mercyhurst. I'd wait out the ban and then return where I belonged. I certainly wasn't going to let them beat me. Of course, getting kicked out was my fault, but I saw this as a challenge. Being a fighter has kept me alive, but sometimes I don't know when to stop. Anyone who knows me recognizes that I can be unbearable in an argument. I can elevate a debate to the level of life and death. I was going to win this one.

I enrolled in classes at CCAC, the Community College of Allegheny County in Monroeville. I also sold suits on commission at the Monroeville Mall. I worked part time and lived at home, but things remained strained with my dad.

The Currys were a nearby family who knew about our tensions. Bill Curry had coached midget football when I played. Years later, I watched his team practice when he asked me to help him coach the 10-year-olds. Eventually, I was invited to dinner at their home. Sandy, Bill's wife, is an amazing cook. They had three kids: Billy, who is six years younger than I am, and Wendy is a year younger than her brother. The littlest, Adam, is ten years younger than I am. Adam was my buddy, following me around all the time. I called him my little brother. To put space between my dad and me,

I moved in with the Currys. They were such a loving family and it was generous of them to open their home to me.

Of course, I went back to Woodland Hills to talk with Coach Novak. I visited him in his office, told him what had transpired at Mercyhurst. In the fall of 1992, he had two openings for position coaches. He hired me as quarterbacks coach. Joey Samsa, a classmate and close friend during high school, was hired as defensive backs coach. I was only nineteen, about to turn twenty. I like to tell people I'm the youngest assistant coach ever in the Western Pennsylvania Interscholastic Athletic League.

My job was to coach ninth-graders. After their practice ended, I walked over to the varsity field and helped out. I knew many of the students already. I was three years removed from being a player on that very field. I was a young punk and dressed like the kids. Part of that was practical. We didn't have many quarterbacks on the roster, so I'd throw warmups with them then change into different clothes before kickoff. Heading into games, an opposing coach mistook me for a player more than once.

There were future Division 1 athletes on that 1992 team. I learned more from them than they learned from me. The challenge was to get them to buy into a system and embrace a style. Coach Novak's mentality is to treat every player like he's your son. I wanted to be a drill sergeant, but I was too young to pull it off. Later in my coaching career it became easier, but at this stage it was difficult.

That said, I loved coaching. The first time someone called me "coach," I knew it was special. Until then, I had been a son, a brother, a nephew. None of those were relationships I had chosen. I was too young to be a father or a husband, so at nineteen years old, I thought "coach" was the best title to have.

Mercyhurst's fall trimester ended at Thanksgiving, then after a ten-day vacation, classes resumed for three weeks heading into

Christmas break. I took my coaching salary and drove back to Erie to secure an apartment. The football bug still burned and I wanted to play. Sadly, that was my primary motivation to return.

Once I walked on campus, things just weren't the same. I had lost track with many classmates because they were at a different point in their academic careers. Upper classmen had first choice for campus apartments, but due to my suspension, I wasn't allowed to live there. The system left me behind—deservedly, I can say in retrospect.

The football team had a new head coach, Joe Kimble, a good man who had played college ball and wrestled at Syracuse. My position coach was a first-timer who had played at Duke. I had just been a first-year coach at Woodland Hills. I watched our coach take things personally and hand out random discipline. He told stories that began with "when I was your age." In him I saw all the things I had done wrong while trying to lead young men.

Until then, I had loved playing football. One day, I realized that I no longer did. The season was underway, and I walked onto the turf for a weekday practice in pads. An unfamiliar feeling overcame me. I dreaded starting the session. That had never happened before, regardless of where I was on the depth chart. I didn't want to play football halfway. I wasn't good enough to give a partial effort. I had maxed out my potential—and I never had too much to begin with.

I turned around, strode back to the locker room, and got undressed. I walked away from playing. It was a decision that reflected so much about my life around that time. I was disillusioned and lost.

A few years ago, I was typing the word Mercyhurst but misspelled it as "Mercy hurts." That gave me a chuckle. I wanted to have a positive experience there, but that's not how I remember it.

I could have done well, really drilling down into academics. But I was young and made mistakes. If I knew then what I know now, I shouldn't have even played college football. I wear it proudly, but committing to that was not a good choice.

And then there was my pride. I didn't want to "lose" after being kicked out. At the time, I thought Chrissy would become an integral part of my life. Those feelings were false. After my suspension, I should have moved on, but I didn't know any better. So really, the bad feelings about Mercyhurst are all on me.

My life seemed to be whirling away. In the spring of 1994, I was twenty-one and had already experienced so many things. But as my college classmates were scheduled to graduate, I lagged behind. I planned to return that summer and remain on campus until I earned my degree.

Then I connected with Tony Scarpino, an old friend who played college football in Memphis, and that goal was knocked sideways. Life took a completely different turn.

CHAPTER 6

That's How I Got to Memphis

ON THE NIGHT OF FRIDAY, June 17, 1994, I sat in a banquet facility west of Pittsburgh, in Aliquippa, watching with fascination as the White Ford Bronco rolled along a California highway. Helicopters filmed a squadron of police cars in slow pursuit while people lined the streets and overpasses, cheering "Juice! Juice!" Like the rest of the country, I was riveted by the O.J. Simpson saga. Could this really be happening?

Tony Scarpino, Dave Mike, and I were three eager twenty-one-year-olds. We sat in a conference room behind the bar, nursing drinks. A few other guys played cards. Employees paced, serving food and keeping a watchful eye on the TV. We didn't know anyone there, but between the O.J. chase and Mike Ditka's anticipated arrival, the room hummed with excitement.

Mike Ditka. The former Bears coach and star tight end. We knew he was coming. He was an Aliquippa native, and this party was the kickoff for his weekend golf tournament. When he walked in, all eyes pivoted toward the door. Everyone paid attention.

With his square hair and bushy mustache, Ditka looked every bit like a legend. He wore loafers and light socks, as if he belonged on the cover of a magazine. The man had a presence. He was only six feet one or six feet two. I had expected him to be taller. But Ditka had the broadest shoulders I had ever seen. They were like a refrigerator. He must have been three feet wide.

Why were we there? Our friend Dave Mike had been a star high school quarterback from Aliquippa and now attended Maryland. He was golfing in the tournament that weekend, so he invited Tony and me to accompany him on Friday night.

As we talked, Tony Scarpino lobbied hard for me to spend the summer in Memphis. I had known Tony for years. He attended Gateway High School in Monroeville, just up the road from Woodland Hills. Although we both played football, we first met at a track meet as high school sophomores when I lost my footing in mud while throwing a javelin. It veered off course and nearly impaled a star athlete from Tony's school. (I apologized up and down, and was quickly forgiven. But everyone kept an eye on me the rest of the day.)

"Man, that was crazy," said the dark-haired kid behind me. "You could have killed him, bro."

Tony and I have been friends since. Our paths crossed at football camps throughout high school, and my senior year I dated a girl from Gateway, so we attended the same parties and formal events. Tony stands at six foot four, has dark skin and dark eyes, and his arm was a cannon. He has a magnetic personality and has always been down to earth. He attended Maryland to play football, then transferred to Memphis, where he served as backup quarterback. The prior fall, when the starting QB was injured,

Tony had taken the field against Miami. The Hurricanes—featuring my high school teammate Tirrell Greene—had a monster defense in 1993, only allowing four passing touchdowns all season. Two of them came from Tony, who threw to future NFL receiver Isaac Bruce.

After watching that performance, I reached out to Tony to congratulate him and reconnect. While we started hanging out, I mentioned that I was hoping to find a summer internship in marketing.

"Come to Memphis," he suggested. "Work for the university sports department. I'll make some calls."

"Sure," I agreed, not thinking much about it. Charming as he was, how could Tony land an internship for me?

Meanwhile, the three of us kept an eye on Ditka. When we saw him across the room, we giggled like schoolgirls, impressed that grown men flocked to him. It was exciting and a little intimidating. We were just kids and he was a major celebrity. Yes, I had befriended famous people, but many of them were still playing football, only to be elevated into sports history years later, after they retired. Ditka was already a legendary player and coach. Working his way around the room, Ditka ended up at our table, where he nodded then sat down next to Tony.

"Hey boys, where's the party tonight?" he wondered.

Shaking his hand was like grabbing a brick. He asked about each of us and chatted for a few minutes. This was another brush with greatness. I beamed, knowing I was spending time with an iconic coach. It remains one of the unique moments of my life.

A few days later, Tony called to pass along the phone number for John Bowers, the director of marketing for Memphis State University. I hadn't put much faith in Tony's promise to land me a summer internship, but through the good-old-boy network, I was offered a job on the spot. Traveling to Memphis hadn't been my plan, but the more I considered, the more it made sense. I could live in a dorm cheaply, so I packed enough clothes for a five- or six-week stint. In a short time, everything had come together.

My biggest success that summer came when I secured a Nike sponsorship for a "meet the team" event hosted by the Memphis football squad. We expected several hundred kids to attend with their parents, and sought sponsors to help defray the cost. I had always been drawn to Nike products, developing several mock advertising campaigns for them during business classes at Mercyhurst. I also knew the company had a distribution center in Memphis. I began making contacts through "The Finish Line" store at the local mall. First I found a buyer rep, who eventually put me in touch with Nike's community relations department. I learned that Nike had a program called P.L.A.Y.—Participate in the Lives of American Youth. Our event, I explained, was about exposing kids and their families to exercise through our student athletes. The representative was intrigued, asking what he could send us.

"What have you got?" I asked boldly

They offered 500 T-shirts and mini-footballs with their printed logo. We were allowed to silk screen our own image on the back of the shirts. In exchange for their gifts, we agreed to hang a Nike banner at our event and send them publicity pictures.

My boss, John Bowers, was thrilled, as was the assistant director of marketing, Bill Lansden. I had just secured my first sponsorship, adding glitz and sparkle for the kids visiting the university. No money changed hands in the trade. The project had been a home run. I was young and cocky, confident that everything in my career would run this smoothly.

There were two newsworthy events on campus that summer: Memphis State University officially changed its name to the University of Memphis, and star basketball player Anfernee "Penny" Hardaway spent time practicing with the team. Hardaway had been born and raised in Memphis and attended the university before being drafted into the NBA third overall the year before. He had finished a strong rookie season with the Orlando Magic and had been named to the league's all-rookie team.

There had been dozens of Penny sightings throughout July, but I had yet to see him. I laughed when southerners pronounced his name "Pinny." I knew that the basketball team practiced during the day at the campus arena, which was really just a glorified high school gym. Games were played in The Pyramid, located downtown.

After spending lunch hour distributing student ticket information at the Union, I headed to the gym. My plan was to arrive early, sneak a nap in the last row of bleachers, and hope to see Penny participate in the afternoon shoot around with the men's team. Crossing the parking lot, I noticed a new maroon Lexus sedan with an Orlando Magic license frame. Could it be? Could Penny be there already?

In the lobby, the smoked glass gym doors were locked, but I heard dribbling inside. It didn't sound like a team. The echoing bounce suggested only one ball. Yes, doors were barred, but the edge of one was crooked. I gave a good tug and it swung wide, screeching loudly. At the far end of the court, Penny Hardaway sank a three-point shot, then turned toward the sound. I was nervous, and must have looked out of place framed by the doorway.

"Hi," I said tentatively. "I work in the athletic department and I just wanted to meet you."

I knew it sounded corny. We each strolled halfway across the floor and he shook my hand. He was long and lean, standing at six foot seven.

"Anfernee, my name is Joe. Tony Scarpino is my cousin."

Tony and I are not related, but we told everyone that we were. Football players referred to me as "Scarpino's cousin."

"The quarterback?" Hardaway asked.

I nodded. "I've been working here for the summer, and before I head back to school I just wanted to meet you and shake your hand." I paused, aware of how empty the gym was, then looked toward the basket where he had been shooting. "Since there's no one else here, want me to rebound for you?"

"Okay."

Penny shot from all over the floor, and put a backspin on the ball so that after it swished through netting, it bounced back to him. I hardly needed to rebound. He drained nearly every shot. When you're one of the top point guards in the NBA, you don't miss often.

After a time, he passed the ball to me. "Your turn," he said.

I moved out to the shooting circle and made my first shot, then proceeded to miss the next three. Laughing, I made two more, followed by another that bounced off the rim. I could miss shots on my own time. I didn't want to waste his.

"Back to you," I said, sending him a bounce pass.

He kept making baskets until Memphis players entered through the rear locker room. Some of the guys recognized me. As they lined up to practice, I knew it was time to leave.

"Hey," Penny called as I walked away. I turned toward him. "You got anything you want me to sign?"

"No," I shook my head. "I'm good." He was only a year older than me, but Penny was already an international star, and we had just shot hoops together. I knew his autograph would never measure up to this memory. "But thanks for the shots."

Memphis' large campus was a good fit for me, and I loved the sweltering heat. It would require another year to finish my degree at Mercyhurst, but as August progressed, I dreaded heading north to "dreary Erie." Most of my friends there had graduated already, and I wasn't going to play football, so I didn't expect to have much of an identity. I even looked different. Because I stopped lifting weights that summer, I had lost mass and muscles.

John Bowers sensed my reluctance to leave. He brought me into his office and stared at me across the desk.

"Why are you going back to Mercyhurst when you love working here?" he asked.

I didn't have a good answer, but knew he was suggesting that I stay. It was a compliment, the result of a job well done. But money was a factor. Yes, I loved the Memphis sports department, but I hadn't been paid during my summer internship. Nor was I a Tennessee resident, so enrolling at Memphis instead of Mercyhurst would amount to an extra $10,000 per year. There was no way to remain. Unless...

"Find a way to get me in-state tuition, and I'm yours," I said.

I never thought it could happen, but John promised to look into it. When I registered for classes a few days later, I was designated as an "in state" student. I don't know what strings were pulled to make that happen. I accepted a minimum-wage position with the athletic department and made up my own title: Athletic Marketing Assistant. I even had cards printed. There was low pay, no office, no desk, no phone line. But working a job I loved and holding my own business card made me feel legitimate. I was a Memphis Tiger now. Yes, this was Elvis' town, but I felt like a king.

That fall was exciting and momentous. There was always something going on. Between the draws of college sports and Graceland, celebrities regularly passed through Memphis. I often found myself in the right place to interact with many of them.

I performed a variety of tasks with the athletic department. John and Bill loaned me out to coaches they didn't want to deal with, mostly in women's sports. I stuffed recruiting letters into envelopes, hurled T-shirts into sparse crowds, even served as lifeguard when the women's volleyball team trained in the pool.

I loved working men's basketball games at The Pyramid. The iconic building opened in 1991 along the shore of the Mississippi River. Although it has since transformed into a Bass Pro Outlet, my time behind the scenes there was intoxicating. Each game was a spectacle, featuring a live tiger in a cage. Sometimes, we would invite two celebrities to shoot foul shots at either end of the court. Whichever person won, that side of the arena was given free T-shirts. Other times, we navigated a blimp that flew above the seats, dropping gift certificates to fans below. We even commandeered a sling shot that had been used at football games, launching prizes into the crowd.

The Memphis Dance team had won national championships, and they entertained fans at halftime. I had a friend who coached young girls in dance competitions, so one night I organized an exhibition of nine- and ten-year-old dancers to perform after the college team. As I stood on the floor watching, someone tapped my shoulder. I turned to see Loren Roberts, one of my favorite professional golfers, extending a hand to me.

"You're Joe, right?" he asked. "I'm Loren and two of those little girls are mine. I've been told you're the guy to thank for making this happen."

I had followed his career on the PGA tour, admiring his calm demeanor. I thanked him, then gave credit to the varsity dancers who had coached his daughters. He asked where I was from.

"Pittsburgh," I told him. "In fact, I don't live far from the Oakmont golf course." He chuckled and asked if I ever played there. I confessed I wasn't much of a golfer.

When I arrived back at my dorm, friends who had watched the game on TV told me that the camera followed Roberts while announcers delivered halftime stats, and they had seen our exchange. It was only a brief conversation, but to me it was another notable encounter.

Before sporting events, media members gathered in the press room for a pre-game meal. One day early in my tenure, my boss, Bill Lansden, introduced me to an older gentleman with frizzy brown hair. He had a pleasant face, resembling a better looking version of Gene Wilder. He looked like he might have been a 1950s actor.

"This is George," he said, and we shook hands. "He works in radio." I was polite, but there was food on the other side of the room, so I didn't think much about George. During the next several months, we said hi to each other and shared simple banter. He always seemed to be in a good mood.

In the middle of the season, John Bowers held a meeting to brainstorm new promotions. One was to find the best Elvis impersonator to shoot free throws in conjunction with the King's birthday on January 8. We bantered ideas about who the imposter should shoot against.

"Another Elvis?" I suggested.

"Maybe we can convince George to shoot against him," John mused.

"George?" I asked. "Why George?"

John looked at me with lowered brows.

"George Klein was Elvis' best friend. In fact, he was best man in his wedding."

My jaw dropped. No one knew that when Elvis Presley died in 1977, I was about to turn five years old. I was so upset that I insisted to my mom that we send his parents a sympathy card. I later received a return card signed by V. E. Presley, Elvis's father. I have always loved Elvis Presley and still do.

I thought John was toying with me. He frequently called me "Yankee Bastard" as a term of endearment, so it wouldn't surprise me if this was a joke at my expense. Later that day I crossed campus to the library, seeking proof that George was the man they claimed. After ten minutes spooling microfiche, I had it. George and Elvis had met in eighth grade at Humes High School in North Memphis. There was a photo of them standing beside each other, smiling. George had become a disc jockey.

At the next home game, I couldn't take my eyes off him. George didn't know that I watched him the entire night. I never said a word to him about Elvis. That was his past life, I reasoned, and George had continued his career in radio. He probably didn't want to be defined by the old days. (George later published two books about his friendship with Elvis.) Maybe, too, I felt a little dumb for not knowing. I still can't fathom how much history he experienced. To think I had considered him just an ordinary guy.

George did end up shooting foul shots against Joe Kent, who played the third Elvis in the movie *Honeymoon in Vegas*. It's said that if you spend time in Memphis, you'll come away with an Elvis story. I think mine is pretty good. In fact, the first time I shared it was with the actor Ethan Hawke. One good story led to another.

While I was running around for the athletic department, I transitioned into several side jobs. One was at Silky O'Sullivan's Irish Pub on Beale Street. I had already hung out in the bar, and decided that I could earn extra cash by working there. Silky, the owner, was a heavyset guy with a lively personality. He could be found hunched atop a barstool near the front door, acting like he knew everyone. When I approached him about a job, he asked why he should hire me.

"Because my name is Joseph Patrick Michael Lafferty," I said. "I'll be a server or bar back or mop floors. Whatever you need."

Silky looked me up and down. "You're hired," he said. "Go inside and talk to my wife." I started as a waiter, and tended bar on Sundays.

One hot afternoon I was assigned to the patio. I was inside appreciating the air conditioning when two customers walked straight through the seating area and went outside. There was no one else around. A waitress nudged me and said, "That guy looks like Ethan Hawke."

I went through the door to take their order. Both guys removed their sunglasses, and one sure did look like Ethan Hawke. He had already starred in *Dead Poet's Society* and *Reality Bites*. I giggled, looking down, certain it was the actor. When I turned sheepish, he asked if something was wrong. Then they ordered beers, so I asked to see their IDs.

"I'm sure you get this a lot," I said. "But do you know you look like Ethan Hawke?"

He smiled. "Yeah, I hear that often."

"Is that because you're him?" I asked. I already knew the answer.

"Yeah. My friend and I are driving cross country and wanted to see Graceland. Do you still need my ID?"

"No," I said. "I know how old you are."

His friend protested. "Forget that! If I have to show mine, you better look at his too!"

So I checked both their IDs. At the mention of Graceland, I relayed my story about George Klein. Maybe he was acting, but

Hawke thought my adventure was the coolest thing. I didn't spend a lot of time with him, but before leaving, he personalized the check: "Hey Joe, take care. Ethan Hawke." I thought it unusual that he printed everything, even his name.

Later that spring, I was off duty one night at Silky's with some guys I knew from the Memphis football team. A new kid sat down at our table, and I noticed the beautiful girl accompanying him. His name was Peyton Manning, a young college quarterback from the University of Tennessee trying to step out of the shadow of his famous father, Archie. I can't say we got to be friends, but we did hang out with a group that night. Now Peyton is a two-time Super Bowl champ.

There was one more brush with fame that left stars in my eyes. I admired Rick Pitino, the head coach of University of Kentucky basketball. While my Irish ancestry got me a job at Silky O'Sullivan's, I'm also aware of the Italian heritage on my mother's side. Pitino was a smooth Italian who knew how to motivate players and always said the right thing. The movie *Wall Street* features Gorden Gekko as an iconic character. Pitino was the Gordon Gekko of basketball. I had already read his autobiography when his team visited Memphis to play Mississippi in The Pyramid in mid-January 1995. The Wildcats were having a shoot around, so I walked right up to Pitino and extended my hand.

"Coach," I said. "I just wanted to say that I read your book and I'm a big fan. My name is Joe and I work in sports information here with Memphis."

He asked where I was from originally. Pittsburgh, I told him.

"I've recruited plenty of boys from Pittsburgh," he said.

As energized as I was during our first meeting, a few years passed before I spoke with Pitino again. By 1998, he had captured a national championship with Kentucky and moved on to coach the NBA's Boston Celtics. He had also written a second book, the motivational "Success is a Choice." I had read that one too.

I was working for Seton Hall University by 1998, and one of our basketball players, Al Harrington, was getting serious looks from NBA scouts. The team's gym was right outside my office. One day, as I went to the water fountain, Pitino stood by the gym door, watching Al practice. I went right over to him.

"Coach Pitino," I said. "You won't remember me, but I shook your hand a few years ago when you coached Kentucky. It's sure good to see you again. My name is Joe."

"Hi Joe," he said, turning toward me. He radiated sincerity. "Where did we meet before?" I told him we had talked on the floor during a shoot around in Memphis.

"Oh, do you miss The Pyramid? That was such a unique venue."

By then, The Pyramid had closed. I knew he was busy, so Pitino and I didn't talk long, but I remain impressed with his personality and his ability to engage people, making them feel welcome.

While living in Memphis I developed the art of networking. I learned how to read people and interact with them, and how to manage relationships. I was young and eager to please, willing to try anything. As I worked longer hours, classes became less important. I believed my job was more educational than anything I might learn from a book.

Spring progressed, and I stopped attending class. I had been hired as an outside marketing representative for Sam's Club, logging regular nine-to-five hours. Marketing was my career goal anyway, so why waste time with college? I had given up on school. When the university discovered my ruse, the job in the athletic department was terminated. Along the way, I picked up extra work. From 6:30-10 p.m., I earned money as a package handler for UPS, and on weekends, I waited tables. I loved being busy, but often felt stretched to the limit. My social life suffered, and long hours began to take their toll.

It was around this time that I visited Bellevue Baptist Church.

Rival, "Cousin," Friend
—Tony Scarpino

TONY SCARPINO'S ISUZU HATCHBACK DID not have air conditioning. So in July 1994, when he and Joe made the twelve-hour drive from Pittsburgh to Memphis, they kept windows rolled down and vents open. Slowed by traffic around Louisville, Tony used the car ride to confess there was one little white lie that Joe should probably maintain.

"I may have told the athletic director you were my cousin," Scarpino grinned. "I thought it would give you the upper edge. Hey, it worked, right? You got the job. So make sure you stick to that story."

Scarpino, a Monroeville native who played quarterback at Gateway High School, had already known Joe for several years. With the formation of Woodland Hills just down the road, an instant football rivalry was created. Scarpino was a star athlete with a strong arm and enough talent to earn a college football scholarship, but Woodland Hills' team was better.

"Yeah, they always beat us," he lamented.

Off the field, however, his friendship with Joe was genuine.

"Joe lived right over the hill from where my father grew up in North Braddock," Scarpino recalled. "It's an old rust belt-type area, very blue collar. When I first met Joe, we hit it off. We had a lot in common. He had his group of friends and I had my group of friends, but we'd meet up sometimes. We both liked sports."

Each boy dreamed of football glory. Scarpino admired Dan Marino and Joe Montana, childhood heroes who had been raised around Pittsburgh. He longed to follow in their footsteps. Scarpino earned a scholarship to play quarterback at the University of Maryland. After two seasons and a coaching change, Scarpino transferred to Memphis State University. During his junior year with the Tigers, he backed up quarterback Steve Matthews until an injury thrust Scarpino into the limelight. (Matthews was later drafted by the Kansas City Chiefs and spent five years in the NFL, largely as a backup himself.)

Scarpino's talent was on display when he led Memphis against the Miami Hurricanes on November 27, 1993. Although Miami won, 41-17, Scarpino threw for two touchdowns against a stingy pass defense.

"I got to play on prime time on ESPN," he said. "That was a great experience."

Joe was proud of his friend, and told him so.

"We kept in touch," Scarpino said. "I'd run into him on summer breaks from college. It was just a natural friendship. Joe's a tough, tough guy, especially when you consider what he's been through and the things he's overcome. He was never the best athlete, but he compensated with his brains."

As June turned to July, a plan began to take shape.

"The summer before my senior year, Joe said he wanted to intern in an athletic department of a major university," Scarpino said. "I called some folks I knew, said I had a great guy that I can vouch for. I told them he was my cousin."

The pair roomed together in Memphis during summer 1994. That fall, Scarpino moved into a dorm reserved for athletes, but Joe visited regularly and they shared the same group of friends. Like most young men in their twenties, conversations revolved around sports and girls.

"During the drive to Memphis, Tony knew I would be his wingman," Joe said. "So he gave me the lowdown on girls that he knew and liked. One was from Ole Miss. Tony had dated her a few times, but he sensed something was missing. The second was a party girl he met at a bar. And the third was Tricia, a nursing student from Memphis who lived at home. When Tony described her, it was with a different tone. I sensed that love was about to take hold. I encouraged him to date the girl with the hottest friends, but that was just me being selfish."

Months later, after Scarpino had lost interest, Joe spotted the party girl at a bar, where she won the "best buns" contest on the dance floor.

"She deserved to win," Joe deadpanned.

It was Tricia Scarboro, the nursing student who became Tony's wife, who invited them to accompany her to Bellevue Baptist Church. That service changed Joe's life.

In 1995 Scarpino joined the U.S. Navy to learn to fly. He wanted to become a commercial pilot when his enlistment ended. But the September 11 attacks altered those plans, and he chose to remain with the military. Based in Tampa, he was recently promoted to Captain. Now studying for a master's degree in strategic studies, he expects to be named commanding officer of a base sometime in the future. He and Tricia have three kids: Madison, Mia, and Anthony.

Scarpino and Joe no longer call themselves cousins. The ruse didn't last long, although they fooled everyone for a while, even Tricia. Decades after their initial meeting, the connection between Scarpino and Joe remains genuine.

"Joe is so mentally tough and strong willed," Scarpino reflected. "And he's one of the most loyal people you'll ever meet. Great guy and a great friend. I admire the hell out of him."

CHAPTER 7

Awe and Shock

THE SPACIOUS CHURCH LOBBY WAS like a five-star hotel, painted in muted hues, featuring a staircase leading to the second-floor balcony. On Sunday morning, a crowd hummed like a buzzing hive with many people carrying Bibles. Everyone smiled and greeted one another. Worshippers entered one set of doors; some left through another. Tony Scarpino and I dressed well, scanning the faces until we found Tricia. With so many people, it wasn't easy. No other church I had visited seemed so bright or vibrant. I was familiar with dark stone mid-century churches. This was modern, not English Tutor or gothic.

Bellevue Baptist Church, outside of Memphis, was the first mega church I visited. It was palatial, the size of a high school, new enough that the baseball and soccer fields on the surrounding property weren't graded or seeded yet. There were sand pits for volleyball too. Once the campus was finished, it would serve as a religious and community center. Bellevue had begun in the metro area and with the congregation exploding, it sought a mecca in the suburbs, where people moved for newer schools, chain restaurants, and strip malls.

Tricia Scarboro was a nursing student who lived with her parents in Memphis. Tony had been interested in a few girls when I moved there, but when he talked about Tricia, I sensed that something special was happening. She was blonde, lean and fit, wholesome and sweet as cornbread. Her family attended Bellevue, and she had invited Tony and me to worship with them, aware of our Catholic upbringings.

The sanctuary held several thousand people, and an immense theater-style balcony spanned the arena seating. There were risers for the choir that climbed halfway up the back wall; the entire room was carpeted. As music began, lyrics scrolled along giant screens on either side of the altar. I was in awe and no one had even mentioned God yet.

A speaker welcomed us, asking who was a first-time visitor.. I raised my hand and an usher hurried up the aisle, handing over a packet that contained information about the church, Bible study groups and recreation opportunities. The envelope also contained a pen and name tag, which we were asked to wear so people could address us properly. What a friendly marketing campaign, I thought.

Looking around the room during announcements, this didn't feel like a church. In addition to their Bibles, several fellow worshippers carried spiral notebooks, pens, and neon highlighters. After blessing the newborns, the pastor stepped to the altar and stood behind a clear podium.

Dr. Adrian Rogers looked like a preacher. Dressed in a suit, he was tall, and his voice was deep and booming, with perfect diction.

He was comforting and exact with his words, carrying a trace of Southern accent. He spoke with authority, but was a humble showman. His face was thin, with dark hair parted on the side.

Today, Dr. Rogers' biography is available online. Born in 1931 in West Palm Beach, he entered the Christian ministry at nineteen. After attending Stetson University in Florida and New Orleans Baptist Theological Society, he was ordained by Northwood Baptist Church in West Palm Beach. He served as pastor in Merritt Island, Florida, between 1964-72, when he became senior pastor of Bellevue, remaining there until 2005. During his tenure, membership more than tripled, from 9,000 to 29,000. He also served three terms as president of the Southern Baptist Convention.

Dr. Rogers reminded me of a priest from St. James in Wilkinsburg, the first church I attended as a child. My parents had been married there, my sister and I were baptized there and my grandfather was the head usher for thirty years until his death. St. James's pastor was kind old Father Murphy, grandpa's good friend. To have him at our house for dinner was normal and he served as a second grandfather to me. There was another priest at the church, Father Ragni, who was a fire and brimstone preacher, complete with the yelling. His voice echoed in that big stone sarcophagus and frightened many kids into a fear of sinning. I always considered Murphy as the kind patient voice—a finesse guy—while Ragni was a grip-it and rip-it type. Likewise, Dr. Rogers had many tools in his belt, and he used them all.

He asked everyone to open their Bibles, naming the book and verse. As he began preaching, I was mesmerized, lost in a swirl of ideas and concepts. Dr. Rogers made me consider things I had never thought of before. Next thing I knew, the service was over.

I've been a fan of public speakers all my life. I had been speaking myself since I was twelve. Hands down, Dr. Rogers was the

best public speaker I ever heard. At that time, I wasn't overly familiar with God or the Bible, but I was confident that Dr. Rogers was
great because he had great material to work with.

Televangelists like Jim Bakker and Jimmy Swaggart give
Southern preachers a bad name. Charlatans begin from the same
place as true men of God, but their words wither while the truth
wins out. I believe the fault is never in the word but the way a
person uses it. I was confident that Dr. Rogers was genuine. (He
died in 2005, but his sermons are still played on radio broadcasts.)

Back in the car, Tony was skeptical about what we had experienced. He was a devout Catholic, but I was lost, not sure where
God fit into my life. I sensed something important was about to
happen. That morning, I felt like someone had removed my heart,
scrubbed it clean, then popped it back into place. I assured Tricia
that I would return to Bellevue. A few months passed before I
made good on that promise.

My next visit was triggered because of a camping trip with
young people from the Baptist Student Union. There was a building on campus near fraternity row where Christian kids of all
denominations hung out. I knew people there and was invited
to spend an overnight with them in the foothills, an hour from
Memphis. I was never much of an outdoorsman, but thought it
would be fun to ride the trails on horseback.

That weekend I met a real Memphis Belle. She was a pretty
Southern girl with curly brown hair and hazel eyes. She reminded
me of a young Andie McDowell. We spent most of Saturday
together outdoors, and she talked fast and seriously about God.
She was so enthusiastic and committed that she began to sell me.
Being a salesman myself, I like being sold to. Belle's happy attitude drew me in. Between this, riding horses, and reading scripture with the group, I felt elated. It was only the first day I knew

her, but I found myself telling Belle things that I rarely shared with close friends, let alone someone I just met.

When I was a teenager, I had visited a psychologist. Many of my issues were triggered by normal teen angst. But the doctor rooted through the past, my feelings, and my struggles and suggested that I was burdened by guilt: I lived through cancer when others had not. Some days, it was difficult to accept. I was also raised Catholic, so guilt was not a new experience. I now understand that most kids go through a period of not fitting in. I was no different. Having survived should have been a point of pride. It was, but it felt better when I was volunteering among adults instead of walking the halls during high school or college.

Much of this I shared the first day I met Belle. She owned an amazing spirit. It was easy to talk with her because she was so positive.

"You don't have to feel guilty," she assured me. "God is in your life already and you don't even realize it."

Her words got me thinking. Back on campus Saturday night, she asked where I attended church.

"Nowhere regular," I admitted.

"I go to Bellevue," she said. "Why don't you come with me? I'll pick you up tomorrow for the 9 a.m. service."

I like to say that girls in the South recruit boys to their church. Belle did it with me; Tricia did the same thing with Tony. Part of me thought I was getting a date, but girls bring guys along to church because they're happy to be Christians and they want you to share the experience.

The second time that I entered Bellevue, I felt moved. Near the end of their service, an altar call was conducted. Dr. Rogers suggested that if anyone wasn't saved and wanted to walk with Jesus Christ, come to the front and everyone would pray with him. His commanding tone was like a tractor beam pulling me down the sloped aisle. I felt that God was calling me home.

As I approached the altar, I started to cry. Very few times in my life have I shed tears, but this was one of them. As I strode toward the sanctuary, my cheeks were wet. I tried to choke back, but sobbed more. I was asked to repeat a prayer, and as I did, the congregation echoed the words. They were literally and spiritually behind me. As I spoke, a feeling washed over me. It was a tidal wave of absolution and grace.

There is a special tank at the top of the sanctuary where the congregation could witness events. Dr. Rogers immersed me there. I'm very proud to say I was part of that. For the first time in my life, I didn't feel the guilt of surviving cancer. I believed that God had blessed me no matter what. There was a lot of cheering and hugging afterward. I was led to the lobby, given a pin and a new Bible, and encouraged to talk about the experience and what it meant.

This was a turning point in my life, starting me down the road of true faith. I didn't have all the answers. I didn't know what came next. But I knew I wanted to be part of something bigger than myself. I had gotten away from religion, and being saved started my trek of studying the Bible every day.

This spiritual faith still drives me. I know it's gotten me through the darkest times.

Years later, when I underwent severe medical challenges and awaited a transplant, I was back coaching at Woodland Hills. Even then, I stayed happy and positive. I remember being at practice, standing on the sidelines with Mike Yezovich, a father of twelve children. Five of his boys played football for Woodland Hills. We had a "Yezie" on the team for thirteen consecutive years. They are a devout Catholic family, really wonderful people.

A player's mom who knew about my struggles walked over and asked how I was feeling.

"I'm great," I told her. "I'm taking dialysis, waiting for a transplant."

"And you're still coaching?" the woman asked. "That's a lot."

"It is, but I'm blessed. I can handle this."

"You're so strong to go through this," she beamed. "Joe, I'm so proud of you. You're the strongest person I've ever met."

She walked away. She meant well, but her words left me hollow. It felt wrong to receive such undeserved praise. Mike and I stood in silence for a time.

"Mike," I finally said, "You know that's not me. I'm not that strong."

"No one is," he said softly. "It's God in you. God is that strong."

I was called back to the moment at Bellevue when I was saved. The conversation reminded me of the last line of the poem "Footprints," when God told the narrator, "When you saw only one set of footprints, it was then that I carried you."

∞

Belle and I dated for a time, but her mother could not stand me. She was open about it too, in a syrupy passive-aggressive manner. I never knew why there was so much animosity, but as time passed I reasoned that it had little to do with me. It must have been difficult for Belle to live with her mom.

That spring, just after I'd been saved, my sister Tara phoned several times and asked me to fly home for a weekend. With three jobs, I logged long hours, so I didn't foresee returning to Pittsburgh anytime soon.

"Mom and Dad will pay for your flight," Tara prodded. When I kept saying no, she flipped the script and said she was flying down on a Saturday. It was nice that she missed her baby brother and wanted to tour Memphis.

I think I'm a smart guy, but sometimes I can be pretty stupid. I had no sense of what was coming.

Belle drove me to the airport that spring morning. I was so excited to see my sister that as I bound into the terminal, I accidentally bumped the sliding glass door with my shoulder and knocked it off track. Once Tara arrived, Belle drove us to a car agency then headed home. Tara rented a ride and I navigated her down American Way, the highway where Sam's Club was located. I wanted to show her where I worked.

"Hey, I've got something to tell you," Tara said without preamble. She was getting married in October, six months away, so I expected her to mention something about wedding plans. Her voice was sober and serious. "Mom and Dad are getting a divorce." Her expression made it clear that this wasn't a joke. For emphasis, she added, "I'm not kidding."

Confused, my mind whirled, then I grabbed the dashboard and started to hyperventilate. She pulled into a gas station and I got out of the car, steadying myself against the hood. A kaleidoscope of sights and sounds swirled around me. There was a pay phone at the parking lot's edge. I rushed there, punching in digits memorized from my calling card, then quickly dialed Mom's number.

I didn't know that Mom and Tara had made an arrangement. Mom would not answer her phone until my sister called first to give the all clear. Mom needed to know that everything was okay on our end. When I got no answer, a red haze washed over me. I grabbed the phone's metal base and released my rage. I pushed and pulled, rocking the pole. Although bolted to the ground, I was going to rip it from the concrete. It had started to loosen when my sister pushed me back into the car. We drove a little longer before going into a restaurant named The Brown Derby.

I was a rookie drinker. I had tasted alcohol before, but that day Tara and I went hard. We both ordered Long Island iced teas while my sister revealed the full story.

Mom and Dad had intended to sell the house where we grew up and build an empty nest home where they could grow old. It would be small, with only two bedrooms. They had even bought property in Churchill, so the site was ready. While those plans were underway, Dad came to Mom and said that he was in love with another woman. It had been going on for four years. Stunned, Mom didn't yell or scream. She just turned cold.

"Dad, Dad," I repeated, shaking my head as Tara narrated the facts. It was all I could say. Anger and betrayal washed through me.

I had never expected this. My dad raised me in a black and white world. It's the same world I often live in today. There is a right way and a wrong way, and I knew from my health issues as a boy that life and death choices are real. I have strong convictions, and at that moment, those teachings crumbled. Had everything been a lie?

"Dad wanted to come and tell you himself," Tara said. "But I convinced him that wasn't a good idea."

Tara was right. His presence would have been a disaster. Had he sat before me and shared the news, I'm certain I would have tried to kill him.

The next few weeks tested my boundaries. Thank God for my faith. While I struggled in Memphis, I knew Mom had it worse in Pittsburgh. It wasn't long before I got an itch. Mom had taken care of me so many times. Now, after twenty-seven years, she was alone, angry and bitter. I needed to head home and be there for her. I spun all kinds of stories about why I left Memphis. I had stopped attending class already, so I wasn't walking away from a 4.0 average or a guaranteed diploma. The people closest to me knew the truth: Tony, Dan Gomez, and Joe Borich. But no one else did.

I had met Dan and Joe through Tony, because those guys played football too. We all became good friends. While Tony started spending more time with Tricia, I hung out with the other guys. We called Dan "the world's largest Mexican." At six-six and 315 pounds, he played left tackle for Memphis and started forty college games. He should have made the NFL, but scouts thought he appeared stiff. I never understood that. He was athletic and fit, with a flat stomach. He didn't fit the view of a stereotypical lineman. After college, Dan remained in Memphis and began selling cars. He had a side business working in concrete. Then he met a girl who was a hairdresser. They married, he learned to style hair as well, and they opened several hair salons. Joe was Tony's backup quarterback. He went on to coach college football in several different places, including Cornell University. We've lost touch over the years, but I remember laughing when we watched *The Office* and Andy Bernard's character boasted about Cornell.

Although Belle and I dated, I couldn't bring myself to tell her what was happening at home. When I left Memphis, Belle's mom was thrilled. Belle and I stayed in touch, and she visited me a few times in Pittsburgh. We never had a conversation about remaining a couple or breaking up, but in my mind, I was transitioning to a different point in my life. While she may have considered us together, I dated other people. I walked away from Memphis and Belle with no ill feelings. But both were as dead to me as Elvis. Like a song from The King, you play the memory in your head and smile. The most important thing from that time was that a seed of faith had been planted deeply.

In July of 1995, I moved back to Pittsburgh to live with my mom.

My sister's wedding plans helped to distract us all. Tara and her fiance Jimmy had already bought a house in Churchill. Jimmy moved in early, while Tara waited to join him there until after their vows. The pending divorce reverberated for everyone.

Neighbors were stunned too. The Alton family lived across the street. John Alton was ten years older than me and we had known each other most of our lives. One day, John crossed the road and spoke to my mom.

"Is Mr. Lafferty around?" he asked. He wanted help with a car repair, knowing my dad was an expert.

My mom has always been no-nonsense. "Oh John, we're getting a divorce," she said simply. "He doesn't live here anymore."

His face fell. He stood there, dumbfounded. "What? No... no... no. You can't do that. You're the Laffertys."

CHAPTER 8

Marketing Pitt

BACK IN PITTSBURGH, I FOUND myself without direction, harboring few thoughts about the future. I languished in several part-time jobs, and often getting through the day became my goal. In Memphis, my faith in God had begun to grow. Now, with my parents' divorce, the foundation of who I was had broken apart.

Today, I recognize and acknowledge that my father is an amazing man. I say that knowing people are flawed and that he is flawed. I didn't feel this at the time. Resentment boiled. He had raised me to believe that doing something halfway was the wrong way. It was difficult to discover that he didn't live that credo himself. Had he told my mother, "I don't love you anymore and want a divorce," it would have been far less traumatic. To learn that he kept part of his life hidden from us simply rocked me.

Their marriage ended the day he revealed himself. Dad didn't sleep in the house another night, moving out immediately. He suggested Mom find an attorney, tell the lawyer what she wanted, and Dad would agree without contest. They owned rental income properties together, dividing them up evenly. Their divorce never went to court or turned contentious. Because he didn't put up a fight, the whole process played out in a very short time.

In many ways, Mom didn't have an opportunity to absorb it fully. Her emotions came in waves. There was a crash followed by an undertow. Living with Mom left me feeling like rocks on the beach. Sometimes I got pounded with her anger; other times things remained calm for long stretches. She was pleased to have me back mowing the lawn and caring for the house. With my sister's impending marriage, there was plenty to do, so Mom was often on the move. I coined an abbreviation that Tara and I both understood: B.W.C. It stood for "bitter wife comment." Mom would claim she was okay and happy, then something would trigger her and she'd snap, flying off the handle. When that happened, we gave her space. Considering what she had been through, she had every right to behave this way.

To earn money, I undertook a variety of jobs. One was installing fences. Another was delivering the Pittsburgh Post-Gazette overnight. My neighbor, John Alton, stuffed 350 newspapers into boxes around Churchill every morning, beginning at 2 or 3 a.m. and finishing before daybreak. He earned good money—$100 a day—but the job was constant, 365 days a year. There were times when he needed a reliable substitute, so he taught me his route. Once I mastered it, another woman asked me to sub for her as well. I also went back to selling suits at the Monroeville mall. My title was "visual merchandiser." I folded sweaters, dressed mannequins, and changed window displays. My job was to keep the store looking nice. It was always a thrill when the late Kaye Cowher, wife of Steelers' Head Coach Bill Cowher, came in to pick out clothes for her husband.

With so much change, I needed structure. Woodland Hills has always been a safe place. Coaching football is a year-round job. I knew the schedule for camps and practices. On Monday, Wednesday, and Friday, for example, kids lifted weights after school. On a weekday afternoon in July, coaches could be found on the field while athletes worked on bag drills. I saw Coach Novak and explained what was happening with my parents. He hired me back. I was welcomed again and fell into a regular routine.

We played a game in early September, right around my birthday, and during the bus ride home, I felt apprehensive. I was about to turn twenty three, had no footing, and was convinced my life was lost. I unloaded all this on Denny Damico, a strength coach and trainer who is twenty-one years older than me. We're still friends today.

"What are you talking about?" Denny asked. "You moved to Erie then Memphis and lived in a brand new city. You're not afraid to try new things. You have courage, Joe, whether you recognize it or not."

His words propped me up. It was what I needed in the moment. Denny helped me realize that my life wasn't as dark as I made it out to be.

I also reached out to Barry Joncour, a teacher who had been the quarterbacks' coach when I played at Woodland Hills. He was open about his Christianity, and used fake swear words like "Jiminy Christmas," "gosh darnit," or "heck bent for election" instead of "hell bent for leather." He ran a fellowship for Christian athletes. I attended meetings and Bible studies with the group, but didn't go to church. With so many changes, I was clinging to faith by my fingertips.

The Woodland Hills team featured accomplished seniors who went onto play football for Notre Dame, Kentucky, and West

Virginia. We had talented juniors as well, but didn't get far in the playoffs. It was disappointing because we expected more.

One of the greatest blessings in our family is that Tara married Jim Reis that fall. Jimmy is a good man and I've never had any worries for my sister. All these years later, they are the proud parents of Adam and Reilly. I go to sleep each night confident that he cares for Tara and their children with great joy. Jimmy helps complete the Lafferty family.

The wedding went smoothly. Our extended family wanted to avoid any mention of my parents' divorce. In fact, there is a photo of Mom and Dad standing together that tells the story of their calm demeanor. They both realized that this was their daughter's moment, so any lingering animosity needed to be swept aside for the day. Tara mattered most.

The University of Pittsburgh holds a coaching clinic every spring. High school coaches are invited for food and beer, then observe a Saturday practice, learning techniques from the college staff. It's a great way to exchange information and ideas. The night before, while at a social gathering, I talked to Jim Earle, the football operations guy at Pitt.

"Last year I worked at the University of Memphis in the sports marketing department," I told him. Sports marketing was coming into its own in the mid-1990s. "Do you do anything like that here?"

"We just hired an associate athletic director named Tim Fitzpatrick," he said. "He's going to oversee all that. Want me to introduce you?"

I didn't meet Fitzpatrick that night, but left with his office phone number. I saw this as an opportunity, and excitement took hold. Maybe this was a chance to work in my field while staying home to care for Mom.

On weekdays I held a part-time job taking cash at a parking lot in Oakland. My buddy Brian had let me in on this sweet deal where I sat in a tiny booth for several hours and was paid under the table. Brian often came by with lunch and we hung out and laughed together. From that booth, I left messages for Tim Fitzpatrick every day, telling him I was eager to sit down to talk, and included phone numbers at the parking lot and home. I even reached out to an old contact from the Dan Marino Open who was a Pitt booster. Denny Palmer was a successful insurance salesman and had co-founded the Pitt Golden Panthers, an organization to promote the athletic department. Denny knew Tim and could speak on my behalf.

Tim finally called back, probably because he noticed that I was a coach from Woodland Hills and because Denny told him to.

"I have thirty minutes a week from tomorrow," he said gruffly. "Come to the athletic department and we'll talk."

So in late March, I went there with my resume, expecting a brief meeting. Two hours later, we were still deep in conversation. Tim was new to Pitt and didn't know many people there. He was seeking a young employee who was familiar with the city, could be loyal to him, and would work his butt off. I displayed all those traits.

The catch: there wasn't money available to pay me until May 1, when I would be given an office in Pitt Stadium. May seemed a long time away.

"I want to start tomorrow," I told Tim. "I don't expect to be on the clock. I'd like to hit the ground running and learn the lay of the land. If you see me standing next to a coach talking about hoops, understand that I'm getting to know him and what he does."

For more than a month, I arrived first thing in the morning and stayed late. I educated myself about the different personnel and their responsibilities. I familiarized myself with work done by Tim and Rex Hough, director of ticket sales and marketing. I talked to everyone. I wanted to be on the front end, implementing a new vision.

On my third day, Tim pulled me aside. "Many people here represent the old guard. The direction we're taking is going to shake them up. Be compassionate, be nice, but don't let their ideas about the way things used to be affect our goals. If I have to correct you, I want to slow you down, not the reverse."

This was just what I needed to hear. It was a blank check to promote Pitt. Hours and money didn't matter—I was twenty three, excited for the opportunity, and felt arrogant. Our work brought money in to the college, and that money paid people's salaries. Sports marketing was important.

We focused on football's home opener against West Virginia that was scheduled for broadcast on ESPN. Both teams wore the same colors, so regardless of allegiance, everyone in the stadium would don blue and gold. We knew there was pressure surrounding this game. We needed to sell out and put on a great show.

Ticket sales were key. I stuffed fliers into mailboxes for U.S. Air because Pittsburgh was one of their hubs. I met several sponsors, including Three Rivers Cellular. I had watched boxing and liked Michael Buffer, the man who's voice boomed "Let's Get Ready to Rumble!" I thought it would be cool to bring him in for the game. Michael's brother, Bruce, booked his events, so I got Bruce on the phone. The cost of having him in Pittsburgh was $10,000, a hotel room and flight out. While we were preparing the paperwork, Michael received an offer to perform in Malaysia the following night for $25,000. There was no way he could do both, so we lost out. But Bruce was a nice guy who educated me on trademarks. After we talked, any time I heard the phrase "Let's Get Ready to Rumble!" I called Bruce to let him know. His lawyer then sent a cease and desist order. A few times he even passed along a small compensation check to say thanks.

We sold out the West Virginia opener, and made our yearly ticket sales budget in a single game. The rest of the season didn't go as well, but that Saturday, I was in charge of the game script. Tim was in the press box and I patrolled the sidelines, coordinating music piped into the stadium, announcements, and marketing promotions, like cheerleaders shooting T-shirts into the crowd courtesy of a slingshot. Just like coaches planned plays on the field, the game script is very rigid. No one wants the band to hit their notes when we're supposed to read a paid advertisement over the public address system.

As fall progressed, there were so many great experiences, despite the football team's lack of success. Once, on the sidelines during homecoming, I went in search of the assistant cheerleading coach. She was talking with a man whose back was to me, but I needed to coordinate something and time was short. Because I was in a hurry, I approached them quickly.

"Excuse me, sir," I said curtly. "May I interrupt you for one minute? I need to speak with her."

The man turned. Under his hat I saw it was running back Tony Dorsett, an Aliquippa native, Pitt alum and former star of the Dallas Cowboys. In 1994, he became a member of the NFL Hall of Fame.

He stepped away, and the cheer coach was furious with me. Through clenched teeth, she hissed, "Nice." Later in the game, I circled back to Dorsett and introduced myself. We talked for a few minutes.

Often, scouts showed up at games, so another time I ran into Doug Williams, the Super Bowl winning quarterback of the Washington Redskins. I also got to know Dick Groat, who did radio broadcasting. As a former Pirate from 1952-1962, he was one of Pittsburgh's favorite sons. Forty-year-old men in the stands pointed to him and giggled with glee.

Each year, everyone from the athletic office traveled to an away football game to build group camaraderie. On Nov. 16, 1996, senior officials and coaches' wives traveled to Notre Dame. Our team wasn't expected to beat the Fighting Irish, but the trip was something to look forward to.

I promised Adam Curry that I'd take him along. At thirteen, he was both a Pitt and Notre Dame fan. Although we weren't related, I called Adam my little brother because I had lived with the Curry family and we remained close.

But someone needed to oversee the exhibition basketball game that Pitt hosted on Friday night. Very few high level athletic department officials remained in town, so I was named game manager along with a fellow staffer, Jason Lener. It became comical because we both kept telling people the other guy was in charge. Also that night, Woodland Hills battled in a playoff game. There was so much going on in a short time and I didn't want to miss any of it.

After the basketball game wrapped, I picked up Adam and we drove through the night, bunking in a hotel outside South Bend. We slept briefly, then made it to the stadium before kickoff. We planned to sit in the stands, but Sam Scuillo, one of the assistant sports information directors, asked me to work in the booth as a spotter for the NBC broadcast. The job paid $90, although I don't recall ever getting a check. I had never done this before, but it wasn't hard. Every play-by-play announcer sets a chart in front of him called a "two deep" that lists each player's name, size, position and a few interesting facts, like where he played in high school or whether his brother is an athlete too. A spotter stands behind the announcer with a laser pointer. When a player carries the ball or makes a tackle, the spotter aims the laser pointer at his name on the chart. The announcer looks down, sees who it is, and shares a detail about that kid with the audience.

Adam was allowed to watch the game from a different part of the press box, and as we waited for a creaky old elevator to take us upstairs, a booming voice carried through the crowded hall.

"Excuse me, son," a man said. I turned to see Paul Tagliabue, the NFL Commissioner, walking by with his wife. I nudged Adam. We were both impressed.

Upstairs, Adam and I grabbed a snack, then I headed to the perch, where I was introduced to Charlie Jones and Randy Cross, the announcers calling the game. My job was to spot for Pitt players; another guy spotted for the Notre Dame team. Before kickoff, Charlie was fooling around and laughing. Once they went on-air, he popped a lozenge in his mouth. "Welcome to Notre Dame football," he said smoothly. It was riveting to watch the transition. Just like that, he snapped into character, sounding like a pro.

The Irish demolished Pitt, 60-6. After the game, Adam and I headed down to the Notre Dame locker room. I wanted to see a few people: Rob Mowl, an offensive lineman, was a Woodland Hills alum, and Pitt's former offensive line coach, Joe Moore, now held the same position for the Fighting Irish. I wore a Pitt jacket and Adam wore my black Pitt baseball cap, complete with cross stitching. We each had passes that read "All Access." At the door, two college-age equipment managers noticed our clothes and told us we couldn't enter. I pointed at the pass.

"It's all access," I said.

One shook his head. "That doesn't count here. You can't come in the locker room."

It did count there, and I knew it. These guys just didn't like that we were from the opposing school. I believe when you're pushing for something, you just have to go for it, so I made sure my voice sounded serious.

"All right, young man, you tell Joe Moore that Joe Lafferty is here. He wanted me to come see him after the game, and now you're telling me I can't come in. So you head inside and explain to the coach that despite an all access pass, you won't let me through. I'm sure he'll love that."

The two equipment managers glanced at each other, vanished inside for ten seconds, then came back to wave us through. They weren't gone long enough to speak with anybody, but I'm sure they realized that if this went much further they could get in trouble.

The Notre Dame locker room was tiny, with dark blue carpeting. Adam's eyes were huge as he watched the college players. One of them approached with a smile.

"Hey little man, I like your hat," he said. "I've got a brand new Notre Dame hat. Want to make a trade?"

It was my hat, so Adam glanced at me for permission.

"Go ahead and trade," I told him. I found a sharpie and urged him to ask the quarterback, Ron Powlus, to sign his new cap. Powlus was one of Adam's favorite players. Ron treated him so well. In fact, a reporter interrupted them for a quote, but Ron put up a hand.

"I'm talking to Adam right now," Powlus told him. "Can you stop back in a few minutes?"

I chatted with Joe Moore and we chuckled about the score. Suddenly I heard a high voice bellow, "Who's wearing a Pitt jacket in my locker room?" I turned around to see Lou Holtz, Notre

Dame's coach, standing in shorts, socks, and a T-shirt while smoking a pipe. It was the funniest looking outfit. I introduced myself, explained that I work for Pitt, and complimented him on the game. I said I enjoyed his quotes and had read his books. After a few minutes, he said I was welcome in his locker room anytime, wearing whatever I wanted. Holtz only coached two more games for Notre Dame, then left for reasons that were never disclosed.

A day full of memories, for sure.

Because I was so busy at Pitt, I didn't coach Woodland Hills that fall, but followed the team and attended all their games, helping out when I could. I had spent time with the boys during workouts the summer before. On a July weekend, Coach Novak and I had taken a group to Philadelphia for a combine at Temple University. In the heat of summer, we roasted on the field, then afterward visited historic places around the city, like the Liberty Bell. One location I knew the kids would love was the Rocky steps at the Philadelphia Museum of Art. Amid pouring rain, we pulled Coach's Ford Explorer to the foot of the stairs, turned on the four-way flashers, and all the boys and I sprinted up the steps. One of our players, Joey Sperduto, lost his footing. As he fell, he put his hand out for balance and accidentally pushed my hip, knocking me over. I landed in a puddle so deep I had to swim to the edge. Everyone had a good laugh.

Joey apologized, but I told him it was an accident and not to worry. We scrambled up, ran to the top, and did our Rocky impression with arms raised overhead. It was fun, because I'm still just a big kid at heart. Soaking wet, we piled back into George's van. During the drive back to Pittsburgh, one of the kids mentioned winning the championship that season. I laughed to myself. There was no way this band of misfits was going that far. My senior year hadn't done it, nor had the team the prior year, with three Division I athletes.

Woodland Hills started the season with a rocky record, going 3-4. They had lost to New Castle, which plays in a division of smaller schools. Although no one expected them to be champs, everyone was frustrated that they weren't winning, because there was a decent quarterback and receiver. During week eight, they faced undefeated North Allegheny. I arrived at the Wolvarena thinking the game might turn ugly.

Woodland Hills scored two quick touchdowns, then gave up a score. After halftime, North Allegheny scored again to draw within three points. I wasn't their coach, but at this point, I huddled with the offensive linemen on the sidelines.

"Don't let up," I yelled. "Go back out there and take control of this game! This is the moment! Don't let up!"

The center, Larry Vogel, started screaming "Don't let up!" They drove down, scored a touchdown, and won the game. All the players started chanting "Don't let up!"

An hour later, I walked up the hill toward my car, happy for the boys. An ambulance siren grew louder along a road behind the stadium. I remember thinking it was a tough time to need an ambulance amid the postgame congestion. There were still people everywhere.

The next morning, Coach Novak called to tell me that Joey Sperduto's mom, Trish, had died of an aneurism after the game. I knew her because I had coached Joey when he was younger. She was a nice woman, in her early 40s, with flaming red hair.

Driving to Pitt on Monday, I hatched an idea. I knew a guy, Chuck Bonasorte, who played for the Panthers in the 1970s. By 1996, he sold Pitt apparel every day at the corner of DeSoto and

Forbes Avenue, in the heart of Pitt's campus. That morning I approached him.

"Any way to get a block of shirts printed by Wednesday?" I asked.

"The only way to turn it around that quickly is if you get me a proof positive screen," he said. "You need artwork."

I didn't know what a proof positive was, but immediately started phoning people. I found a design shop that did work for Pitt. I explained what I wanted: lettering that read "I WON'T LET UP" and "Wolverine football 1996." I learned a proof positive is clear film with one color so it can be run through a screen. Ninety minutes later, I came back to Chuck, design in hand.

"Will this do?" I asked.

He stared at me, dumbfounded. "Joe Lafferty, who are you?" When I requested white shirts with turquoise lettering, he told me I could pick them up Wednesday morning. As I told him the story, he said we'd haggle over prices later.

Thursday was Trish's funeral, and the entire team attended. I had a meeting at Pitt, so could not be there, but I had spoken with Coach Novak about hanging a printed t-shirt in every locker while the boys were on the field.

At the end of practice, the kids were kneeling on the grass. Joey Sperduto was right there.

"A few weeks ago, you guys lost to New Castle, and my faith in you was gone," I told them. "I thought you were going to get demolished by North Allegheny. But I came to the game because I support you no matter what."

They stared back at me, confused. Some probably thought I was kicking them while they were down.

"But you showed me something," I continued. "The offensive line knows what I said after halftime. What was it, Larry?"

The center, Larry Vogel, nodded. "Don't let up."

"Don't let up," I repeated. "Coach Novak just said that this has been a hard week. I'll make you a promise if you make one back to me. I'll never give up on you guys again if you promise that you won't let up. If you make me that promise, I have one of these for every one of you." I held up the T-shirt, then told them that these were hanging in every kid's locker right now.

"I won't let up" became their rallying cry. Boosters used the T-shirt design and printed sweatshirts. Everyone started wearing them. And the team disproved anyone who doubted them. They didn't lose again until the state championships.

CHAPTER 9

Beinvenido a Miami

FOR THE FALL AND WINTER, I worked all over the Pitt Athletic Department. I was lead marketing guy for teams that didn't generate revenue, such as volleyball, gymnastics, and womens basketball. I met many people, logged long hours, and racked up great experiences. I even had a chance to attend a party with Sports Illustrated swimsuit models.

Before I arrived at Pitt, during spring football practice, a receiver named Damale Stanley bobbled a catch, tripped, and tumbled head-first into a wall. Tragically, he was paralyzed from the neck down. The university held a benefit, with people calling in favors from all over the country to contribute auction items. One was roundtrip airfare to New York City and two VIP tickets for the unveiling of the 1997 Swimsuit Issue.

Rex Hough won that bid. He summoned me into his office, complimented my good work, and told me that because of his busy schedule, including the coming Big East Tournament, he could not attend. Did I want to go in his place? As a red-blooded American male, I certainly did.

I traveled with Eric Ridgley, an intern from Slippery Rock with whom I had played football at Mercyhurst. We chose nice sport coats, and upon landing in New York, hired a car service to transport us to the location. A receiving line formed outside the door. Inside was model Tyra Banks. Next to her was a giant blow up of the magazine cover photo featuring her in a red polka-dot bikini. Tyra was polite—her parents stood alongside her—but I got the vibe that she wasn't happy to be there. She was doing her job, greeting every schlepp in line, ninety-five percent of whom where male.

Inside, drinks were free, and other models walked around while photographers roamed snapping candids. These were stunning women, some of whom went on to pose for the Victoria's Secret catalog. I'm glad to say I went, but the night was a little anticlimactic. I had expected something like a cookout at the Playboy mansion, but it was really just a bunch of dudes drooling over beautiful women. Eric and I were more relaxed afterward, when we left and found a neighborhood bar.

By the spring of 1997, there was a chance that my work in Pitt might not lead to a full-time position. I had signed up as a one-year assistant, hoping the job might develop into something permanent. Rex Hough was only six years older than I was, so he wasn't going anywhere. We thought Tim Fitzpatrick was a shoe-in for promotion when Pitt's athletic director was fired. In his mid-thirties, Tim had been the number two guy in the department for almost two years, but instead of moving up, his role diminished when a new athletic director was brought in through the old crony network. Anyone with foresight could see that Tim was going to be a short-timer.

Once the new guy came on board, nine people were fired in one day. The remaining staff had a meeting with an agency that coordinated marketing and ticket sales for the 1996 Olympics in Atlanta. While we were impressed by their credentials, none of them were Pennsylvania natives. These so-called marketing geniuses wanted to rebrand Pitt, suggesting the school adopt its full name to sound more formal. Pittsburgh natives understand that the school is called Pitt, but soon the change was underway. The colors and font were changed to read "Pittsburgh." I saw Pitt losing its identity. (It wasn't long before the college realized this was a mistake and changed back.)

Both Rex and Tim didn't foresee my work turning into a full-time job. While I appreciated their honesty, I grew worried, and began looking for new opportunities, updating my resume and drafting cover letters to other schools. I wanted to get out sooner rather than later.

Keeping my eyes open for any other sports marketing jobs, I stumbled across a help wanted ad in an NCAA newsletter: a one-year position was available to develop licensing and marketing at the Orange Bowl in Miami. Right away, I knew I had to land that job.

The closest I had ever been to South Florida was watching *Miami Vice* on TV, but the city hovered before me like a land of dreams. There were so many things to love. Dan Marino sat on his perch as the NFL's greatest quarterback there. I've always despised cold weather, so I expected to thrive in the heat. (Having been gone from Mercyhurst for decades, even today I joke that parts of me are still not thawed from winters along Lake Erie.) It would be amazing to work in Miami and see the diverse culture. Plus, it was a huge, growing market, and I was certain that networking would be as easy as gathering shells on the beach. Oh, and beaches were everywhere!

The Orange Bowl sought a full-time employee for a one-year contract. The short time wasn't cause for worry; I planned to work so hard that they would have no choice but to retain me when that year was up. I was versed in marketing, and would commit to learn the ins and outs of licensing. After a solid phone interview with Dale Schoon, the Director of Merchandising and Licensing—and a letter of recommendation from Dan Marino—I was offered the job. Pay was $800 per month, but that wasn't enough to live on. I negotiated a higher salary; the Orange Bowl agreed, but stipulated that I had to begin immediately. In spring 1997, all my dreams were coming true.

Accepting the job meant leaving home again. Nearly two years after her breakup, my mom seemed tougher. She always put on a brave face, but it wore her down to do that every day while we lived together. During my time at Pitt, whenever I traveled for work, she didn't have to act like a mom all the time. I sensed that she wanted to be alone and overcome this by herself. More than a year earlier, her father passed away as well. That was another blow, but Mom kept moving forward and taught me to do the same thing. She would be okay when I left. There was never a question of "should I go?" Mom is a strong woman who could handle herself just fine.

Needing a place to stay in Miami, I reconnected with my old friend Dennis Atiyeh, who had family in Hollywood, Florida. He arranged for me to bunk with his relatives until I found my own living arrangements. I couldn't afford a new car, so Dad secured me a used sedan, cautioning that I might be inheriting someone else's problem. I didn't worry. Dad was a car expert, and I trusted his judgement. With the trunk packed, I pointed south and drove away.

My first stop was Atlanta, where I visited Corey Taylor, a friend from Mercyhurst. We played basketball our first morning together, and that afternoon, while Corey napped, I discovered a tattoo parlor near his house. With a fistful of dollars, I went inside and paged through their designs, asking how much each one cost. It was a slow day, so they agreed to cut me a deal, but Georgia state law required identification before anyone could be tattooed. I had left my license back at Corey's. I took that as a sign that I shouldn't get a tattoo.

When I told Corey the story, he admitted that he wanted a tattoo himself. So armed with ID, we trekked back. Corey had been a Division I basketball player, so he was inked with Foghorn Leghorn cradling a basketball beneath wings. I got the Superman logo tattooed on my right shoulder. We laughed all day, went out Saturday night, and the next morning I woke early and got back on the road.

Dad must have had a premonition, because my used car died in Macon, Georgia. I walked along country roads until I was finally able to hail a ride, then sought the nearest Hertz office to rent a car. Driving the rental back to my broken down sedan, I repacked everything and set out again. When I crossed the state line into Florida, excitement bubbled. I thought I was nearly there, but I-95 along the east coast of Florida is brutally long. Miami was another eight hours away. I drove through the night, knowing I was scheduled to work in the morning and that I had a good story to share on my first day.

The Orange Bowl offices were located on the second floor of a beautiful building on Brickell Key. That neighborhood of Miami has been featured in countless movies and TV shows. In fact, our building was shown in the movie *True Lies* when Arnold Schwarzenegger was chasing terrorists. While I worked there, George Clooney and Jennifer Lopez filmed *Out of Sight* across the street.

On the same floor of the Orange Bowl office, a talent agent rented space, so during my first day at work, I walked into Jon Secada, the singer, and another guy who looked familiar. It was

Emilio Estafan, husband of Gloria, the lead vocalist for the Miami Sound Machine. Secada had been a backup singer for the band before recording solo material. We didn't talk that day, but during my time in the office, I spoke to Secada on a couple occasions. Once, I was carrying Burger King bags with Bonita Whitehead, an office secretary, when she whispered under her breath "There's Jon Secada in a baseball cap coming this way." Secada had just inked a contract to perform at halftime, so that was the opening to introduce myself. He was a nice guy; surprisingly short. I don't think he was five feet tall. You could put him in your pocket. Seeing him cemented that I was living in Miami.

Being in Florida wasn't a smooth adjustment, although I might not have admitted it at the time. I tried to learn the city and embrace its Hispanic influence, but I knew almost no one there. It's not like I hung out with Marino any longer, and Dennis Atiyeh's relatives who allowed me to stay with them were busy leading their own lives. I didn't realize I was homesick until a month passed and I was summoned to my boss's office.

"What's up with all these phone calls?" he wondered. He showed me a list of long distance numbers that had been dialed from my extension. There was a call to Pittsburgh almost every day. The frequency startled me. I didn't get in trouble, but my boss wanted to be sure I wasn't wasting Orange Bowl money on phone conversations during hours I should be working. It was a wake-up call. From then on, if I needed to speak to friends or family, I did it from home.

That feeling of loneliness is why I reached out to Art Kehoe, the Miami University offensive line coach whom I first met at Woodland Hills when he recruited my teammate Tirrell Greene seven years earlier. Art was a link to life in Pittsburgh, so I wandered over to the Miami Hurricanes offices one day and asked around until I found him. I reminded him who I was, but it wasn't long before recognition dawned. Art has an amazing memory. He was surprised to see me again. Tirrell had left school two years before, and I explained that I was working at the Orange Bowl. Our relationship really grew from that point. He quickly became a valued friend, and we remain close today.

Soon I moved into an apartment in Coral Gables with Dave Murphey and Scott Carr, two guys from the Orange Bowl. We were a few blocks away from some of the richest people in Miami. But because our hours were so varied, we drove to work separately. All of us plugged away. I logged twelve- and fourteen-hour days as part of an initiative to open Orange Bowl-themed stores that sold merchandise year-round. Past practice was that tables and booths were assembled the week before the game, but that limited sales opportunities. So we secured space at Bayside Marketplace, a downtown mall, and developed a system for numbering inventory. I took shifts there, working the register and folding clothes. It seemed like every other day I was troubleshooting in that store. We also marketed a plush toy around the Orange Bowl mascot, Obie. Every employee had taken a turn wearing the mascot suit, which was a giant orange wearing a crown. You wore big Mickey Mouse gloves and once in the costume, elbows couldn't be bent. Little kids hugged you and grabbed your hands. The littlest ones cried because they were so excited and scared.

By Memorial Day weekend, I had been on the job for two months and hadn't had a day off yet. I circled the calendar, excited to head for the beach. My roommate Dave wanted to come too. He was an Oklahoma native, so the sand and open water were a new experience for him.

The day was sunny, in the 90s, and Dave slathered sunscreen over every inch of himself. I used his SPF 30 too, but I was sloppy. Most of me was covered, but I was more interested in the scenery.

The beach was packed with women from around the world. We heard different languages and kept our eyes open for swimsuit models, figuring they must be everywhere in Miami. We strolled along the water's edge, looking backwards and forwards at the thousands gathered along the shore. Once, when we stopped, I almost tripped over a woman lying on her back without a top. Dave and I stared like teenagers until she noticed us. We giggled and moved along. Approaching Ocean Avenue, we acted like tourists, checking out cool hotels and cafes. My shoulders began to sting from the sun.

That afternoon, we passed an elegant house that resembled a castle with hedges and a black iron fence in front. The gate was open, and we noticed three men sitting and talking on the front steps. One of them was in his fifties, tanned with salt-and-pepper hair. His appearance was striking, but I had no idea who he was. He nodded to me. Several weeks later his story made headlines.

Back home, after showering, I realized my mistake. I should have been more diligent about sunscreen. I should have used something stronger than SPF 30. Blisters formed along my chest and shoulders. I hadn't thought it was possible to burn the scalp beneath my hair, but I had done that too. Despite drinking water all night, I woke the next day too cramped to walk. I had to phone my boss and confess I needed a day off to recover from my trip to the beach. Dave wasn't much better. Two days later, he was still home sick. We were the two young guys in the office, so this was comedy fodder for everyone else.

Later, when we sat around the sales bullpen one morning and recounted that day, everyone grew interested when I described the castle we passed. It was the Versace mansion. They pressed me for details about the man I had seen on the steps. I described him, and someone grabbed a glossy magazine from a desk, holding up a photo.

"Is this him?"

"Yeah," I nodded. That was Gianni Versace, the fashion magnate. Seven weeks later, he was murdered on the same stoop at age 50 after coming home from a coffee shop with the morning paper. Andrew Cunanan, a serial killer who made the FBI's Most Wanted List, was linked to the crime. Cunanan committed suicide that summer, and his story dominated TV and tabloids for its mix of celebrity and murder in high society.

∞

Before moving to Florida, I promised myself that I would find a church there. Being saved in Memphis had affected me, but I had drifted away from faith after my parents' divorce. It was time to get back to God. Once I arrived in Miami, work swallowed so much time. When I could squeeze out a rare quiet moment, I recognized that I had good friends and found purpose in my job. Yet that feeling of being alone still lingered, as it had for much of my life. It was okay, but I wanted more.

I used to drive home after a long day and listen to the song "What You Won't Do For Love" by Bobby Caldwell. I owned the cassette single, and played it often, admiring the great horns. The best love songs deal with unrequited love. No one wants to hear that a person is happily in love. Moving toward love or losing love makes for an interesting song. I was young when I realized I wanted to be part of a lasting love. Now in my mid-twenties, I wondered if I had missed the chance with one of my former girlfriends. Or was real love still to come? I sometimes prayed that God would show me whether love existed, that the potential for love was out there. I had adjusted to being alone, but these thoughts weighed on my mind.

When football season began, work ramped up even further. Young staffers attended games in what was then Joe Roby Stadium to familiarize themselves with the surroundings. As I sat in the press box for a Dolphins' Monday night game, a door marked "Emergency Exit—Do Not Enter" swung open, and a guard moved aside to let two guys pass. One was Ben Stiller, the actor. He apparently had special privileges.

I attended many sporting events and was given a press pass for the NBA's Miami Heat. Often, rather than sit on press row, I chose a vacant seat in the arena. Once I noticed tennis star Boris Becker not far from me. Another time I recognized two actors from *Martin*, the sitcom starring Martin Lawrence. Perhaps the most memorable encounter came when I sat next to a woman with her young son. He was boisterous, jumping around and having fun. His mom asked if the boy was bothering me.

"He's fine," I said. We started chatting. "What brings you to the game?"

She explained that her husband, Pat Riley, was the Heat's coach.

"Wow," I said. "That's great. I'm a big fan of his."

The media needs to be fed, so the press room served food and drinks prior to tipoff and again at halftime. Once, I waited there in a long line to order a drink. When I neared the front, the servers reacted, looking past me. Their eyes lit up and they nudged each other, giggling. I pivoted to see Cameron Diaz and Matt Dillon standing right behind me. Stiller and Diaz and Dillon were in Miami to film *There's Something About Mary*, which was released the following year. I smiled, nodded at them, and ordered my Diet Coke, then sat in the crowd and watched the stars just like everyone else.

Because of my long hours, I kept a change of clothes in the trunk of my car. I had a pair of Nike flip flops that were so comfortable. After spending twelve or fourteen hours a day in dress shoes,

I would come home and walk around the apartment in them. I used to gauge how good my day was by how much time I spent wearing my trusty flip flops. One night after work, I wanted to attend a Heat game, but the only clothes in my trunk were a blue cotton sweater, faded jeans, and those flip flops. The sweater and jeans were passable; the footwear was questionable. I decided I didn't care. Exiting a bathroom, I emerged in a hallway near the players' dressing room. Alonzo Mourning came through a door, took one look at me, and chuckled, shaking his head. Miami is unique because rich people can dress shabbily and normal folks like me can dress to the nines. I fit in, because anything goes.

Because Miami is an international city, stars were everywhere. One weekend, with friends visiting from Pittsburgh, we went to The Clevelander, a hangout in South Beach where Jamie Foxx was shooting pool with a group. They were all very animated. He noticed us watching him, so he jumped over the table, approached us and extended a hand.

"How are you folks doing tonight?" he wondered. "I don't mean to bother you."

He had flipped the script on us. We all laughed, including his friends, and he resumed shooting pool without anyone pestering him.

In early December, a month before the Orange Bowl game, our staff swelled when temporary employees were brought on board. One who impacted my life was Joyce Aschenbrenner. She was in her late thirties or early forties and had worked for my boss, Keith Tribble, at the University of Nevada Las Vegas. Joyce had an electric personality, quickly becoming a big sister to low level grunt workers like me. With her experience, she had seen everything in sports. She knew how to tell great stories; was always cool, and wasn't impressed by big names.

She and I had an instant connection because she was born in Pittsburgh and still had family there. Her uncle, Tom Bigley, was the athletic trustee at Pitt. I had spoken to him when I worked there. He had a full head of white hair and drove around campus in a Mercedes with personalized license plates that read "Biggs." I told her stories about him and she laughed. I had known him as a VIP, but she knew him as her uncle. In the short weeks we worked together, it wasn't long before I relied on Joyce for career advice.

In 1998, there was no true college national championship game. Our selection committee invited teams to play. We knew there would be two great ones. On New Year's Day in the Rose Bowl, Michigan—with Brian Griese and Charles Woodson—defeated Ryan Leaf's Washington State, 21-16. Some argued that was the national championship, but we believed our matchup the following day represented a better balance: the No. 2 Nebraska Cornhuskers against the No. 3 Tennessee Volunteers, led by Peyton Manning. It required a huge staff and extensive planning to make sure things went smoothly.

Some issues were a logistical challenge. Nebraska's strength coach, for example, demanded that his players eat immediately after leaving the practice field. Most teams let players shower, then bussed them to a restaurant or banquet hall. Dr. Boyd Epley wanted his team to be fed right after they took off the pads. I'm sure the coach had science to back up the importance of protein loading after a workout, but that was tough to arrange.

Both teams arrived in Miami five or six days before the game, and then things really kicked into gear. We met players at the airport tarmac. Nebraska's linemen weren't tall, but they were wide and thick. Tennessee drew fanfare because of Manning, who most experts pegged as the No. 1 NFL draft choice. Our job was to provide anything players and coaches needed while showcasing the best of Miami. We scheduled activities for both teams, but tried to keep them separate to avoid any animosity. There were times, however, when players from each side attended an event simultaneously.

The Miami Seaquarium put on a show with a dolphin named Flipper. Nebraska's quarterback, Scott Frost, threw a pass that the dolphin caught in his mouth. Everyone applauded, but Tennessee players booed in jest. I ducked out early, reaching the food tent before players arrived. Events were an opportunity for interns to eat while everyone else is busy. Catering stations had been set up and teams would enter at opposite ends. Considering this was the Seaquarium, I found it odd that seafood was on the menu.

I sat by myself under a giant tent, head down, eating quickly. Soon players began filtering in.

"Do you mind if I join you?" a voice asked. I looked up to see Peyton Manning.

"Please do," I said. "Have a seat."

Although I knew who he was, he extended a hand and we introduced ourselves. He noticed my ID badge, which read licensing and merchandising, and asked if the work was fun. Soon Manning's teammates sat near us, diving into heaping plates.

"Peyton," I told him, "I'm sure you don't remember me, but we've met before." I recounted that night at Silky O'Sullivan's in the crowded Memphis bar. He didn't recognize me, of course, but recalled being on Beale Street, and the friend who had brought him to the city. We didn't chat long, but Peyton proved to be a gentleman.

Once players arrived, I didn't want to linger. This was their event and I figured I might get in trouble for sitting among them. Staff were supposed to remain in the background and not engage players or coaches unless spoken to first. So I finished eating and offered my seat to a Tennessee athlete walking past.

For the record, Nebraska won the 1998 Orange Bowl, defeating Tennessee, 42-17. It was the culmination of nearly a year of intense work, and the relief was evident. I had to figure out my future, but first, I needed to relax.

On Martin Luther King Day weekend, my roommates and I drove south to Key West. Living in Florida, I had become part of the bar culture. During the occasional nights that I was free, I nurtured my social life by going out for drinks with friends. It was the first time that I drank alcohol regularly. I did it to unwind, knowing I needed to pay attention and manage my blood sugar.

Key West was great. We ate a seafood buffet for twenty dollars and watched the sunset on Mallory Square. Looking back on that weekend, if I was awake, there was an eighty percent chance I was drunk. Scott grew up in Gainesville and knew Key West, so he became our travel guide. Our first night there, we sang karaoke at a bar called Rick's. Filled with liquid courage, the three of us got on stage and began belting out *You've Lost That Loving Feeling*. We knew we sounded awful, and laughed hysterically. People in the crowd smiled and booed.

"Your boos don't affect us," I slurred into the microphone.

I noticed a familiar face at a nearby table, so when the song ended, I approached him with the brazenness of a drunken man.

"I know you and you're booing me," I said incredulously.

"You know me?" he asked. He had dark hair and dark eyes. "Okay, who am I?"

"I don't remember your name," I declared. "But you're on *Third Rock From the Sun*."

"I'm Joseph," he nodded. "But call me Joe." It was the actor Joseph Gordon Levitt.

"I'm Joe too," I smiled. "Hey, I don't want to bug you, but I have to ask you something. This is serious. I watch that show all the time, and you're the shortest person in the cast. But looking at you here, you're not that short."

"We have a tall cast," he grinned, then pointed at the stage. "I have to tell you, you did a really horrible job up there."

The next day, we snorkeled off a catamaran in frigid water. Afterward, walking up Duval Street, we passed Margaritaville, Jimmy Buffet's bar, and considered going in. But we were shivering, so continued toward our room. Later, we met a group of girls who claimed that Jimmy Buffett had shown up, locked all the doors, and played a private concert for the patrons in his restaurant.

After seeing so many famous people in Miami, this was a near miss.

Coaching and "The U"
—Art Kehoe

ART KEHOE AND UNIVERSITY OF Miami football go hand in hand.

Kehoe arrived in Coral Gables, Florida, in 1979 as an undersized offensive lineman who transferred from Laney Junior College in California. He blocked for quarterback Jim Kelly, who went on to a Hall of Fame NFL career, and roomed with Jim Burt, a nose tackle who later won Super Bowls with the New York Giants and San Francisco 49ers. When Kehoe's playing career ended, he became a student assistant at his alma mater, working his way up the ranks. From 1985 to 2005, he coached the offensive line and recruited players to "The U."

A native of Conshohocken, Pennsylvania, outside Philadelphia, Kehoe first met Joe Lafferty when Kehoe wandered into Woodland Hills High School on a visit to recruit Tirrell Greene, one of Joe's classmates.

"Kids from Pennsylvania want to play college football in two places: Penn State or Pitt," Kehoe explained. "I was a young guy, just starting out. I thought I knew everything, but needed to get kicked around a little. Even though I was from Pennsylvania, people viewed me as an outsider. It was hard to build a bond of trust because Miami was out of state."

Joe liked Kehoe. And Joe was friends with Tirrell.

"Joe gave me an in," Kehoe said. "He was like my agent. I knew Tirrell had interest from other good schools. Joe warned him not to talk nonsense in front of Coach Key. It's good to have a guy like that. I think without Joe I might not have gotten Tirrell, and Tirrell was a good kid and a decent player for us at Miami."

That was just the beginning of their relationship. Joe later coached at Woodland Hills, and stayed in contact whenever Kehoe visited Pittsburgh.

"He'd say, don't you come into this town without calling me," Kehoe laughed. "If I was hitting five high schools in a day, I'd schedule my stops so we had time for lunch. Or I'd try to finish early so Joe and I could go to dinner. Sometimes, he'd come to other high school games to scout with me. He kept me in the loop about kids in Pittsburgh. Joe was always there, and later I ran into him at coaching clinics. We just stayed in touch."

Their connection ran deeper than simply football, however. Kehoe's father, also named Art, endured a transplant as well.

"My dad was the best," Kehoe said. "He was the ninety-ninth heart transplant at Temple University. He lasted more than ten years. I remember all the medical things he went through. That kept my dad going from his mid-fifties until he was sixty seven. That's still too early, but the transplant kept him alive. Joe Lafferty could have died in his thirties if it wasn't for a transplant."

Kehoe speaks with the cadence of a football coach. Each sentence is important, dispensing wisdom. During his time with the Hurricanes, he coached seven players who became first-team All Americans. Twenty three of his offensive linemen played professional football, including Bryant McKinnie, Leon Searcy, and Vernon Carey.

When matters turn serious, Kehoe's voice lowers.

"Joe is tough, mentally tough," Kehoe reflected. "This guy had diabetes, was on dialysis, and he didn't bitch about anything. This guy is a dude. I'm lucky to have him as a friend. When he came down to Miami, he wanted to come to practice. I said, hell yeah. I'd bring him into my meetings. He loved that stuff."

Today, the two men trade text messages and inspirational quotes. When Joe had a recent health issue, Kehoe texted him about the power of prayer, combined with positivity. Joe's alliterative response: "Proof of the power of prayer, especially when peppered with positivity, Sir Arthur."

Kehoe took it a step further, texting back: "The propensity of such powerful prose punctuated in a prolific prayer has unlimited precision and potential, so one must heretofore point to Pluto and settle for any and all possibilities of peaceful coexistence permeated by positivity."

"One of the biggest themes I learned was from Jimmy Johnson," said Kehoe, who worked under six head coaches during his tenure at Miami. "We had a walkway from the weight room to the training room. On the other side of the wall was our locker room. Painted there in big black letters was the phrase 'Be positive. Work hard. Have fun.' He must have engineered 200 lectures around those words."

During a team meeting, Johnson talked about various challenges for a student athlete: the wrong girlfriend; a failed test; an ailing parent. Those things affect a player, and in turn the player affects the team. Johnson preached the importance of overcoming obstacles, working hard, and living in the moment. Have fun playing football.

"When Joe was in the hospital, I told him hang in there, I'm praying for you, and I don't know anyone tougher," Kehoe said. "Then I told him be positive, work hard, and have fun every chance you get. When I don't do those things, it's a recipe for a bad situation. When I use that formula, things get better more often than not."

After a long career, Kehoe left Miami University after 2005. He coached offensive line for two seasons at Ole Miss and spent time in the United Football League before returning to the Hurricanes in 2011. In January 2016, he was dismissed by new coach Mark Richt, a former Miami teammate.

"I don't want to sound like woe is me," Kehoe said. "I've had a good life and I love my family. But I miss coaching football. I've got five national title rings and we played for eleven of them. I've gone to clinics in thirty states, so I have connections everywhere. I got fired by a head coach who used to be my teammate. This whole deal that I've been through near the end of my career, Joe was calling me, saying 'hey bro, I understand. You'll get through this.' Sometimes I get by myself and I start to dwell on the fact that I haven't been working. Then suddenly a text pops up with a motivational shot by Joe. I jab back at him, and pretty soon we're laughing and it's taking my mind off the dark stuff."

Kehoe claims that Joe always signs his texts "I love U." The U has a double meaning—a tribute to Kehoe's pedigree.

"I don't have a problem repeating it back to him," Kehoe said. "I feel that strongly about him too."

CHAPTER 10

Viva Las Vegas and Sugar

AFTER THE NATIONAL CHAMPIONSHIP GAME, I knew the Orange Bowl would scale back its staff. The year-round store that we piloted had been a wash. We didn't lose money, but we didn't make any either, so the project had failed. It was clear that more people were needed if it was to be run correctly, and management was going to shut down the operation.

It was likely that I would be let go. I was hired as a temp, after all. I had been through this same routine a year earlier in Pitt, and part of me wanted to escape before the ax fell. I thought I had done good work in both jobs. Certainly, no one could say I didn't give it my all. I stayed positive, convinced that moving on is moving up. I'm a salesman; sometimes I have to sell to myself. I didn't relish the thought of waiting around to see if there was a job or not.

Joyce Aschenbrenner provided advice for the next step in my career. She previously worked as a consultant in Las Vegas, and

knew people who staged the Western Athletic Conference basketball championship. She suggested I apply for a temporary job
there. I could spend a few months out west and gain experience
quickly.

So in January 1998, I interviewed over the phone with Tina
Kunzer-Murphy, a manager for Las Vegas Events, which staged
the WAC championships. She and Joyce had been young staffers
in the University of Nevada Las Vegas athletic department years
earlier, when the Runnin' Rebels basketball team was coached by
Jerry Tarkanian. I was offered a three-month job that came with an
efficiency apartment and access to a company car.

Upon leaving Miami, I only lugged a few bags to the airport.
There weren't any complicated farewells, because my co-workers
expected me to return after a brief hiatus. But it felt like I was leaving Miami forever, and it turned out that was true. On the day of
my flight, my boss had me clock in for the morning shift because
the plane didn't take off until afternoon. I had worked exceptionally hard since my arrival, so it seemed odd that he wouldn't grant
me that half-day off.

There was a two-hour layover in Pittsburgh. In the pre-Sep-
tember 11 era, my family met me at the airport for dinner. Then it
was off to Las Vegas, a city I had never visited. I was nervous and
excited. The first few days were a whirlwind of activity. There was
a car waiting for me when I landed, and I was driven to my apartment, where I unpacked.

That evening the Thomas & Mack Center hosted a basketball
game. I wanted to talk my way in. My co-workers would be there,
and I was eager to meet them. Taking a cab, I asked the driver
to drop me at the arena's media entrance. I didn't realize what I
was walking into. Entering the building's bowels was like stepping
backstage with lights and glamour out front. It was a Big Monday

game, featured on ESPN, which meant it was one of the country's hottest matchups. Everyone in Las Vegas is a showman, and that night the pep band played "Viva Las Vegas" with zeal during TV timeouts. The band director resembled Elvis, undergoing spasms as he shook his arms to the music.

At the press booth, I explained who I was. A pass was available for Tina Murphy's people, but I needed to wait in a different line. On the other side of a nearby table was sportscaster Dick Vitale. Although I had never spoken with him, my first foray with Dickie V occurred when I worked in Memphis. I recalled a six foot six player who was building a reputation, and during warmups, Dickie V called to him from the sidelines.

"Michael Wilson," he boomed. "I heard you got springs. Show me something, baby!"

Wilson jumped straight up like he wanted to bust his head through the tip of the Pyramid, and the crowd went crazy. Dickie V went crazy too. He has an electricity about him. He's friendly, and strangers flock to him.

As I waited for my pass, he looked me dead in the eye.

"What are you doing here?" he wondered. There was a big, surprised smile on his face.

I froze, dumbfounded. Sure, I knew who he was, but how did Dickie V know me?

Someone tapped my shoulder, followed by a voice behind me. "Excuse me, son." He passed me on the right, and extended a hand to the broadcaster. It was Jerry West, former Los Angeles Lakers great, nicknamed "Mr. Clutch." That's who Vitale was speaking with, not me. My heart thudded with excitement at being close to two legends. This was life in Las Vegas!

Still on East Coast time, I arrived early to work the next morning. The Las Vegas Conventions and Visitors' Authority, abbreviated as the LVCVA, helped coordinate conventions around the city, hoping to fill hotel rooms. The LVCVA was the umbrella under which we worked. As I waited in an office, a gentleman came down and asked me to drive him to the airport. He was with the Professional Bull Riders, and we talked as I loaded his bags and navigated roads. He had been a champion bull rider in the 1970s, and dazzled me with stories about his career.

Back at the office, I finally met Tina, describing to her all the excitement since my arrival.

"Don't get caught up in the glitz," she cautioned. "We have a lot to do and little time. You work for me, and this is an opportunity to run a tournament and learn operations. With three months, don't act like you're only here to network for your next job."

The warning brought me back to reality. It was her version of a drill sergeant's introduction. I said "yes, ma'am," but she wouldn't let me call her "ma'am." From that point forward, we spent every day working out details of the upcoming tournament. We assembled backpacks as gifts for players. We spent time making travel arrangements and dealt with sponsors and licensing. I prepared for every meeting, and often was pleased to encounter people who had performed these tasks five or ten times already. I'd give a direction, and staffers around the table would nod and say, "Oh yeah, we know how to do that."

Despite Tina's warnings, networking would be important. At the time, the WAC had sixteen teams, and all were heavily into basketball. That meant there would be sixteen athletic directors at the tournament. My job was to glad hand them, so I planned to tell my story, hoping to make an impression on someone.

"Here's my card and phone number," I would say. "Let me know what you need while you're here. And if you're looking for someone in the future, I'm on the market."

Soon I learned the ins and outs of the city. A young quarterback I had known at Memphis, Chad Reed, had transferred to UNLV, so we reconnected and I tapped into his base of friends. If I wasn't working, we went out occasionally.

Tournament week was fun, but stressful. I met people besides players and coaches. There were liaisons and operations people checking in. Joe Borich, who had been Tony Scarpino's backup quarterback in Memphis, now coached in Utah. He came down for the tournament and brought friends. A guy he knew, Tariq Ali, had family members who owned a restaurant called Marrakech. We dined there, then hopped into clubs as VIPs. It wasn't difficult to get my friends into basketball games. After working all day, Borich and his crew wanted to party at night. It was exhausting, but I was ramped up.

The tournament was set up so men and women played on alternate days. Rather than handing out week-long passes, we gave most of the participants a day pass, because their team might lose and they would no longer need access. I carried a walkie-talkie and two cell phones, positioning myself in a certain area so anyone looking would know where to find me.

On the first day, a women's game was scheduled to begin at noon. We planned to open arena doors at 11:15. That morning, the Utah men's team was working out on the floor. Their practice was supposed to end at 11, which would give us time to wipe the court down, clean up any debris, and get the players' benches ready. From an opening in the bleachers, I watched coach Rick Majerus run drills with Utah athletes. It was highly organized and disciplined. But by 11 a.m., it didn't appear they were wrapping up. At 11:05, they were still practicing. Same thing at 11:10. My walkie-talkie chirped.

"We're ready with the doors. Let us know when to have people in."

"Give it a few minutes," I said.

Then one of my phones rang. Tina had learned what was happening and instructed me to clear Utah off the court. I gulped. Wearing a headset like Janet Jackson, I approached an assistant coach.

"Um, excuse me," I said. "You're supposed to be done at 11."

He half-turned, meeting my inquiry with skeptical eyes. Perhaps he thought I scouted for UNLV, Utah's first-round opponent. "I know," he said.

"Well... are you going to leave?"

"Not my call," he shrugged, nodding to Majerus on the far side of the floor.

I circled the perimeter, trying not to step in front of anyone or appear confrontational. With the scorer's table between us, I called, "Coach Majerus, excuse me, sir."

Rather than pivot in my direction, he looked over his shoulder. "What?"

"Practice ended at 11."

"What time is it now?" he growled.

"Eleven fourteen."

He nodded. "We'll be done soon."

"Uh, Coach, I can't let people in until you vacate the court. Fans are waiting."

It took another five minutes, but Utah finally left. I thought the disaster was averted, but Majerus didn't leave. He sat courtside and waited to watch the first game. Someone brought him McDonald's burgers. No one was supposed to bring food into the arena. It was an odd choice because Majerus had access to a hospitality room with free food and drink.

I didn't have anything against the guy, but at that moment, I cursed Majerus. He was frustrating me at every turn.

Once the tournament was underway, I expected things to run more smoothly. But during the first TV timeout of the opening game, there was an injury. Cheerleaders from each team alternated floor routines during a break in play. One squad dressed in blue had a girl at the top of a pyramid who lost her balance, teetered, and fell. Everyone in the Thomas & Mack Center heard her smack the ground, watching her writhe after dislocating a knee. An ambulance carted her away.

The tournament wasn't ten minutes old, but between Majerus and the EMTs, this was a tough start.

Over the next few days, I was busy all the time. During a packed UNLV game, I stood in my area, exhausted, sipping Diet Coke. I'm not a fan of coffee, so I hoped the caffeine would keep me moving. It was the final game of the night. By then I had removed my sport jacket.

Tina came by and scowled. "You're standing around with a drink?" she wondered. "Hey Joe, this isn't a cocktail party."

"I've been moving around all day," I told her. "I haven't even had time to sit down and eat."

She stared at me. "So sit down and eat."

At first, I thought she was slamming me. She was suspicious of an old boy's network whose fingers stretched deep in the tournament. She didn't want to see me become part of that. But I soon realized that Tina was being maternal. She cared and didn't want to see me pass out from hunger.

After making my way to the hospitality room, I had just started eating when my phone rang. Tina needed me in one of the lounges on the far side of the building. I rushed over to find her standing in the hallway.

"Tark is inside," she said. "I want you to sit with him."

Tark was Jerry Tarkanian, former coach of UNLV who had led his teams to four national championships and was legendary for biting towels during a game. He now coached at Fresno State. I thought it strange that Tarkanian couldn't sit by himself for ten minutes, but I wasn't about to cross my boss. I entered a classy room with a big TV and saw the coach sitting alone.

"How's it going, Coach?" I said. "My name is Joe and Tina sent me in to see if you need anything."

He nodded. "Sit down."

I was thinking that I had fifty five things to do, and wasting time here wasn't one of them. But of course I concealed those emotions. Tarkanian turned out to be a nice, regular guy, a grandfatherly figure. He asked about me, so I told him I was from Pittsburgh and had recently worked in Miami. It was just one of the times when I realized that famous people have different personalities than their public image. There was "Tark" and then there was Jerry Tarkanian. Spectators only know the persona, rarely the human being.

UNLV went on to an upset win that night. On the second men's day, they defeated Majerus' Utah team in a major upset. Utah was so good that year. During the game, the band played "Viva Las Vegas" every chance they could.

The WAC has a travel office set up just off the court. From there, losing teams make arrangements to get home. The plan for every defeated team was that players returned to the hotel, spent the night, and were put on the first available plane the next morning. It was standard procedure.

Majerus was having none of it. After the loss, he demanded his team board a bus immediately and be driven back to campus. It was a huge inconvenience for everyone, but we made it work. There may have been something to his methods, because a month later, Utah ended up playing for the national championship, losing to Kentucky.

∞

When the tournament ended, I left Las Vegas with a good feeling. I had interviewed for a long-term job with LVCVA and liked what I was told. Contacts at the WAC office in Denver suggested there might be an opportunity to work there. I grew excited, keeping options open for the next leg of my career. Returning to Pittsburgh temporarily, I waited, confident that I would soon return to either Las Vegas or Miami.

But time stretched. During frequent phone calls to the WAC office, I was told something was coming, just be patient. It started to wear on me, so I searched the NCAA newsletter for a job. I saw openings for director of marketing at University of Texas El Paso, and another at Seton Hall marketing for Host Communications, an outside vendor. I pursued both vigorously.

By April, each offered a job simultaneously. UTEP's salary was $40,000, and Seton Hall was $5,000 more. I tried to stretch out the offers, but Seton Hall needed a decision quickly. I had never been there, but conducted a phone interview with a guy named Sandy Diamond. It seemed great, but soon I would have a different feeling. Right around this time, the top eight teams in the WAC withdrew from the conference to form the Mountain West Conference. Apparently, they were tired of sharing revenue with the bottom eight. That was the reason my job prospects there were delayed.

I accepted the job at Seton Hall, but in retrospect, I probably should have gone to UTEP. Seton Hall is in South Orange, N.J., just outside of Newark. I located an inexpensive third-floor apartment in a grand old home in Montclair. The house was owned by an Italian family whose matriarch lived on the ground floor, while her son and his wife and kids lived on the second floor. I had a separate entrance, and was instructed not to play loud music or host parties. That was no problem because I didn't know anyone in the area.

As soon as I arrived on campus, I felt resentment toward my position. Because I had no history with these people, it couldn't be personal. The setup was a little different from Pitt. The university hired Host Communications for a three-year contract to run their marketing department. It was a way to skirt around Title IX. An outside vendor doesn't have to market women's soccer or volleyball because those sports aren't profitable. Instead, they can concentrate on generating revenue.

Sandy Diamond was a regional vice president who worked at the corporate office. From the day I arrived, he was on me. He embodied all the negative stereotypes of an aggressive New Yorker. Rather than ask me perform a task, he jabbed sarcastically: "Don't you think you'd want to try it this way?" His instruction method was annoying, sometimes even contradictory. He told me to keep the client happy at all times, yet I needed to run every decision past him.

Two months into the job, working every day, I sat down with Jeff Fogelson, the new athletic director. As we talked, he said he wasn't sure how long the relationship with Host was going to continue.

"What do you mean?" I wondered. Because of the three-year contract, I figured the job was safe for a while, provided I kept everyone happy.

"This is year three, and you're the fifth person in this position," Fogelson said.

Color drained from my face. The guy who held the job before me, Tim Roth, had jumped ship after a short time. My mistake was that I never asked when the contract began. But neither had Sandy volunteered that information. I went back to him, irate.

"It's true this is year three," he said. "But you're going to work hard and get us a renewal."

So I dove in, determined to earn that extension for the college. I inherited an assistant named Rob who had recently graduated from Seton Hall, so he knew the ins and outs around campus. The problem was, he thought he knew everything else too. What I didn't realize was that Rob was calling Sandy regularly with updates about what I was doing. He kept referring to his past boss, saying "Tim did it this way." He said it one too many times, and I erupted in frustration.

"If you have a question, you ask me. You think Tim was Jerry Maguire? Well if he's Jerry Maguire, I'm Bob Sugar," I yelled, referencing Jerry's nemesis from the movie. "I fire Jerry Maguire. Tim's gone, and I'm what's left!"

From then on, my nickname around the office became "Sugar." I sensed there were happenings behind the scenes that I didn't understand. I kept plugging away, but I didn't know who to trust. Things didn't feel right.

I didn't do much other than work and hang out in my apartment. This was a lonely time. I didn't even have a TV at home because it cost extra to wire cable to the third floor. So I listened to Yankees games on a clock radio. Fortunately, that was the year they won the title. There was a pizza shop two blocks away, so after parking my car, I'd walk up there. Soon I began talking to the owner, and that was a nice diversion. Besides him, I didn't converse with too many people outside of work.

Each morning, driving to campus, I listened to Howard Stern on the radio. His material is fairly mindless, so my thoughts wandered to the coming day and the tasks before me. Once in awhile, I felt a twitch in my eye. Sometimes it lasted longer than the car ride. I did my best to cover it up when it happened around other people, but it was a nervous reaction to the stress and bad feelings of my job.

That said, not only did I reach my sales goals, but I bettered them, performing at 125 percent of my target number. I tried to connect with higher ups as well. Richie Regan had been a basketball legend at Seton Hall in the 1950s. By 1998, he was nearing retirement, but still roamed the halls as a fundraiser. He lived in the same neighborhood as football coach Bill Parcells, and many days, the two met for a morning walk before heading to work.

Richie took me under his wing, inviting me to lunch with Paul Huegel, a fellow fundraiser. Paul talked about a local businessman who sold office machines and wanted to donate money to Seton Hall. Yes, it was a gift, but his goal was to form a long-term business relationship with the college.

"Really?" I asked. "Because our office needs a new fax machine. Nothing too expensive." I was authorized to spend up to $200 for a new one. I figured that if I could help Paul grease some skin along the way, it would be good for everyone.

The dealer gave me a floor model to save some money and promised a full service plan. But the cost was $250. I believed that Host Communications could afford a little extra to further that relationship. Besides, I had exceeded my sales goals. Shouldn't I be granted some leeway?

Later that day, Sandy called me with an edge to his voice.

"I heard you bought a fax machine," he said. So Rob must have told him, because how else would he know? "I thought you were going to discuss prices with me before you committed to anything."

I explained the situation and why I made the decision. I said there was no shame about going over budget in this instance.

The next day, in our tiny little office, Rob's phone rang. He grunted, then laid down the receiver, stood, and declared that he needed something at the bookstore. Almost immediately after he left, the door opened and in walked Sandy Diamond with another manager from Host, a guy nicknamed Rosey. He had never visited the office before. My eye began to twitch.

"So is this the fax machine?" Sandy asked, running a palm over its shell. God, I hated his sarcasm. Sensing what was coming, I remained silent.

"Joe, this is a tough conversation," he began. "I asked Rosey to be here because I can't do it by myself."

"Don't say another word," I told him. "I quit. I can see what you're doing, and I don't want to be part of it. I don't want to be treated this way. I'll walk out of here, but you can't say I didn't do my job. I made all my sales goals and then some."

Shuffling papers into a folder, I felt myself getting hot. I'm a fighter and didn't care for being subservient here. This whole situation was frustrating.

"Joe, you know—" Sandy started to say.

I stood up and stepped toward him, invading his space. I'm taller, so I stared down at him. "You should leave now and not say another word. Rosey can stay and watch me pack up." I felt tough, but it was little consolation. As Sandy scurried away, I turned to Rosey. "I know you have to put up with him because he's your boss, but that guy is a rotten human being."

At the end of 1998, another employee at Host Communications splintered from the company to form his own sports marketing firm. He brought Sandy with him. They soon landed the Seton Hall account, along with a few other colleges. Suddenly all that transpired made sense. Sandy had mismanaged me so that Seton Hall wouldn't extend their contract with Host. I had been making inroads with people at the college, but that conflicted with Sandy's plans. So when I bought a fax machine over budget, that was convenient grounds to fire me. At the time, none of that information was available. Knowing that probably wouldn't have given me comfort anyway.

So after leaving campus, I trudged home to my apartment, broke the lease, and packed up my car. The next morning I was back in Pittsburgh. The seven months in New Jersey had been a bust, and I had little idea what to do next.

CHAPTER 11

Connecting in Dallas

BY EARLY DECEMBER 1998, I was back in Pittsburgh with
no clue about what my future held. It felt like I had been stuck
on this wheel before. I talked with Bill Curry, who had given me
a place to live years earlier. Bill was like a second father to me.
He had built a happy life selling plumbing supplies, raising a
family, and staying active in youth coaching. He suggested I
come to work with him. It was a generous offer, but I couldn't
see myself in that role. Selling plumbing supplies wasn't for me.
I didn't know what to do. I examined my life up until that point.
The only thing I really knew was that I had felt happiest when I
was in Florida.

"Danny Vargo has a place in Pompano," Bill told me. Danny
was a childhood friend whom Bill had mentored. Although he was
four years older, we had known each other our whole lives. "You
should reach out to him."

I phoned there, and before the conversation concluded, Danny and his wife Leslie invited me to stay with them temporarily while I searched for a job. Their beach condo had an extra bedroom for visitors. I could crash there, get my feet under me, and seek out the next challenge.

Their condo was small, so I didn't have much space. I only kept a week's worth of clothes on hand. Joe Whitehead, a friend from the Orange Bowl, let me store extra things in his office. I quickly landed a job at the Pittsburgh Grill on the causeway at A1A and Atlantic Avenue. The bar had a gift shop with Pittsburgh-themed items, and they trucked down Iron City Beer for customers. They made great cheesesteaks and the place was packed during lunch hours. The Pittsburgh Grill was owned by a father, Craig, and his son, nicknamed Spanky. Although I had worked in restaurants before, being a Pittsburgh native had opened the door for me. I began as a cleaner and bar back.

At this time, *The Sopranos* was the hot show on HBO. Each Sunday night, Spanky hosted a watch party. Friends would come by to tune in. One of them was Tony Siragusa, the defensive lineman for the Indianapolis Colts and Baltimore Ravens. I knew Goose from my days at Pitt. He was a freshman when I was a ballboy there. He said he remembered my face, but he was probably just being polite. Siragusa later won a Super Bowl in 2001, and coincidentally, guest starred as a character on *The Sopranos*. Another familiar face at the viewing parties was Dan Morgan, a former bodyguard for Dan Marino. Craig closed the bar, and everyone except me drank beer while we ate cheesesteaks and watched HBO.

Danny and Leslie Vargo had another guest coming to stay with them, so the clock was ticking on my time as their houseguest. It was a planned eviction. They had been up front about that, but I had nowhere to go. While working at the bar, I met a guy who was a property manager for a former hotel that had been converted to condos. He was struggling to find reliable help. I didn't have enough money to rent a place of my own, so we brokered a deal: I'd live in one of his efficiencies for a reduced rate, and in exchange, work part-time as a cleaner. Doing that bought me another two months in Florida. It was time to go hard pursuing my career.

I paid for a weekly fax subscription of job openings in college and pro sports. The faxes were sent to the Pittsburgh Grill, and the owners were fine with that. But I faxed out so many resumes in response that eventually Craig said he needed to take a little money out of my check as compensation.

One job that caught my eye was a salesman for the Dallas Cowboys Radio Network. It was based out of the CBS affiliate, KVIL, a longtime Dallas adult contemporary station. On football Sundays, they became the Cowboys' radio host. In my former jobs, I had never sold radio other than spots that were bundled with sponsorships. Admittedly, I didn't know the nuts and bolts of radio terminology—things like reach and ratings—but those details didn't apply in this job. Their goal wasn't to target a certain number of people. Instead, it was to sell their association with the Cowboys, considered by many to be "America's team."

I conducted a phone interview with the director of sales, Craig Zurek. It went well enough that they offered to fly me to Dallas for a face-to-face meeting. I negotiated a flight that went from Florida to Dallas on Friday. I'd have an all-day interview, tour the sights on Saturday, then Sunday I'd fly from Dallas back to Pittsburgh so I could see my family.

The flight from Florida landed in Texas at 7:30 a.m., so I hardly slept the night before. I was excited, thinking about the prospects of working in the same organization as Jerry Jones. I got my shoes shined in the airport just to indulge my nervous energy. Once I arrived in Dallas, I took a taxi to the radio station to begin my big day. I first met Craig, then the programming manager. We had lunch with the station manager. It was going well. Late in the afternoon, I interviewed with David Henry, the director of sales. I had seen him walking the halls. He was loud and brash and funny, a real live wire. By this time, I'd been awake fourteen or fifteen hours and had flown back a time zone. Between airports, taxis, and interviews, I sensed that my focus was slipping. I went to the bathroom and doused my face in water. I thought the interview with David went well. I tried to match his energy, ending the day with a good feeling, but I was tired and I knew it. It was a challenge to conceal my fatigue. I shook hands with everyone and was assured they would be in touch.

Greg Bonner, one of the station's salesmen, knew I was single, so he suggested I spent Saturday hitting up bars in Greenville. When I told him that wasn't my scene, he invited me to dinner with his wife and two boys. They were a good Christian family, and it was a kind gesture to include me. On Sunday, I was on a plane again.

Back in Pittsburgh, I stayed with my sister and her husband. At the time, Tara worked selling radio ads, so we spoke in detail about my prospects. Early the following week, I received a phone call from Craig.

"I want to thank you for coming in," he said. "It was really great to meet you."

I knew immediately that I wasn't about to be hired. "Thank you for coming in" is code for no thanks.

"I'm not sure it's a fit. We're going to keep looking," he said.

I was disappointed. "Can you tell me why?" I asked evenly. "I'd like to know if I did something wrong so I can correct it."

He hesitated. "Well, Joe, I really liked you, so I'm sorry, but... it's just that you lack experience selling radio."

When I hung up, Tara offered comfort. I repeated what Craig had said.

"Lack of radio experience?" she echoed. "No way. They knew that when they flew you in for an interview. That can't be the reason."

I thought about what she said. My sister was right. Her words sparked the fighter in me. The guy that I didn't impress was David Henry, the director of sales. I had a good read from everyone else, but I hadn't connected with him. David's was the vote I needed to flip. I thought for a while, then hatched a plan and reviewed it overnight. Tara agreed that I had nothing to lose.

The following morning I phoned the station and asked to speak with David Henry. When I gave my name, the secretary remembered me and wanted to transfer me to Craig Zurek, but I insisted that it was important to speak with David. When he got on the line, I was polite and firm.

"Craig said the reason I didn't get the job was lack of radio experience," I said. "So I called to give you a second chance at hiring me."

It was dead quiet. I told myself he was going to speak next, not me. Silence stretched for twenty seconds. It felt like five minutes.

"I'm listening," he finally said.

I went into a pitch about the timeline of my interview, how I had awoken in the middle of the night to fly from Florida to Dallas. I bullet-pointed everything, down to getting my shoes shined at the airport.

"I liked you but it was the end of a long day," I said. "I didn't match your energy during our face to face. Here's the thing: I know I can. I'm an early riser by nature, so if I move to the Central Time Zone, I'll be awake an hour earlier. I'll be the first person in the building every morning. And my lack of radio experience means that I'll work harder than everyone else to compensate. If you tell me to call five hundred clients, I'll do it and I'll do it well. In fact, I'll do whatever you ask me to. So I'm asking you to reconsider."

I exhaled and waited, knowing it was up to him now.

Again, silence on the line. "If I were you, I'd wait by the phone," he said simply.

David had been a trumpet player in the Southern Methodist University marching band, and talked about it like it was the greatest experience of his life. He quoted General George Patton regularly. He loved explosive ideas, and my phone call to him was like a punch in the gut. He had never heard anything like it before. I didn't know it at the time, but my brash suggestion was exactly the right thing to do.

Later that day, Craig called to offer me the job.

Back in Florida, I loaded my Dodge Intrepid and rented a U-Haul trailer., excited about the new challenge before me. Greg Bonner, the kind station salesman, helped me find an apartment off Route 75 in Dallas. As I unloaded a sleep sofa alone, a guy about my age came by and grabbed the other end to help. He lived in a neighboring apartment. A few hours later, around dinnertime, his girlfriend brought over a plate of food. They were Canadian, and invited me to join them and some friends for a trip to Greenville Avenue that night. Bars and nightclubs lined the street. Although I wasn't much of a drinker, it was a nice opportunity to meet new people and be active.

The first place we wandered by was The Granada Theater. The sign on the marquee read "Bryan Adams Live." I thought it was advertising some cover band, not the singer himself. My new friends, ironically, did not have any interest in Adams, despite their Canadian roots, so I wandered into the little venue alone. The show had already started, so I missed him singing *Cuts Like a Knife*, my favorite song of his. But the rest of the night was a great time. I didn't even mind being by myself.

Because I'm an early riser, I usually got up at 5 a.m., worked out, then headed into the office, where I was always the first salesman there. KVIL had a legendary disc jockey, Ron Chapman, who had been on the air for nearly thirty years. He was a known quantity in the Dallas market. By then he was in his sixties, and was a great storyteller. He was so beloved that later in his career, he broadcast live from his home in Florida but led everyone to believe he was in the studio before passing off to weather and traffic reports.

My desk was behind a glass partition that faced the hallway toward programming. Early one morning, Ron bounded down the hall wearing sweats and tennis shoes. He stopped to look out the window and see the sun rise. We said hi, but he didn't know me. Once on the air, he made a throwaway comment.

"I was just in the sales pen, and saw Larry Parks working bright and early. Larry is everyone's favorite KVIL salesman."

I had the radio playing and barked a quick laugh. I was alone in the room, but because Ron didn't know my name, he spun a tall tale for his listeners. Moments later the phone rang, an unusual occurrence at this hour. I picked up.

"Hey, let me talk to Larry Parks," a voice said.

"Oh, I'm sorry," I replied. "Larry isn't here yet."

"No, he is. Ron Chapman just saw him."

"Oh, okay." I put the caller on hold, and waited thirty seconds to give the illusion that I had left my desk to look around. Then I came back on the line. "I'm sorry, but I can't find him just now. If you leave a name and number, I'll have him call you back."

"Son, I know he's there somewhere. I need to speak with him, and I'll wait until you can find him. How big can that office be, anyway?"

I tried stalling more, but finally had to explain the truth: I was the only one there, and Ron used Larry's name on the air because he didn't know mine. Like any good performer, Ron was able to suspend reality with his audience. That morning, I was forced to draw back the curtain.

When it came to selling advertising, David Henry liked me and told everyone I was brash; I soon earned a reputation as a bull. Except for me, this was a seasoned sales staff. A few other young bloods were brought in as well. Every morning I went into David's office and asked him to teach me something. He wanted aggressive sales people, so promised $500 to anyone who was thrown out of a car dealership for being too persistent while trying to make a sale. I visited Ewing Auto Group, a Mercedes dealership in Dallas. They had previously advertised with the Cowboys, but took a year off. I rolled right into a sales pitch with numbers, asking them to reconsider. I didn't sell anything, but David liked my attitude.

Soon he dangled a big carrot: any business who had not advertised with the network for the past two years was fair game to any salesperson It didn't matter who the original contact person had been. So I and other new salesmen went into full attack mode. The job turned cutthroat.

I approached Acme Brick in Fort Worth. The company ran TV ads featuring Cowboys' quarterback Troy Aikman. Their prior salesman was Larry Parks. The manager asked why I was in his office trying to drum up business instead of Larry. I was forthright.

"My boss has given me leeway to get you better prices," I said. "I'm trying to land clients. Getting you back on the air is very important to me."

Arriving back at the station, Larry Parks jumped up and got in my face. Apparently Acme Brick had phoned him after I left.

"What are you doing talking to them?" he yelled. "They're my client." He was a chubby little guy; I wasn't intimidated.

"Not according to David," I said. There was some back and forth before I said, "If you have a problem with the rules, let's go talk to the boss."

David hemmed and hawed, trying to calm us down. Yet he was vague with any resolution. Two weeks later, Acme Brick bought air time, but the commission went to Larry Parks. I had initiated contact, but the company preferred to deal with Larry. When I complained, David promised he would make it up to me. A similar situation happened with a Jaguar dealership who had been away from the network for three years. I brought them back, but didn't get credit on that deal either. The situation couldn't be sustained.

I became friends with Brent Porterfield, another young salesman at KVIL. Brent had played college football with Barry Sanders at Oklahoma State. He was my best friend in Dallas and later served as my Bible instructor. As young single guys, we spent time talking about girls, both searching for something that we couldn't find.

Radio employees were often invited to CD release parties by up-and-coming musicians. We attended one featuring Jessica Simpson. She was cute, but we couldn't get anywhere near her. She sang one song, then informed the room that her throat was sore. She was really there to schmooze the industry people who buy records. But there was plenty of free food and pretty girls, so Brent and I had fun. As I stood at the bar, I noticed the guy next to me.

"Oh my God," I said. "You're Tommy Mottola," Mottola was the head of Sony Music, famous for having married Mariah Carey when she was just starting out. "You're a legend," I gushed. "I'm Joe. It's an honor to meet you."

He was polite, asking if I was in the record business.

"I'm not, so the fact that I know you just proves how much of a legend you are."

Weeks later, we were invited to another CD release party at a bar on Greenville Avenue. We arrived late, when the only remaining open seats were close to the stage. Country singer Jack Ingram led off his set with a song called *Biloxi*, and I was hooked. After the performance, he went around the room and spoke with fans. He sat down and talked to Brent and me. He thought it was so cool that we worked for the Cowboys and that each of us had played college football. He even invited us to hang out with him after an upcoming concert in Fort Worth. Eventually, someone from the record label came to pry him away. For promotional purposes, Jack needed to move around the room. His manager believed he was spending too much time with us. Years later, when I went back in Pittsburgh, I told everyone how great Jack Ingram was. In 2008, he won the Academy of Country Music Award for best new male vocalist, but I had known about him for years.

That fall, David called me into his office and said that I wasn't generating enough sales. I pointed out that I had sparked sales, but credit and commissions had gone to other people. He understood, but expected me to do more of my own.

My sister was an experienced salesperson. When I relayed this story to Tara over the phone, she cautioned that this was my warning. "You're about to get fired," she said. "The boss said that to you as a courtesy to start looking for another job."

So after ten months at KVIL, I jumped ship to a sports talk radio station called "The Ticket." They liked that I was always eager for the big sale. The highlight of my time there came when I talked with Mark Cuban in the studio's break room. He was a successful Dallas businessman. Everyone knew who he was, although he didn't own the Mavericks yet. I had listened to his interview from my office, then wandered into the kitchen for a Diet Coke. He was there too, wearing jeans and a golf shirt. His dollar was crinkled and the soda machine wouldn't accept it, so I fed one of mine in the slot and asked what I could get him.

He tried to give me his wrinkled bill, but I wouldn't take it. It was funny, because the guy could buy and sell me a hundred times over and still be a millionaire. He protested, "You don't have to get me anything."

"No worries. One Pittsburgh guy to another."

Cuban was from Mount Lebanon, a Pittsburgh suburb. He asked for Diet Coke, and I joked that was my drink too. We talked for several minutes, and I walked him out of the studio to a white Toyota Land Cruiser.

One great thing about working at The Ticket was their annual convention for listeners called "Ticketstock," a wordplay on the music festival Woodstock. The event lasts four days, so I spent time setting up booths and autograph events. There were gimmicks like a marathon contest where people press their hands against a truck, and the last person to remove his or her hand wins the truck. Our DJs introduced bands that played live music; beer flowed.

I was better at selling sponsorships than I was at selling radio ads, so this was right up my alley. During Ticketstock, I met Al Fischera, who worked for Fury Sports. Al was in his early forties—not quite old enough to be my dad, but close. He was a smooth talker who intrigued me as he explained an interesting business model.

Fury Sports had experienced success by introducing club soccer around Dallas. Al had played soccer when he was younger, but Texas was football country, so not many parents were familiar with the game. Because of this, Fury Sports recruited young men from England and Ireland, guys who had played soccer their entire lives, brought them to America, and hired them to coach young kids. The accent lent them instant credibility. Parents heard their foreign brogue, and assumed those guys knew what they were preaching. Some of them did, but most were not semi-pros. Many were simply young men who had played soccer at the high school level back in their homeland. Those that weren't effective went back across the ocean.

Fury Sports went into schools, charged ten bucks per head, and staged an afternoon or after school event for several hundred kids. While building a brand, Fury took a portion of the cash. The guy who coordinated the event made money and paid the coaches. Precision marketing was used to blanket an area. All the elements fed off one another, and everyone helped spread the word.

As I talked to Al during Ticketstock, he shared with me his new vision of opening a sports complex. He had located an abandoned mall in North Richland Hills, between Dallas and Fort Worth, and wanted to reconfigure it so the anchor properties were converted to soccer fields. Inside would be basketball courts. But more than just athletic endeavors, this would be one stop shopping. There would be places to eat healthy food or get a haircut. We even talked about installing a gym with windows overlooking the soccer field so moms could use a treadmill while watching their kids play. I was absolutely intrigued.

Living in Texas had taught me that I wasn't great at radio sales. But I had been successful selling sponsorships. At a radio station, that only took you so far.

"I need a guy like you," Al said. "I'm trying to put together sponsorship money to make this deal happen."

After seven months, I recognized that things were way too cutthroat at The Ticket. People regularly stabbed each other in the back while trying to get ahead. So it wasn't a hard decision to leave there to work with Fury Sports. In retrospect, I should have asked for more up front money in the new job, but at the time was content to work on speculation. I planned to do any and every thing to make this a success. I was ready to swing a hammer and get construction going if that would help. When the sports mall opened, I believed we would be rich.

One of the first things I did was convince Al and his partners that they needed to ensure that the sports training was correct. Being a football coach and former player, I knew the importance of speed, agility, and quickness.

"My coaches run drills like that at every camp," Al said.

But if those elements are taught incorrectly, I argued, a player would never improve. Practicing a flawed technique only reinforced bad habits. I had a name and contact for one of the top speed coaches in the nation. Al and his partners were finally convinced when I suggested that some big name athletes I knew might be willing to invest. Athletes were always on the lookout for a moneymaking venture.

I contacted Bill Welle, a speed guru who I had met in Boca Raton. At five foot ten, with a blond flattop, Bill was only a few years older than me. He was a strong Christian who exuded confidence. His nickname was "Wheels" because he had worked with Cris Carter and several other Minnesota Vikings' receivers, and they all swore by him. Bill had told Randy Moss "I can make you faster," then went out and did it.

Bill agreed to visit Dallas, asking us to arrange lodging in Arlington because he wanted to attend a Texas Rangers baseball game and visit one of his clients there. He invited me along to meet Bucky Dent, who coached the Rangers.

"Bucky Dent?" I repeated. I knew that name. He was a former New York Yankee who was famous for his crucial home run in Fenway Park in 1978. I had never met a professional baseball player, but before the day was over, my head would be spinning with a flurry of names, faces, and memories.

It was a hot Texas day when Bill and I descended a long runway into the bowels of the baseball stadium. This is where players parked, so there were Ferraris, Porsches, and jacked up trucks angled into parking spaces. Standing in a garage beneath the ballpark was a handsome man with gray hair wearing a sparkling white baseball uniform. He was fit and muscled, skin tanned from years in the sun. The clean uniform sparkled like polished armor.

Bill performed quick introductions and Bucky Dent and I were soon talking about the sports mall as we walked toward the locker room. Bucky was curious because he was a businessman himself. He and a partner ran their own baseball school. As time passed, I learned that he practiced an old-school work ethic and understood the value of training. He sought to spread those values to more people.

"Hang on a second, Joe," Bucky said, and turned to a player trying out bats in the clubhouse. "This is Ivan Rodriguez." I shook hands with Pudge, then looked around to see Alex Rodriguez and Ken Caminiti. The 2001 Rangers were a "who's who" of baseball greats. For a moment, I stood in the center of them all.

In a short time, Bucky and I exchanged phone numbers and talked about another meeting. He wanted to learn more about the sports mall. When I called the following week, he mentioned a diner not far from my apartment. We agreed to meet there one morning.

When I arrived, he was already at a table, halfway through the morning paper. I sat down to talk business, but we never got to it. Instead, we just began chatting. I asked him about the famous home run. He still attended corporate events in Boston despite the obscene nickname that fans in Beantown have given him. He enjoyed working fantasy baseball camps with the Yankees. He had the most amazing and detailed stories. With a grin he told me that Dave Thomas, the founder of Wendy's, enjoyed betting when he shot eighteen holes, but was a horrible golfer and nearly always lost money—yet didn't seem to care. Soon he asked about me, so I explained my childhood cancer, the opportunities it afforded me, and the whirlwind life I had led.

Two hours passed when he glanced at the clock and said he needed to head to the ballpark. Over my protests, he insisted on paying for my meal.

"When the team is in town and my family is back in Florida, I eat breakfast here every day," Bucky said. "I arrive by eight, so show up anytime after that."

This man was a legendary player, a Yankee hero and professional coach, and he just gave me an open invitation to continue our conversations. It was another reminder that sports figures and celebrities are ordinary people who have done extraordinary things. Sharing the experiences helps connect as part of a community.

About a half dozen times during the next several weeks, I made my way to the diner. I call these my "Breakfasts with Bucky." Our discussions began casually but soon stretched far beyond the scope of a sports mall and morphed into a genuine friendship which continues today.

Years later, when his twins, Cody and Caitlin, were being recruited by colleges for their athletic skills, he wanted to be sure they could draft a thoughtful application letter, so he asked for writing samples from me because he liked my concise way with words. It was flattering and humbling.

Several years ago, he was approached by the Republican Party in Florida to run for Congress in his district. I was interested in working for him, thinking it might be a way for me to get off disability. I had the energy and wanted to try it. At the same time, he was having conversations with the Yankees about being hired to mentor players in their minor league system. I had a stake in that too because I wanted to help him write a curriculum and develop a private app that would be available to anyone with the organization.

Bucky delayed accepting either job because his wife, Marianne, developed inoperable cancer. He put career goals aside to care for her. In October 2015, she lost the battle. Bucky was relieved that he had not accepted either job offer because he would have had to back out.

Befriending Bucky was life changing. He's a great Christian and remains positive. He frequently texts to ask how I'm feeling and say that he's praying for me. And this friendship grew because two guys shared breakfast.

Breakfasts With Bucky

—Bucky Dent

"I MET JOE WHEN I was coaching in Texas through a friend named Bill Welle," recalled legendary New York Yankees shortstop Bucky Dent. "They were looking to put in a running and training facility. I wanted to know more about making athletes better, and those guys were experts."

Baseball fans recognize the name Bucky Dent. He is most famous for knocking a three-run homer at Fenway Park during a tie-breaker game in 1978 between the Yankees and Boston Red Sox. The winner made it into the playoffs, while the loser went home. Dent's home run flipped the score from 0-2 to 3-2, and the Yankees went on to win not only the game, but the World Series.

Dent's epic homer is still talked about today, considered by many to be one of the top moments in Yankees' history. What made it surprising was that Dent was not considered a power hitter. During a twelve-year playing career, he tallied only forty home runs. On that day, he was buried at ninth in the batting rotation.

Dent instantly became a Yankees hero for the ages. He had already been part of a World Series championship the prior season. In 1978, the Yankees repeated and Dent was named World Series MVP after batting .417.

Retired from playing since 1984, Dent has experienced a varied career of managing and running his own school. He still participates in speaking engagements for the organization and autograph sessions at corporate events. In Boston, it's a different story. Even today, decades later, fans from Beantown have welcomed him back to visit, although they interject a seven-letter curse word between the names Bucky and Dent.

Back in 2001, Dent was in his sixth year coaching the Texas Rangers. It was to be his final season there, although no one knew it at the time.

"My family stayed with me in Texas for the summer, but when they went home to go back to school, I was by myself," Dent said. "I met Joe around that time and liked him. Sometimes you just hit it off with a guy."

During the months he lived on his own, Dent regularly started his day by eating breakfast at a nearby diner.

"So I told Joe, anytime you want, come over and we'll have breakfast together. Once he did, we started talking about our different experiences. We went back and forth as I told him about pro baseball and how I enjoyed teaching. He told me his perspective on coaching football. I was interested in hearing about him. I learned all these amazing things. Despite the physical problems he's had, Joe has a great attitude and positive outlook. He's been blessed. He has this amazing will to win and an amazing desire to live."

Dent has four children. Scott, his oldest, worked as a firefighter and paramedic. The others followed in their father's footsteps and took up coaching. Stacy coaches high school soccer. Cody played baseball at the University of Florida then minor league baseball with the Washington Nationals organization. When his playing days ended, Cody coached softball at the University of Florida. His twin sister, Caitlin, played softball at North Carolina State University, then coached at Hofstra University before moving back to Florida to accept a job at a hospital in Boca Raton.

When Dent first met Joe, the twins were only ten years old. After they left town with his wife Marianne, he was lonely. Even so, Dent doesn't invite everyone he meets to share a meal with him. Something about Joe sparked his interest.

"He didn't want anything from me," Dent said. "I just recognized that he was an interesting and humble guy, so we hit it off quickly. While we talked, we shared ideas about teaching and coaching and philosophy. Conversation was easy."

Over morning meals, Joe and Dent reflected on the parallels between football and baseball.

"Baseball is played year-round, and it's grueling," Dent observed. "Football has a different mentality of toughness. But if you're going to be a baseball player, you have to have mental toughness to play so many games over such a long period."

At the time, Dent ran the Bucky Dent Baseball School in Delray Beach, Florida. He wanted his students to be exposed to up-to-date training methods. Dent was a football fan himself. He played in high school, and followed the Miami Hurricanes and Miami Dolphins. He even portrayed a wide receiver in a late-1970s made-for-TV movie titled *Dallas Cowboys Cheerleaders*. Dent began thinking about how training for football might help his baseball players improve.

"To succeed as an infielder, you have to have first step quickness and great hand-eye coordination," Dent said. "Being that I had my school, I was always looking for ways to be better. I wanted to be a better coach, so I talked to other experts to get their input, even if they were football coaches. What type of training does a wide receiver do to improve his first step quickness? Can that knowledge make my infielders better? I found it interesting to learn those things."

While Dent ruminated on teaching practices, conversation with Joe gradually veered away from sports. Their friendship continued even after both men left Texas. As Dent's children grew, Joe visited Florida, where he met with Dent to watch Cody play baseball.

"We sat in the stands, shared things about ourselves, and talked about religion," Dent said. "He's a religious guy."

Joe's daily text blasts began when Dent first sent him inspirational words. Joe loved the idea and expanded them to include a circle of close friends. As a result, he and Dent exchange messages nearly every day.

"The great thing about Joe is that he wants to make a difference and do things to inspire other people," Dent said. "I still marvel at the guy."

CHAPTER 12

Cyclops

LIVING IN DALLAS REAWAKENED MY spiritual side. Since moving away from Memphis, I had drifted in and out of churches. I read the Bible sporadically, but always found reasons not to attend church on Sundays. Once I was invited to Irving Bible Church, however, I became excited to be part of a faith community again.

The invitation came early one morning when I walked on a treadmill at a 24-hour fitness facility. There I met a couple, Rick and Cindy. They were a few years older than I was and struck me as very confident people. As we talked, they asked where I attended church. I told them I bounced around, so they suggested I visit Irving Bible Church, a non-denominational church northwest of Dallas. One Sunday, I took their advice.

Being an early riser, I found myself at an 8 a.m. service, and have vivid memories of the first time I worshipped there. There was a band with guitars, bass, and drums, almost like Dave Matthews music with a Christian twist. There were two big TV screens on either side of the sanctuary that featured a multimedia presentation.

The video showed a person wearing a sheep's costume shuffling through the halls of the building, stopping at a vending machine and peering into windows. I thought it was corny and silly. Then the pastor, Andy McQuitty, stepped to the altar and began talking in a smooth voice. McQuitty was about forty five, wearing an untucked shirt and khaki pants. He read Psalm 23, which many have heard at wakes and funerals. Below is the King James version:

> The Lord is my shepherd; I shall not want. He maketh me lie down in green pastures: he leadeth me beside the still water. He restoreth my soul: he leadeth me in the paths of righteousness for his name's sake. Yea, though I walk through the valley of the shadow of death, I will fear no evil: for thou art with me; thy rod and thy staff they comfort me. Thou preparest a table before me in the presence of mine enemies: thou anointest my head with oil; my cup runneth over. Surely goodness and mercy shall follow me all the days of my life: and I will dwell in the house of the Lord for ever.

During the next six weeks, we talked about the Psalm line by line. McQuitty broke it down into such plain terms. He convinced me that much of its message is misunderstood.

The first week focused on how stupid sheep are. They eat everything, including rocks and poisonous plants. They won't drink water unless they are led to it. They have horrible vision and poor reactions. If a wolf comes to devour a sheep, others standing nearby won't move. They're even dumb enough to walk over a cliff and fear moving water. If not for a shepherd damning up a stream, sheep wouldn't be able to move across it. If not for a shepherd making sure a field contained no deadly plants, sheep would swallow something toxic. In short, sheep would die if not for a shepherd.

McQuitty convinced me that this isn't a Psalm for funerals. It's a Psalm that should be read in front of a mirror every day. The passage mentions preparing a table in the presence of one's enemies. But if you're in heaven, you don't have any enemies. The earth is the valley of the shadow of death. This earth belongs to Satan. Once you die, you don't need a table prepared for you in the presence of your enemies. This is a Psalm about living, not dying.

Once I heard this new interpretation, it blew me away. I had read the words many times during my Catholic upbringing, but now I saw them in a different light. I realized how lost we are without Jesus, our shepherd. It's insulting, but accurate, to say that we are the sheep.

I was entering a new phase of my life, learning better ways to live and love. I began attending Irving Bible Church every week, and shortly after I had fallen under the spell of McQuitty's preaching, he announced that he was taking a sabbatical. He had not been on vacation for fifteen years, so planned to take fifteen weeks to ride his motorcycle. I was bummed to see him go. But it's amazing how God works. The next Sunday, as I arrived with a feeling of reluctance, a temporary pastor was introduced named Dr. Steve Farrar.

I know that different preachers have their own milieu. For example, Billy Graham deals with salvation. He can preach about other things, but it always comes back to that theme. Adrian Rogers spoke about a love worth finding, living in the moment and working for Jesus. Steve Farrar preached about men's leadership. I was enamored with his message and bought audio sets of his sermons, listened to them, then promptly passed them along to friends.

During my time in Dallas, I became active in Irving Bible Church. I took the job of table leader, and liked being in a leadership role. I attended singles events, giant gatherings for hundreds of people of all ages. Although I met many people, I didn't date anyone. I was surrounded by pretty girls with solid values, but I didn't think I was good enough for them. I was interested in chasing the word, not women.

My friend Brent Porterfield complimented me, saying I spoke in a Godly manner. I'm strong with words, and he told me that my statements reminded him of scripture. But I wasn't any prophet. I spoke with conviction, because I am firm in my thoughts and beliefs.

When my nephew Adam was born in 2000, Tara and Jim asked me to be his godfather. I flew home to Pittsburgh and put on a suit to attend his baptism. But when I returned to Dallas, I told Brent I had a problem.

"I don't know much about God," I lamented. "Sure, I study the Bible, but I'm not really happy with the man I am. I don't know enough to be a Godly influence in my nephew's life."

Brent's response was simple: "I'll help you if you'll let me." He passed along tapes by Kenneth Hagin, a preacher who sounded like Ross Perot's annoying brother. I couldn't listen to that, so I gave them back and asked for something else. He gave me Kenneth Copeland, whose voice was easier. I was soon swallowed by his sermons, and came upon Creflo Dollar, who spun off Copeland. Then I was on to Joel Osteen. It didn't take long to realize that preachers spring from one another like a coaching tree. I supported their books, but never sent them money, largely because none of them ever asked. Six months later, I visited a Christian bookstore to buy Kenneth Hagin tapes and give them another try. By then, my senses were heightened and I craved more. If you study and read, you're being fed different ideas and messages. Over time, I've been influenced by that entire lineage of preachers.

Sometimes when I attend a church, I'll hear a preacher and not feel moved. Because of my public speaking background, I'm arrogant enough to think that I could take over the pulpit in that moment and do a better job. I've never attended divinity school, but I'm convinced that I know God's voice. I don't always listen, which is a failing we all have. But I've never been called to the ministry. God has never given me an opportunity to lead, yet I remain fascinated by the word, God's message, and how it is delivered.

For several months, I worked full time developing the sports mall, but money just wasn't coming in. I had believed there would be a big payoff in the end, but the investment structure seemed shady. I received a clean cut of any money I helped raise—and I was one of the few people bringing in dollars. The money should have been rolled over as an investment for the future. I saw the writing on the wall that this wasn't going to work. The tipping point came when Al Fischera, the developer, vacated the office to work from home. With little cash trickling in, I picked up extra hours doing odd jobs elsewhere. More than once, I was forced to borrow money to pay my monthly rent.

Joel Dyke was a friend from radio sales whose father, David, was a pastor. Joel and I had both left the Ticket, happy to be free from the rat race. He was easygoing, and I loved being around him and his dad. They were renovating a house in the Grapevine area, northwest of Dallas, to take advantage of the financial incentives and tax credits when older homes were redeveloped. I began working for them to earn extra cash.

One day around Christmas, I was helping remove scrub brush from the back yard when I noticed the left side of my head was sore. I didn't remember exactly when it happened, but I was scratched by one of the vines when I stuck my head into the bushes near the garage. There was a little blood. It was annoying, but I soldiered on, working through the day.

But when I got home, it began to throb. I alternated warm compresses and ice packs, even trying to swab the cut with alcohol, but nothing seemed to dull the pain. I wrapped the side of my head in a bandage, hoping pressure would provide relief. Because of the holiday, everyone was taking a few days off. Knowing I could stay in bed late the next morning, I told myself a good night's sleep would cure me and I'd feel better by sunrise.

When I woke, my eye itched and watered. My entire head pounded, and Tylenol didn't help. I was a few days late with January's rent, but I now had money, so I walked to the manager's office. I knew the ladies working there and they had always been nice, offering cookies and water on past visits. This time, however, the property manager seemed shocked at my appearance.

"My God," she gasped. "Your eye is all red and erupted."

I played it off as nothing, but the pain had gotten worse during my short walk. The migraine began in my left socket and spread, radiating all over. The office women suggested I visit an optometrist, but in addition to being late with the rent, my car had died. I started to feel woozy.

I don't remember much of what happened next. I was told one of the ladies phoned her husband, who transported me in a pickup truck. I felt foolish, like everyone was making too much of a bad headache. Yet every bump in the road agitated the pain in my eye. It hurt to talk.

We ended up in Arlington in a store that sold eyeglasses. They kept an optometrist on site during business hours. His diagnosis was sudden.

"You need to see an ophthalmologist real soon, buddy," he said.

"How soon?" I wondered.

"Come on," he said, voice cracking. "Get in my car."

I had grown progressively more scared by everyone's reaction. This was alarming. Slipping in and out of coherence, I found myself in an office, lying on the floor holding my eye in silence. Pain was excruciating. A nurse helped me up, where I was placed before a machine that flooded my eye with the brightest light I'd ever seen. It was all I could do not to cry. Another nurse materialized with a wheelchair.

"I can get up," I assured her. "I don't need a wheelchair."

The doctor insisted. I stood up, then sat before promptly passing out. When I woke again, I lay in a hospital bed with a bandage covering my left eye. It felt like someone had stuffed a golf ball into my socket.

Soon a doctor came in and explained that I was lucky I had arrived when I did. Any further delay might have meant death.

"Death?" I said. "How does someone die from having a sore eye?"

Tests were being run, the doctor said, and he had injected antibiotics into my head.

"I'm pretty sure it's a staph infection," he said solemnly. "But we have to wait for results. If so, you're going to have some tough decisions to make over the next few days."

I was scared, so I called my parents. My dad, who hates to fly, jumped on the first available plane and arrived the next afternoon. In the meantime, I had gotten out of bed and stood in front of a mirror, removing all the bandages to look into my eye. The color was bent; it looked like someone had squeezed blueberry syrup into a stirred drink. I couldn't see out of it at all, and during regular tests from the medical staff, no light passed through.

"We don't believe the vision will return," the doctor said. "The brain is right behind the eye. If the infection spreads there, you'll be dead."

Dad remained stoic, suggesting we wait until Mom arrived the next day before making any decisions. I spent several hours alone, both in bed and staring out the window, feeling sorry for myself and asking God "why me?" Lying on my back, I opened a Bible and draped it over my face, hoping God's grace would drip into me like osmosis. Sometimes a little self-pity helps me take the next step down the rough road. I knew what needed to be done.

By the next afternoon, when mom stood at my bedside, I was calm again. "The infection has ruined my eye," I explained. "They need to remove it so it doesn't spread and kill me."

She looked at me with worry. "Remove the infection or remove the eye?"

I chuckled dully as I pointed to the eye. It was one of the few times I saw Mom cry in front of me. "Oh Joey," she muttered. People think it's tough being me, but it's harder on my loved ones, especially Mom and Dad. When the doctor appeared to ask for my decision, I was direct and succinct.

"Praise God," I said. "Take my eye."

He looked at me curiously. The staff probably expected me to sob or rant and say I need more time, but I had gone through that process the night before. When faced with the choice of my eye or my life, it was clear. Even then there was no guarantee, but I wasn't about to play chicken with a staph infection. I would figure out how to live with one eye.

In retrospect, I'm proud that I said "Praise God." Those two words did not come easily at that moment. They didn't leap or spring out of me. But I knew what I was saying, confident where I placed my faith.

I woke from the surgery, happy to be able to see from my good eye. I felt gauze packed into the empty socket. Mom sat beside me, wearing a terrified expression, but I reassured her it was okay. I had already asked the doctor about an eye transplant, but no such procedure exists. The eye has millions of nerves; too many to graft. A coral ball was stitched under layers of skin so that later, when I was given a prosthetic eye, it would have room to move.

As my recovery progressed, I stared curiously into the empty socket. Some might find this gruesome, but my shame died years ago. I was warned that I would experience problems with depth perception. At first, I was tentative. Along the way I discovered that despite one eye, every night I dreamed in perfect vision. It was one more example of how the "dream me" is often better than actual me.

Once, a year later, I used my empty eye socket to make a point. I was back in Pittsburgh, and Mom took me to her favorite restaurant, an Italian place called Luigi's in White Oak. By then I had adjusted to my limited vision. Restaurants like dim lighting to provide atmosphere, but because I only have one eye, I'm not good in the dark. If it's bright enough to shoot a TV show, we're approaching the level of light where I'm comfortable.

Although it was the middle of the day, Mom and I were led into a dim back room. Near our table was a window with the blinds lowered. I stood up and tugged the drawstring to open them. A shaft of light shined toward our table.

"I hope it's not a problem, but I opened that so we could see the menu," I explained to a waitress when she came by. She assured us that was fine.

As we were reading over our meal choices, a waiter came through and shut the blind, walking away before I could stop him.

Now I couldn't see again. So I stood up, opened it once more, and sat back down. Thirty seconds later, the waiter came back to pull the cord closed.

"What are you doing?" I asked. "I opened that."

"Other customers prefer it closed," he said.

"Well, I'm a customer too, and I want it opened."

Reaching toward the drawstring, he hesitated. I could see he was annoyed. He had no idea of the fighter within me.

"If you close it now," I warned him, "I'm going to open it again. So I'd advise you to leave it like that." There was a momentary stare down before I challenged him. "If that's a problem, why don't you get your manager?"

He scurried away, and Mom scolded me. "What are you doing?" she asked.

I knew exactly what I was doing. It was perfectly logical to me. But to add weight to my argument, I popped out my fake eye and set it on the cloth napkin before me. A manager approached and hovered before us with the waiter by his side.

"What's the issue here, sir?" he wondered.

I pointed at the table. "This is my left eye. The right eye is the only one I have. Because of that, I'm sensitive to light and I need that blind raised so I can read the menu. All the other blinds are closed, but I'd like this one open while we sit here. We're your customers, so I'm not sure who else in this room is more important than us."

The manager was stunned to see my eyeball on the table. He didn't know what to say. "Absolutely, sir," he stammered. He cast a scolding glance toward the waiter. "We'll leave this blind up for you."

My mom was embarrassed. But she knows that I have strong convictions, and I needed to prove my point, even if the method made others uncomfortable. As time passed, she laughed, and today the story has become part of our family lore. I suspect that manager and waiter are probably still telling the tale to their friends.

Fathers and Sons
—Joseph Lafferty, Sr.

"I GOT A CALL FROM his mother, who told me what was happening with his eye," recalled Joe's dad, Joseph Lafferty Sr. "I got tickets right away and flew to Dallas to meet him. One of Joe's friends picked me up at the airport and drove us directly to the hospital. When I talked to the doctor, I asked if there was anything else that could be done. Could we get a second opinion?"

The doctor stressed the sense of urgency. If the infection hit the optic nerve and spread to the brain, Joe would die.

"That showed how serious it was," Lafferty reflected. "You don't have time to think, and sometimes you don't have options. Throughout much of Joe's medical history, you follow what the doctors recommend and trust that their judgment is best. Thankfully, when he was eight, nine, and ten years old we had great doctors in Pittsburgh."

Born in 1947, Lafferty is now retired after working more than thirty years as a union steward at the Pittsburgh Post-Gazette. Part of his job was to create a work schedule, manage employees' vacation and sick days, and handle grievances. Because there was no manager during an overnight shift, Lafferty was the point man when problems arose.

Despite retirement, Lafferty still prepares taxes for some fifty clients. But his true love has always been tinkering with cars.

"When I was nine years old, I started loafing at a gas station in Wilkinsburg," he said. "When I turned nineteen, I bought that gas station in my father's name and ran it for a few years."

Although he was not old enough to drive, at fifteen he paid for a car to work on, but kept his new acquisition concealed from his parents. Over the years, he spent hours with friends in garages, rebuilding and refitting vehicles, increasing their value. By the 1970s, he ran into the route manager from his childhood paper route. Lafferty recognized that working for the Post-Gazette would afford a steady job, good pay, and benefits—the stability he sought for his young family. Within six months, he was working for the newspaper full time.

His son's health issues were met with steely resolve.

"When Joe was going through cancer, the less I thought about it, the better I was," he said levelly. "It was always there. If you stop and think too much it could catch up and overtake you. Sometimes you don't think, you just do what the doctors tell you."

His own childhood was considered old-fashioned by today's standards.

"I never heard my parents tell me they loved me," he said. "I don't ever remember getting a hug. But every day they showed their love by the way they raised us and the way we lived. That generation didn't show their emotions."

Some of that sternness may have transferred to him, although Joe jokes that his father "is like Dr. Phil" compared to his late grandfather. When Joe suffered from non-Hodgkin lymphoma, his father remained strict, insisting that his nine-year old not be afforded any special preferences.

"One time when he was taking chemotherapy, he was a smart aleck, so I reprimanded him," Lafferty said. "A friend of mine told me I was too hard on him. He wanted me to give Joey a break. I said, 'I'm going to treat him like he's never been sick a day in his life. Otherwise when he makes it through, he'll be healthy, and then I'd have a spoiled brat on my hands.'"

Joe didn't notice any difference. Lafferty wanted to be sure his son and daughter were dealt with firmly and consistently.

Lafferty always admired his son's ability to speak in front of large audiences. It is not a trait he possesses. He is shy, displaying nervous tension if he is required to address a crowd—even if the group is composed of people he knows. At the last minute, he insisted that his son act as proxy and give the farewell send-off at his retirement dinner.

"When Joe was young, I saw he was destined to be a salesman. He had the right lines and could talk his way into somewhere. He learned a great deal being involved with the Leukemia Society. When he was ten years old, I remember saying to him, 'you're going to be a salesman. Which would you rather sell, a Rolls Royce or a loaf of bread?'"

"A Rolls Royce," Joe replied.

"That's where you're wrong," his father told him. "A Rolls Royce might sound exciting, but not many people are ever going to buy a car like that. People buy bread every day. That's where you'll make money. He was thinking like a typical kid. I wanted him to know that glamour wasn't always the way to go."

CHAPTER 13

Two Robs

AFTER BEING DISCHARGED FROM ARLINGTON General Hospital, I packed up my belongings, left all my furniture behind, and moved back to Pittsburgh, living with my mom again in the house where I had grown up. It was a cold January in 2002. With one eye, I felt broken. I was twenty nine years old and had been hopping from job to job across the country for the better part of eight years. Now I was back in the same spot I had been as a kid, feeling like a shell of a man. My confidence had bottomed out.

I visited Coach Novak at Woodland Hills, but didn't stay long because I felt self-conscious, worrying that people would stare at my eye patch. Bill Curry, my surrogate father, carted me around town. He could tell my heart was crushed.

"I don't know what I'm going to do," I lamented.

"You're going to keep going," he said simply.

"How? I can't even drive anymore."

Bill paused. "Did anyone tell you that you can't drive?"

I scoured my memory, but didn't recall any doctor saying that I couldn't. Bill pulled into his driveway, opened the door and stood, walking around to my side of the car.

"Let's go," he said. "Get behind the wheel."

It took me a few minutes to become comfortable. We ended up navigating the vacant parking lot at the elementary school in his neighborhood. I'm grateful to Bill for so many things, and this is just one more example added to the list. He shoved me forward when I felt stuck.

The first week I was in Pittsburgh, I contacted an ocularist. I had never heard the word before, and there was only one in the area. Walter "Bud" Tillman's office was downtown, but he also had locations in Ohio and West Virginia. He made custom prosthetic eyes, and they weren't cheap. It took a full day to get fitted and for the prosthetic eye to be painted to match my good one. Insurance did not cover the $1,850, so my parents agreed to split the bill. The receptionist on the phone told me the next available Pittsburgh appointment was in six weeks.

That felt like an eternity. I didn't want to walk around wearing a patch for another month and a half. I inquired about an earlier appointment in a different location. When she said no, I begged her to put me on a cancellation list. I hung up and spoke to the empty room.

"God, I'm giving this to you. I know you'll work it out."

The next day I got a call back. There had been a cancellation the following morning.

I spent that day waiting while Bud Tillman made my eye. There was no school to teach his trade; he had learned as an apprentice from his father. The entire process took seven or eight hours. He stared into my good eye, then matched the color and pattern on the prosthesis. He pointed out I had little gold flecks around my pupils. I joked my eyes were blue and gold, the colors of Pitt. Leaving his office, I felt good again, slowly inching back to myself.

Living with one eye became my new normal. Human nature assumes that people get set in their ways, but I don't buy that argument. If I cut off your foot today, you would learn how to walk with one foot tomorrow. People have an amazing capacity to adapt, adjust, and move on.

I started coaching football again. Woodland Hills had always been my home, and I was welcomed back. That summer, I was heading toward our opening game when fellow coach Joey Samsa saw me on the sidelines. I was wearing a baseball cap and dark glasses to shield my head from the sun. He paused.

"Did you know your hat's on crooked?"

He grabbed my cap and straightened it over both eyes. The bill had been centered over my good eye. I realized that my hat had been canted for the past eight months. In a moment of truth and love, Joey made it okay, and we laughed. Since then I have learned to center a hat over my temples, not my field of vision.

I kept busy by landscaping with Coach Novak's two sons, Tyler and Austin. They were both in college and ran their own business with a friend named Shawn Zetkulic. There was enough extra work for me to mow lawns alongside them. I also helped my friend Ray Fischer with Compliments Custom Clothier, a startup business selling custom-made suits. My marketing experience came into play when we read that Steelers' running back Jerome Bettis was making an appearance at Buffalo Wild Wings. Ray went to the event and gave him a certificate for a free custom shirt if he ever visited the store in North Hills.

A few weeks later, I was working in the shop one afternoon when I noticed a silver Range Rover pull in. Out stepped Jerome

Bettis. When he came through the door, I introduced myself and told him that Ray would return shortly.

"I know he'll want to fit you personally," I said. "Do you mind waiting for a few minutes?"

Bettis browsed the shoes while I phoned Ray, who was twenty minutes away.

To stall for time, I began talking to Bettis, asking if I could call him Jerome. He complimented me on the store, saying he owned a custom suit business in California.

"Can I ask you a personal question?" I wondered. "We're the same age, and you're from outside Detroit, right? How does a kid from Detroit drive past Ann Arbor to go to school in South Bend?"

He laughed. He said he had been named Mr. Football in the state of Michigan, and the coach there had been interested in Bettis coming out of high school. But he was also enamored with another running back, Ricky Powers. Bettis reasoned he had a better shot by playing at Notre Dame. Bettis was a down-to-earth guy, and I enjoyed talking with him. He bought a few shoes to accompany his free shirt.

At Woodland Hills, football is a year-round activity. During summer, we host morning workouts on Monday, Wednesday, and Friday. Tuesdays and Thursdays we do evening sessions. We spend time in the weight room then alternate on the practice field developing agility and practicing plays. Weekends we run seven-on-seven passing drills. It's a never ending process, and anyone is welcome. Boys from youth football show up; we accepted kids as young as seventh grade.

In July 2006, I received an early morning phone call from Coach Novak asking me to wear khaki shorts and a coaching shirt to practice that day. A new kid was coming by, Novak explained, who might attend Woodland Hills. His dad had scheduled a visit. He was supposed to be pretty good.

At first I was skeptical. Our football program has a great reputation, so stories like this were not unheard of. Outstanding young athletes wanted to join the team. A year or two before, a six foot five inch kid came by who was planning to move into the district and live with his grandparents. We gave him a T-shirt, showed him around, even took him to lunch, then never saw him again. I don't know where he ever ended up. The program's winning record, coupled with individual accomplishments of players like NFL Hall of Famer Jason Taylor, Chris Edmonds, Lousaka Polite and Shaentae Spencer, had put us on the football map. Sometimes outsiders wanted to be part of that. The transient nature of under-privileged kids allowed for this, but our successful athletes were largely homegrown talent.

Coach never cared what we wore to practice. We rarely dressed well for a summer session, so this must have been important. Novak picked me up and elaborated during our ride in. The kid was a tight end whose older brothers had played Division I football. He was about to enter his senior season, and his dad boasted that he already had sixty college offers. I didn't believe it. The father was probably lying to inflate his son's case. My doubts increased when I learned he was from Buffalo. No good football players come out of Buffalo. I had my phone out, ready to Google the kid, but Coach was playing it close to the vest and wouldn't tell me his name.

At the high school, there was a buzz of excitement outside Novak's office. Fellow coaches who hadn't dressed up were teasing us, wondering if President Bush was stopping by. But their jabs all stopped when the kid came down the hall with his father. From my angle, I couldn't see them through the window, but one of our offensive line coaches, Tim Bostard, stood in the hallway for a clear view. I heard him mumble "Holy shit!" He dashed into the office and said, "This can't be true. Is this a setup?"

When the young man passed by the glass, the first thing I noticed was his height. He stood at six foot six inches, with blond spiky hair. He must have weighed 240. He had an Eastern European face and nose. He looked like a cyborg, like a young Ivan Drago. His name was Rob Gronkowski.

His father, Gordy, was a big dude too. He was chiseled out of granite, like a Polish Arnold Schwarzenegger. As we shook, I noted that he had giant bear claws for hands. Coach asked me to stay, along with father and son, then cleared his crowded office. Around the desk, I learned the backstory.

Gordy owned a chain of fitness stores based in Buffalo, but planned to live in town for the coming year to renovate a satellite store there. Rob had been misbehaving for his mother back home when dad was out of town. Gordy wanted Rob alongside him so he could keep the kid under his thumb. He envisioned his son as a tight end who would play professionally someday, but many colleges wanted to convert him to an offensive lineman. Gordy had stopped conversations with schools who proposed that.

Coach Novak asked me to take Rob upstairs to the weight room, where our kids were working out. There he could meet some of the boys.

"Sounds good," Rob said. "Mind if I get a workout in?"

The kids had all heard about him, and there was a buzz before we arrived, mumblings of "wait until you see this guy." When we walked into the weight room, the place went quiet. I introduced Rob to our strength coach, Denny Damico.

"I played for him," I said. "He's a guru. You're not going to meet a guy who knows as much."

Rob looked at me squarely. "You played for him?"

"I'm not that old," I joked.

Rob mingled with the other boys, and got along well. He was a funny, respectful kid. After a time, we headed for the turf field behind the school, where agility ladders were spread on the ground. As kids ran through drills, I pointed out areas where they could improve. Rob didn't know the moves we were practicing, but he picked them up quickly. I didn't have to correct him once. My first impression was that he was exceptionally agile for his size. His fundamentals were sound. Good technique had been ingrained in him.

After practice, we brought along a few other boys, taking Rob and his dad to an all-you-can-eat Chinese buffet. Rob wouldn't drink soda. He was very particular about what he put into his body. He drank milk with his lunch. His entire life had been about using the best equipment to train properly. It became clear to me that Rob had been nurtured to play football. I remember looking up from my plate, thinking that coaching this young man was going to be quite a ride.

Rob quickly became friends with Mike Dykes, a smart six foot four inch defensive lineman who ended up at North Carolina, and Rontez Miles, who later played for the New York Jets. Rob was also taken under the wing of Noah Taylor, Jason Taylor's little brother. Noah was highly intelligent too, earning straight As in school. He taught Rob the plays we ran. Noah's older brother had already made it as a pro, and I think Gordy was pleased to have that NFL connection.

There were many Pittsburgh-area schools that wooed Rob and his father, hopeful that Rob would play for them. Gordy had sold fitness equipment all over, so he knew coaches across western Pennsylvania.

"Joe, I'm getting killed here," Gordy told me on the phone from his home in Buffalo. "I sold stuff to these schools, and now they act like it was a favor and I need to send Rob to them. Some of these people promise me the world if I bring Rob to their school."

A phone rang in the background and Gordy cursed.

"Here's another 412 area code," he complained. "Gateway High School."

Gateway, where my old friend Tony Scarpino had played, was a rival just up the road from Woodland Hills. "That's going to be Terry Smith, their head coach," I told him. "Answer it on speaker and let me listen."

I giggled while Smith pressed Gordy, politicking with the hard sell. They had already done business together, Smith said, and he hoped that...

Gordy cut him off. "This is my kid. We moved to Wilkins township and know where Rob is going to school."

Gordy chose Woodland Hills because we could teach his son to drive block. That would be important to his future success. That year, we had strong defensive lineman that most other teams couldn't handle. Once we showed Rob how to tuck his elbows in and maintain parallel feet, he could move anyone. It wasn't long before he was pushing everyone around the field. One time Rob lined up on the left and blocked a defensive tackle clear across the formation, twelve yards downfield. The kid ended up on his back, then popped up. Rob pushed him back down before the whistle. When a flag was thrown, Rob was annoyed.

"Come on," he barked. "I'm just finishing my block!"

Rob had a funny streak, carefree and comfortable with himself. As the process of moving to Pennsylvania continued, I drove around with Gordy, helping him locate an apartment and rent furniture. I've stayed in touch with the family over the years. They've attended our Woodland Hills golf outing. I even sent Rob a birthday card with a ten dollar gift card to Dunkin Donuts, where he has an endorsement deal.

Now that Rob is famous and often spotlighted—he went on to Arizona and won Super Bowls with the New England Patriots—people are familiar with a goofy frat boy off the field. There is that side to him, but he also has a big heart. His charm comes from his childlike passion for life. Take your wildest dreams from when you were a kid. Did you fantasize about being president? An astronaut? A billionaire? Now imagine that you wake up living that dream every day, and that's a slice of Rob's life. He's the biggest twelve-year-old I've ever met.

Around this time, vision in my good eye began to blur. I had a hard time driving, especially at night. To be safe, I would go forty on a sixty mile-per-hour highway. I didn't know that my retina was detaching and flopping around. When I had my vision checked, I was told I could not drive any longer. It was a blow to my confidence, but I understood. The doctor was nervous about trying to fix the detached retina because I only had one eye. He wanted to give it time to heal naturally.

"Why aren't you on disability?" the doctor wondered. "Why are you trying to work?"

Because working and moving forward are what I do. Applying for public assistance felt like quitting, like the ultimate statement that I was giving up. I did accept Social Security, even though doing so left me uncomfortable.

My mom moved to Plum, so I stayed in the basement of my father's home before taking a studio apartment across from the Wolvarena, the stadium where Woodland Hills plays its games.

One day, in 2006, after returning home from a two-mile walk, pain raced up the right side of my chest. It hurt when I took a deep breath. I don't usually complain, but this felt different. It was bad. Could I be having a heart attack?

Just then my mom phoned. She knew something was wrong from my clenched voice. When I told her what was happening, her response was swift.

"Maybe I should take you to the hospital." I agreed fast, so she wondered if an ambulance was a better idea because it would arrive sooner.

"Just get here," I said.

Panic overtook me and I began to pray. After all the medical challenges I had experienced, was this when I would die?

The hospital staff in Monroeville were professionals. Within minutes of arrival there I was lying down with machines attached to my chest. My heartbeat was regular, but pounded fast, probably because of self-induced stress. I was given a calming IV, and blood was drawn. I promptly fell asleep. When I woke, Mom and Dad sat beside me. Dad explained that I had a pulmonary embolism—a blood clot in my right lung. I had been given blood thinners, and doctors wanted to be sure no clots spread to my legs.

"So this wasn't a big deal?" I asked, ever the optimist.

"Well," Dad replied, "you could have easily died."

I grew quiet. It wasn't the first time death had been in my neighborhood, but it was close enough again to knock on the door. I didn't know it at the time, but my organs were starting to fail. Blood pressure and cholesterol medicine became part of my daily routine. Tests revealed that my kidneys operated at forty percent capacity. By the following September, that number dwindled to only seventeen percent, so I began dialysis. My health challenges were moving to a new level.

∞

I wallowed alone in my small apartment, unable to drive, devoid of love. Someone—whether Mom, Dad, Tara, or a friend—had to chauffeur me everywhere I went. Each day, Coach Novak came by my apartment so I could ride with him to football practice. I was a burden on my loved ones. I was uncomfortable knowing that people went out of their way for me.

I began to think about suicide. Being gone would make it easier on everyone else. I even planned the perfect way to murder myself. My friend, Rob Kozub, has a conceal carry permit because of his job delivering pizzas. Sometimes he leaves the gun in his car. I could break into his glove compartment overnight and steal it. He would discover it missing, but not have any idea that I was the thief. Living across from the stadium, I watched the dumpsters get emptied each week, so I knew the sanitation schedule. The night before, long after dark, I could climb into a Wolvarena dumpster, burrow under a pile of garbage, and shoot myself. The gun and I would both be thrown away before anyone went looking for me. No one would ever know the truth, and no one besides me could be hurt or implicated. I might even leave a note in my apartment saying I had fled the country so I didn't trouble my loved ones anymore.

It's morbid, but I ruminated about my own death. That was my mindset at the time. But a fluke injury to my friend Rob brought me back from the dark edge.

Rob Kozub is a year younger than I am. We played football together at Woodland Hills. With his wife, Tami, they four children: Stephanie, James, Ty and Ethan. Rob has made a career for himself delivering several hundred newspapers every morning before sunrise, then delivering pizzas by day. I lovingly call him a mule, because if there's work to be done, Rob is the guy. He's kind and compassionate too. He provided rides when I couldn't drive, and loaned me cash a few times so I could make rent.

During the time I contemplated suicide, I was helping out Joey Samsa at his pizza shop up the road from my apartment. That was where Rob worked. He was making a delivery when he lost his footing on a staircase. He slid along his back, gripping the railing as he fell, tearing his rotator cuff. The next day, in the kitchen, his arm was in a sling. Tami and I both listened as he complained that he couldn't afford to miss work for any surgery.

"Rob," I told him, "you have to get the surgery done."

Tami agreed with me, but Rob dug in his heels. We argued as friends do. Our conversation turned heated, punctuated by raised voices.

"If I go for surgery, how are the newspapers going to get delivered?" he shouted.

I yelled back almost before I knew what I was saying. "Tami is going to pick me up overnight, and she'll drive so I can deliver the papers. We're going to do that every morning until you're better and can resume your life!"

He told me I was crazy. I told him I was serious. Calming, he spoke in low tones.

"I can't afford to pay you," he said.

"I don't remember asking for money. You need surgery. I'm willing to put my time in to help. We're going to do this together."

So that's exactly what we did. Tami drove for a few days. Once Rob was out of surgery, he assumed the role of driver. I folded the newspapers, tossing them out of the right side window. Rob is such a warrior that he learned to throw with his left hand. Sometimes I had to exit the car to lay a paper on someone's porch. A few mornings, between the hills of Pittsburgh and running back and forth, I experienced motion sickness. Rob stopped long enough for me to vomit before we resumed the route.

Helping Rob gave me a purpose. It pulled me up and erased my bout of not wanting to live. In a very real sense, it saved me.

I'm blessed with many friends. Rob, however, is reluctant to view people that way. So I was honored when he turned to me one day and declared that I was his best friend.

"We're not friends or best friends," I told him earnestly. "It's true we don't share the same blood, but let's put it out there: you and I are brothers."

"Coach Ha-ha"

—Rob Gronkowski

ROB GRONKOWSKI IS RECOGNIZED AS one of the premier tight ends in the National Football League. Drafted in the second round, 42nd overall, by the New England Patriots in 2010, he posted ten touchdowns his rookie year, and set a league record for touchdowns by a tight end the following season, with eighteen. Football insiders agree that Gronkowski has redefined the position. In his first seven seasons, despite missing time with injuries, he scored sixty eight touchdowns in eighty eight games and amassed more than 6,000 receiving yards. He has also played in two Super Bowls.

More than that, Gronk is a cultural phenomenon. As disciplined as he is on the field, away from stadiums he is known for his goofy, party boy antics. "Gronking" entered the American vernacular as a verb, meaning to slam something into the ground, the same way Rob winds up and spikes a football after he scores.

He has appeared naked in ESPN magazine's "The Body" issue with a strategically placed football concealing his private areas. He made a cameo appearance in the movie "Entourage." By age twenty seven, he had cooperated with outside writers for not one but two biographies, and was the subject of a romance novel titled *A Gronking to Remember.*

Before superstardom, he was a high school athlete from a Buffalo suburb who transferred to Woodland Hills for his senior year.

"I wasn't sure what to expect when I arrived at Woodland Hills, but I was excited," Gronkowski recalled. "It felt like a good opportunity. I basically treated it as my freshman year of college. It was my first time away from home, so it was definitely an advantage when I got to college. By then, it felt like my second year, because I was used to changes."

Head coach George Novak was among the first people Gronkowski met in Pennsylvania. Right alongside him was Joe.

"Coach Lafferty was the man running around, making sure everything went smoothly. He was Coach Novak's right-hand man. He made sure everyone was there on time, that everything was organized right, that practice drills went as planned."

Amid the social challenges of moving to a different state to attend an unfamiliar school, Gronkowski immediately noticed the level of competition was more intense.

"The transition to a new program was one thing," he recalled. "Overall, it was adjusting to a new atmosphere and the speed of the game. There were ten guys on the Woodland Hills team that ran under a 4.5. We were super fast, so I had to adapt to the speed everyone else had."

On a roster stacked with talent, Joe was impressed with Rob's football skills immediately. He also worried about bragging rights.

Joe's graduating class, in 1990, saw seven seniors earn scholarships to play Division I football. With Rob in the mix, everyone expected the class of 2007 to be offered more.

"The competition level for football was extraordinary, probably one of the best in the country," Rob said. "So there's no question that helped improve my game. We had eight guys who were approached to play Division I. Later, six guys were in the NFL at one time who had played for Woodland Hills."

Some of the Division I athletes from the 2007 team stumbled. Two boys started in Division I, but after a year transferred to Division II schools. Another was set to attend college, but that plan was derailed when he was arrested for stealing a car.

"They got four Division I athletes," Joe said, "but they should have had eight."

While the entire team was impressive, Joe believes that Gronkowski was more advanced than most of his classmates.

"In my time as a coach, I've only seen two players who I thought could make the jump from high school football directly to the pros," Joe said. "One was LaVar Arrington, who I coached against in Pittsburgh, and the other was Rob. While there would be a little lag physically, they had the frame and an ability level that was so much higher than everyone else."

Amid the daily grind of practice, boys on the Woodland Hills team garnered special respect for Joe.

"Everyone had a nickname," Gronkowski said. "We called him Coach Ha-ha because of his last name. At that age, in high school, everyone giggled. Coach Lafferty was cool, and when someone called him Coach Ha-ha, it put smiles on our faces."

Gronkowski was not privy to Joe's challenges off the field. Around this time, Joe's health problems began to multiply, but they never distracted the team.

"I was just a high school kid, and I was also the new guy trying to adjust," Gronkowski admitted. "I was in college and beginning my NFL career when I became aware of the things he went through. That was when I learned about his lifetime struggles: having cancer, diabetes, open heart surgery. It was remarkable, the things that were going on with him. I definitely respected his perseverance for going out and coaching us. It showed what kind of heart he had. His heart was so big. Despite everything he went through, he wanted to be out there helping kids."

After leaving Woodland Hills, Gronkowski attended the University of Arizona for three years, then moved to the NFL. Yet he and Joe have remained in touch.

"He texts me quotes every day about life lessons, things like taking one day at a time," Gronkowski said. "I love reading them because they offer good advice. It helps me out."

"Rob told me once he likes when I text religious quotes," Joe recalled. "That way he doesn't have to go to church. I told him, no, you still have to go to church!"

Their paths continue to cross. Recently, Gronkowski appeared on the Home Shopping Network to promote Gronkball Bluetooth Wireless Speakers, an audio speaker shaped like a football. Joe watched this and realized he hadn't spoken to Rob for a while. So he picked up the phone.

"He called in and talked to me live on the air," Gronkowski laughed. "It was classic. Hilarious. Perfect timing. I didn't expect that."

CHAPTER 14

Flatlining

REID CARPENTER HAD BEEN IN my family's life since before I was born. Working in Pittsburgh's eastern suburbs, he ran a group called Young Life, which gathered teenagers and introduced them to Christ, teaching them how a relationship with God could affect the community. In many of the churches I attended over the years, I noticed that women seemed willing to participate. Recruiting males, however, could be a challenge. So when Reid pulled up to my grandparents' house all those years ago, he must have been pleased to have four Lafferty boys pile into his car. My dad and his three brothers went off to a meeting. The connection among our families continued through generations. Reid's second-youngest son, Don, sat next to me in high school Spanish class, and his daughter, Christy, knew Tara from cheerleading.

When I returned to Pittsburgh, my uncle Jim suggested that I contact Reid, who always needed volunteers. Unfortunately, Reid was working in Florida by then, but he recommended I look up John Stahl-Wert, who ran the Pittsburgh Leadership Foundation that Reid had spearheaded. The organization helped connect smaller non-profits to develop leadership initiatives.

John and I spoke on the phone. He passed along a book he had written, then invited me to meet him at the Omni William Penn hotel. We shared coffee and conversation. John is a smart man, and he probably sensed that I was spinning. There wasn't much going on in my life. I had resolved that I wanted to be alive, but nearly everything else was uncertain. My health was deteriorating. I was on public assistance, limited in what I could do in everyday life. I didn't have a mission, but offered myself to John, explaining honestly that I only had so much to give.

"What are you doing tonight?" John wondered. "Why don't you come to a dinner where I'm speaking?"

I had no plans that evening, but transportation would be a problem. It was always a problem. Because I was unable to drive, finding a ride became a recurring struggle. Despite the generosity of friends and family, I hesitated to continually impose upon others. I bargained with people, offering to walk part way so they wouldn't have as far to go. Often I was told, "I can pick you up, but it won't be for three hours." So I posted up to wait. It left plenty of time to think and read and reflect on my inability to drive.

"I'd love to come," I told John. "But it's going to be hard to get there."

When I explained that I needed a ride, he instructed me to phone a young friend of his, David Paul. When I called, David could not have been nicer. He lived in Wilkins Township, not far from my apartment in North Versailles, so picking me up wasn't a major inconvenience. The dinner was wonderful and John gave a powerful speech, but the lasting memory is that I got to meet David. We had an immediate connection.

David grew up in the South Hills of Pittsburgh, attending Upper St. Clair High School. He is two years older than I am, and during the first year of Woodland Hills in 1987, we played them in football. We talked about high school, and I learned that David was an offensive and defensive lineman. Nearly twenty years later, he was still 240 pounds of muscle. Recounting our pasts, we determined that we had taken the field against each other. He boasted that his team had beaten us early in the season. I countered that we had defeated them in the playoffs—a major upset for our first-year team.

"Pure luck," he insisted.

David went on to study psychology at Northeastern University and earned a master's degree from the Princeton Theological Seminary. As a Presbyterian minister, he is fluent in Hebrew and Greek. His wife, Jennifer, is a neonatal ICU nurse. I learned very quickly that David is big-hearted and brilliant.

He stopped by the Pittsburgh Leadership Foundation nearly every day. I told him I was eager to begin volunteering there. He offered to drive me, so we worked out a schedule. He couldn't do it every day, but when he could, he went a step further, agreeing to pick me up from dialysis. This was the first time I was able to go somewhere regularly besides Woodland Hills.

I've said before that my old high school was a second home. It was a safe and easy place to be, because everyone there knew my story. I kept returning to gain my footing, but looking back, I wonder if I used it as a hiding place. Should I have stretched myself, maybe even given college another try? Sometimes I think about what I didn't accomplish during this time, and reflect that I should have done more.

The Pittsburgh Leadership Foundation afforded a new challenge, providing an outlet for me to serve and grow. They weren't easy days there. One side effect of dialysis is constipation, so sometimes I'd be sick and vanish into the bathroom for forty-five minutes or an hour. Twice I had to phone Mom or Dad to come get me. Occasionally David brought me home when I wasn't feeling well. Yet I was grateful for the work and the beginning of my friendship alongside David Paul.

∞

I took dialysis every Monday, Wednesday, and Friday. A bus transported me from my apartment early in the morning, and once I arrived at the facility, treatment lasted between two-and-a-half to three hours.

Dialysis replaces the function of kidneys. It removes impurities in the bloodstream. Functioning organs allow a person to urinate toxins out of his system, but someone with failing kidneys loses that ability, so fluids gather and remain until dialysis filters that off. Before a treatment, I felt like a water-logged washcloth; by the end, I had been wrung out.

I was regimented about what I put into my body, determined to have very little fluid on me so I could easily return to "dry weight." I couldn't have fruit or cola or anything with too much phosphorus. Salt causes fluids to be retained. I couldn't eat leafy green vegetables, and had to be careful how much water I swallowed. It was a restrictive diet.

My mindset was that I would not miss a dialysis treatment, but many patients who rode the bus with me were cavalier. One guy even came in intoxicated. At the end of three hours, all the alcohol had been removed from his system. It's a horrible thing to do to your body. Another guy I met, Marlon, was about my age, and had been taking dialysis for fifteen years. I asked why he didn't seek a kidney transplant, and he confessed that he was afraid to die if anything went wrong. He was filled with fear.

I would have risked my life because I didn't have much to live for. I needed life-sustaining medication to survive. I fought every day to move closer to a transplant. It would be a long process. In my head, I estimated that dialysis would span five years.

In the fall of 2007, I met the team at the Thomas E. Starzl Transplantation Institute at UPMC Montefiore. They ran a series of tests, filling more than twenty tiny tubes with my blood. When I interviewed with Dr. Ron Shapiro, the clinic chief, he identified me for a solitary kidney transplant or a kidney-pancreas block. I needed a kidney first, and would later require a new pancreas. Which path we took would be determined by organ availability. Due to my health and age, these two options were the best chances for my survival.

My pre-op transplant coordinator was Amy Singh. With all the tests and specific instructions I underwent, she monitored everything that happened. Amy was only a few years older than I was, and we connected right away. We traded funny emails, and I eventually met her husband and daughters. She became like my sister, educating me on the procedure and its aftermath.

"What are your goals following the transplant?" she asked during an early interview.

I thought before answering. "I'd like to continue to help the world."

"That's a little vague. Can you be more specific?"

I reflected more. "I'd like to be a public speaker, talking about the benefits of cancer research and transplants."

"Any super lofty goals?"

"Well, I always had this dream of going to Africa to work with children there. That might be something to pursue."

Amy raised a hand to halt me. "This is why I asked. You can't do that because of the potential for infections. There are many things you'll be able to do, other things you shouldn't do, and certain things that you can't do. Traveling to Africa is too risky."

I assured her that I would follow the rules. There were plenty of other ways to help improve the world.

Even though twenty-five years had passed since I received chemotherapy, an oncologist needed to confirm that I was cancer-free. Once that hurdle was cleared, after Thanksgiving, I underwent a heart work-up. Amy explained that this was routine. From there, my case would go before a review board so my name could be added to the transplant list. It was here that we ran into a roadblock.

My mitral and aortic heart valves were leaky. My cardiologist, Dr. Angel Lopez-Candoles, suspected the radiation I endured as a child had caused the valves to gradually deteriorate over the years. When he listened to my chest with a stethoscope, he heard a murmur. I gave permission for his students to listen as well. A parade of them marched through the room. I don't know how many cardiologists are in training at UPMC, but I'm certain all of them listened to my murmur. Dr. Lopez-Candoles said they would never hear anything so distinctive in another patient.

I learned that heart valves are measured on a scale from one to sixteen. Lower numbers are better; anything above eight is unhealthy. One of mine was twelve and the other was eight, so they both needed to be replaced with steel valves. "You don't replace just one spark plug," my dad said dryly. Because the transplants could not occur until this problem was solved, I lobbied for surgery at once.

But that wouldn't come easily thanks to other health complications. The fistula in my arm had not matured. Throughout the process, I had been taking dialysis via a PICC line near my neck's jugular vein. PICC is an abbreviation for "peripherally inserted central catheter." Mine was meant to be temporary, allowing intravenous access. Doctors believed the better option for me was a fistula, so they went into my arm and stitched together an artery and vein, essentially creating a jugular there. You could feel a heartbeat in my arm. During dialysis, I needed a good wide channel for blood to be sucked out then pushed back in. But despite wearing out a foam squeeze ball (shaped, coincidentally enough, like a kidney), the fistula refused to develop, probably because my veins were so constricted from chemotherapy.

Meanwhile, I kept getting infections from the PICC line. They manifested as flu symptoms, where I would throw up, then have to stay in a hospital for seven to ten days and receive intravenous antibiotics. That would be followed by another six weeks of prophylactic antibiotics administered when I went to dialysis. Between October 2007 and the following July, I was admitted to the hospital seven times for this recurring issue.

It reached a point where a balloon was inserted into the fistula so it would stretch out. This was done four times, and the pain was intense. Finally, at the end of June, the fistula had widened enough to take dialysis. That was a great day.

The medical challenges took their toll. I slept horribly, only able to doze if I was sitting upright. At football practice, I was accustomed to walking around during drills to demonstrate technique, but often I had to take a knee or sit down. Sometimes I ducked into the training room hoping to sleep. Fellow coaches and players were understanding. I didn't have much in the tank.

It all came to a head in July 2008. I had framed pictures and memorabilia that I loaded into Coach Novak's van. It was a Tuesday, and I wanted to move everything to Woodland Hills. The pictures weren't heavy, but I grew winded. The simple act of picking them up took a lot out of me. I struggled to regain my breath.

"You okay?" Novak asked. "You don't look so good."

"I'm fine," I assured him. "It's just really hot out."

Once everything was unloaded at the field, I knew I was kidding myself. I didn't experience sharp or shooting pain, but I was tired in a way I hadn't been before. Something wasn't right. I used the office phone to call my dad, whose house was just over the hill.

"I need to go to the hospital," I told him. "It's my heart."

After being admitted to UPMC Montefiore, doctors examined me and determined that my valve replacement surgery needed to happen soon, so it was fast-tracked to take place on Friday. On Thursday night, the procedure was explained to me: the doctor would saw through the middle of my breast plate, attach me to a heart and lung bypass machine, and swap out the faulty valves. It was presented as pretty standard stuff.

Friday morning I felt good, eager for the next step. The anesthesiologist wore a multicolored surgical cap. He kept things lighthearted, so we shared a few laughs before he administered the IV that put me under.

That was the last thing I remembered. The next six days are erased from my memory. I was unaware that my heart stopped or that I flatlined or that my mom was called to the hospital believing that her son died.

∞

I heard the beeping machines before opening my eyes to see Dad slumped in the chair next to me, half asleep.

"Who let you in the recovery room?" I asked softly. His face sagged, hair disheveled, clothes askew. "By the way, you look terrible."

I hoped he would smile at my ribbing, but Dad just sat up and blinked. "Hey. This is the cardiac ICU, not the recovery room. You've been out a while."

I felt stiff and foggy. "How long? Is it still Friday?"

"No. Today is Thursday."

Thursday? He must be groggy too, because he was wrong by a day. I had undergone surgery on Friday. Popping in and out of hospitals so often, Dad probably got confused. I started to argue with him, but he cut me off.

"You've been out for six days, Joe."

I didn't believe him at first, although eventually I pieced the story together. I have no memory of this missing time. Surgery had proceeded well Friday, then Saturday and Sunday I insisted on getting out of bed to use the urinal. I've never liked bedpans. Sunday night, I even stood up so the staff could put down fresh linens after my sponge bath. On Monday morning, however, things went sideways. I had requested a banana for breakfast, but the potassium in bananas can be deadly to a post-op heart surgery patient.

"I'll bring you something else," the nurse said with a smile, then left the room.

Apparently, I didn't like her answer, because right after that, my heart stopped beating. Alarms sounded. Wires gauging my pulse went flat. Medical professionals who were nearby raced in.

I died, and remained dead for seven minutes.

Early that morning, the phone rang at Mom's house. She answered to the news that I had taken a turn for the worse. Although no one told her outright what had happened, Mom is astute. She recognized the tone. She had received similar calls twice before, when both her mother and father passed away. This, perhaps, was a call Mom had expected at one time or another for the past twenty-seven years, since I was first diagnosed at age eight.

Mom knew her son had died.

She didn't yell or scream or break down and sob. She nodded, hung up, and dialed my sister.

"Tara," Mom said. "I'm picking you up in twenty minutes. Joey flatlined this morning. I'm coming to get you now."

Mom was at peace, trusting in her faith. She reflected on her own mother's caution years earlier that all children were gifts on loan from God.

"It was the calmest I'd ever heard my mother in my life," Tara recalled. "My husband was lying right next to me in bed, and he couldn't even hear her voice on the phone."

By the time they reached the hospital, I had been revived. They were overjoyed to learn I was alive, but no one could calculate the damage. Going forward, would I be brain dead, or could I respond and heal? If so, how much of my memory would be erased?

I was in surgery again, this time to install a temporary pacemaker. Upon completion, I was placed in a medically induced coma, laid on a cold bed to lower body temperature. My skin was icy, hair was wet, and my arms and legs were strapped down.

"It was disturbing," Tara said. "He was on a gurney, and his friend David Paul was talking to him, saying 'it's okay, buddy.' I didn't think Joey could hear anything. Then he kept trying to sit up and his eyes got big. He looked like Frankenstein."

Watching me strain and tug against the restraints must have been a gruesome scene for my family. Friends came by, too, despite limited visiting time. Besides David Paul, regular visitors were my fellow coaches George Novak, Denny Damico, Larry Whitehearse and Joe Shaffo. Rob Kozub hates hospitals, but he phoned for updates each day. My friends knew I couldn't speak with them, but they came to cheer up my family and waited patiently to spend the last fifteen minutes of every hour by my side.

Novak has a coaching mantra: "you know who your friends are when you lose." I learned who my friends were when I lost my life and got it back. I'm humbled by the love they demonstrated.

∞

Back in the ICU with Dad, I fought against sleep. Knowing I'd been unconscious for six days made me fearful of drifting off again.

When Dad left, Tara arrived, sitting to talk with me. I asked about her kids, Adam and Reilly. Who was watching them now? How was her trip to Virginia? Tara answered patiently, but my brain was still cloudy. She told me later that I repeated the same series of questions over and over. My memory was a mess, but it was a good sign that I remembered anything at all.

When night fell, the nurse asked Tara to leave. She refused.

"My brother has been non-responsive for six days," she said politely. "Thank you for taking care of him, but I'm not leaving. Call security if you have a problem with that."

My family closed ranks to provide me with a sense of normalcy. The next morning, Mom returned, dressed well, like she had reservations at a fancy restaurant. She wanted to look her best as she spent the day with her son, recounting who had visited, who had phoned offering well wishes. Despite her brave front, I read the worry on her face, her concern about my long-term prognosis.

My chest had been stapled shut, atrophy burrowing deep into my muscles. I stared at the staggered lines of the heart monitor, read my pulse and oxygen and heart rate, wondering how much time was needed for the long road back.

"Understanding Mr. TC"

—Tara Reis

"OKAY, SO LET'S TALK ABOUT the whole dying-for-seven-minutes thing," Tara Reis said irreverently. "I've told Joe a person could hold their breath that long, so it really wasn't a big deal. And another thing: he never saw the light! Don't you see a light when you die?"

Years later, Joe's sister can joke about her brother's death. At the time, however, she recognized how serious it was. She and her mother rushed to his side upon learning the news.

"It was uncanny how Mom never got hysterical," she recalled. "I had planned a trip to meet my best friend in Virginia with our kids. I didn't know if I should go, because Joe wasn't out of the woods. Then I thought, if I stay, I'm just waiting for my brother to die. I called the hospital every hour overnight, and in the morning they told me he was awake and responding to commands. When I heard that, I knew he would make it, so I decided to go."

Born in 1971, fifteen months older than her brother, Tara is a typical big sister, knowing how to nurture, bully, or tease depending on the situation.

"We were ordinary kids. I'd boss him and he beat me up. We were either best friends or wanted to kill each other. My parents used to get mad, tell me to stop ordering him around, that I wasn't his mother. But as he got older, when he got in trouble or did something wrong, they'd ask if I could talk to him. I'd say: wait, didn't you tell me I'm not his mother?"

Since 1995, Tara has been married to Jim Reis, who she describes as "the best man on the planet." They have two kids: Adam, born in 2000, and Reilly, who arrived 361 days later. Having children close in age was something Tara and Jim planned, paralleling their own upbringings.

"Joe and I had a great childhood, never wanting for anything. We went on vacation every year. My father and mother were very good at living beneath their means and were always smart with money. They say you want better for your own children than you had, but I don't know that my kids are going to have it better."

Growing up with a sick brother affected Tara's childhood because of how everyone acted around them.

"Because of dad's job in the union, we had specific instructions for how to answer the phone." Falling into cadence, she recites: "'Lafferty residence; Tara speaking.' People would hear me answer and lower their voice and say, 'Oh Tara. How is Joey feeling?' It was how every single conversation went. It became so commonplace it was funny."

Once, her father's colleague phoned. Upon hearing her voice, he said "Hi, Tara. How are you today?" She was stunned, because no one ever asked about her before.

Tara believes that Joe's attitude as a boy was key to his recovery. He never felt sorry for himself, and the special attention he received throughout the Pittsburgh community helped him push forward. In fact, those connections landed Tara her first job in radio. While a freshman at Pitt, she learned that B94, a contemporary hit station, was seeking interns.

"I happened to mention this at the kitchen table, that the person in charge of hiring was the news director. Joe looked up and said, 'Shelley Duffy? Want me to make a call?' Next thing I knew, he dialed seven digits and he's talking to her. 'Shelley? Joe Lafferty. I'm good. How are you? Oh, it's nice to hear your voice again too.' He's a high school senior, having a conversation with this on-air personality that he knew through the Leukemia Society. They set up my interview right there. When I met her, the first thing Shelley Duffy said was how much she loved my brother. So I got the internship."

From there, Tara's talent took over. She worked hard, undertaking a series of moves across and up the ladder. After gaining experience, Tara shifted into TV, where she edited video and produced promotions. Then she worked sales, zigzagging between stations, selling ads for Penguins and Pirates games before landing a job at the famous radio station KDKA.

Today, Tara's passion is the Woodland Hills School District. She has served on its school board since 2011 and spent the past two years as board president.

"People say it's a thankless job, but I get thanked a lot. When kids do something that get us in the news, I write it off because they're kids. When grown-ups misbehave, I want to hurt somebody."

As adults, she and Joe remain close, talking almost every day.

"Sometimes I wish we didn't," she lamented. "He tells me too much. When he gets moody I call him Mr. TC."

The reference comes from the movie *In the Line of Fire* starring Clint Eastwood and John Malkovich. In a scene where Malkovich reveals himself, his character says, "I don't even remember who I was before they sunk their claws into me... Now they want to destroy me because we can't have monsters roaming the quiet countryside."

Tara saw that and turned to Joe. "That's you! You're the monster roaming the countryside. M-R-T-C. It became Mr. TC."

Tara understands her brother's outbursts and their roots. She appreciates that his prickly attitude is often born of frustration.

"His mind is brilliant," she said. "I don't just mean book stuff. Most people will leave a situation and think, oh, I should have said this. Joe never does that, because he always has a line or a response ready. There's not much that he doesn't understand or grasp. When you have that type of knowledge and experience and genius, people can frustrate you. I don't mean stupid people, I mean people in general. If he interacts with someone who shows a sense of entitlement or doesn't understand history, he gets frustrated, and that's when Mr. TC comes out."

CHAPTER 15

Redemption

THREE DAYS AFTER WAKING UP, I was downgraded and moved out of the intensive care unit, although I remained in the hospital for five weeks while medical professionals struggled to regulate the level of Coumadin in my blood. Receiving the proper amount of Coumadin, an anti-clotting medicine, was vital to my recovery. I was assured that once a target number was met, I could be released. Despite adjusting the dosage, results fluctuated. First it was too high, then too low. Each day, I was told "maybe tomorrow." When I zeroed in close to the target, it still wasn't good enough. The amount needed to be precise. Eventually, after being informed yet again that I needed to remain in my hospital bed longer, I erupted.

"Stop telling me I'm going home!" I shouted, and hurled a tray of food at the wall. It wasn't a pretty scene. The poor nurse who witnessed my outburst scampered away, then complained to my sister that I was unruly. That was true, but I had been stuck inside UPMC all summer. I hadn't inhaled fresh air for four and a half weeks. Every day they kept dangling hope in front of me before pulling it away. Tara likes to say that I morph into Mr. TC in those situations. Considering the circumstances, I believe my anger was justified.

My dad visited every day. We fell into a routine where he gave me a sponge bath daily, and washed my hair every other day. While I stood, he knelt to clean my legs. Once, when I struggled, he told me to place my hand on his shoulder and push until I was steady and balanced. Dad was at my feet, serving me.

Then came the time I wanted to walk. This was a big deal, because I had been too weak to move on my own. I couldn't sit still any longer, and needed to take the literal first step. Dad organized two nurses' aides, one for each arm, and a nurse in front of me, pulling the IV stand. He stood behind with a wheelchair in case I could not continue. After ten feet, we paused, and someone asked if I wanted to turn back. But I pushed ahead, in ten-foot increments, refusing to give up.

These were tough days, but the real blessing during this time was that the gap closed with my father. For a long time, our relationship had been strained, and the divorce broke part of us. I respected men like Bill Curry and George Novak for the father figures they were. Until then, I told myself that Dad and I were too different, never fitting into the same box. He'd rather watch a car race than a football game. He never read or thirsted for knowledge like me, yet he's fiercely knowledgeable, brimming with brains and common sense. He was the one who set me on the path of my life by telling me that cancer didn't need to slow me down.

When I was eventually released, my good feelings toward him grew. He came to my apartment every morning to cook me breakfast and be sure my medicines were in order.

His commitment opened my eyes. He was still working then, but made time for me each day. I realized that Dad, like Mom, had always been there. The strain in our relationship was because of me. I had failed to recognize him and everything he did. Growing up, I should have listened to him more. He was exactly the man he should have been during the time I needed him most.

One of the first places I visited after leaving UPMC was a Woodland Hills football practice. Moving like a ninety-year-old man, I gingerly stepped onto the field greeted by applause from my fellow coaches. Kids patted me on the back. Watching the team run around, I avoided direct sun. I had a bigger goal in mind. Ten days after my release, Woodland Hills kicked off the season in Texas Stadium. It was a rare national game against a team from outside Dallas. Our school can only travel with a limited number of people, so not all coaches were scheduled to go. While I was hospitalized, Coach Novak had assured me that if I were out by then, I was going. That became something to aspire to.

My dad does not like to fly, but he offered to purchase a flight for himself so he could come along to look after me. It was such a kind act. When Larry Whitehearse heard the plan, he asked for my father's phone number.

"Mr. Lafferty," he said, "I'll take care of Joe. He won't leave my side. You know he's going to try to do more than he can, but I'll punch him in the head when he does."

Dad drove me to the airport, where Larry waited with a wheelchair.

"Are you sure you can handle this?" Dad asked. "I brought a travel bag for myself just in case." Larry reassured him, so Dad stayed behind.

In Texas, I reconnected with my pal Brent Porterfield, but the big event was the game in Irving. It was late August, and temperature hovered in the high 90s. The Texas Stadium locker room was air conditioned, but it was too cold for me. I could only remain there for a few minutes before I needed to step outside to warm up.

I had no responsibilities other than to keep myself upright and alive. On the field, a thermometer read 112 degrees. I stood as much as I could, walking the sidelines. Every few minutes I needed to sit. After the first quarter, I headed to the locker room to cool off and get water, ducking in and out, but it was back to the field after halftime.

We lost the game to Northwest High School, 14-12, but that wasn't catastrophic. Coach Novak never emphasized national games. They provided good experience but didn't affect league standings. We flew back to start the 2008 season, and had a decent year.

The new heart valves worked well and my body began to recover. By November, I was finally added to the transplant list through UPMC and the Pittsburgh Center for Organ Recovery and Education, abbreviated CORE. I was excited. The estimated wait time for a solitary kidney was three to four years; the kidney/pancreas block might take two years. The block was faster because solitary kidneys are in greater demand. There weren't as many patients who needed both, but the pancreas was tricky. Doctors had to cut a person open to know for sure if their pancreas was viable for a transplant.

Many friends and family offered one of their kidneys, including Dad, Tara, Bill Curry, and David Paul. We learned that David couldn't donate because he had contracted malaria while serving as a missionary in Africa. He was fine, but the past infection might cause problems down the line. Had I been dying, his kidney would have been acceptable, but my situation wasn't that dire.

Around this time, feelings of guilt welled up again. I've never been ashamed to ask for help, but I grew uncomfortable to be inconveniencing so many people. I wasn't plotting my own murder like I had before, but I kept thinking it would be easier if I was dead.

Any patient who moves closer to number one on a transplant list gets phone calls from CORE. When I was number five, then four, they contacted me to share information about someone who died. The person's name wasn't used, but I was given details like their age, cause of death, and where they lived. I could deny those organs if I deemed the deceased too old or was concerned with past medical history. I once received a call about a young man who had succumbed to a drug overdose. Two people on the waiting list ahead of me had refused those organs. There might also be concerns on the recipient's end. If I had a cold or a cut, I would be unable to receive the organ. Then the person on deck would move up. So despite not being number one on the list, I needed to be informed whenever an organ was available, because there were many factors that entered into play.

By the summer of 2009, all this information began to weigh on me. I realized that I was waiting for someone to die so I could have his or her organs. That became more than I could bear. I found myself thinking about it all the time. Home alone, rather than do something productive or even put on the TV, I sat and stared out the window. Sometimes I watched the wall. When I finally noticed the clock, three hours had passed.

I phoned David. With his psychology degree, he served as my de facto counselor.

"Something's wrong," I told him, explaining my thoughts.

"You're depressed. We've talked about all this, Joe. Are you thinking of killing yourself?"

"No," I said, and I really wasn't. "I just don't want to be a burden to anyone. I don't get a kidney and pancreas unless someone else dies."

"It's not like they're dying for you. It doesn't work that way."

"That's exactly how it works!" I argued. "For me to get a kidney and pancreas, someone has to die! They have to die so that I can live. I know God loves me, but I'm not sure it's worth it anymore."

"You need help," he said. "You need to talk to someone."

"I'm talking to you."

He convinced me that I needed an unbiased professional. After examining my insurance plan and consulting Amy Singh and the transplant team, I contacted the Western Psychiatric Institute and Clinic at UPMC, colloquially known as Western Psych. Immediately they asked if I was suicidal. When I said no, an appointment was scheduled four and a half weeks away. That seemed too far off, so I complained.

"Are you sure you're not thinking about suicide?" they asked.

I hesitated. "Do you want me to say yes? Does it get me in faster?" Despite the temptation, I remained honest with them.

David knew people in the field, so was able to recommend a doctor in Oakland who was available sooner. He drove me to the first appointment and waited outside for the fifty-minute hour.

"What am I supposed to talk about?" I wondered aloud during the ride in.

"You back the truck up and dump it all out," David advised. "It's up to him to sift the garbage."

The psychiatrist was a big man who looked like a football player. I felt comfortable with him right away. After talking for thirty minutes, I declared, "I'm not sure why I'm here."

His response was a classic cliché. "Why do you think you're here?"

"Well, I died last summer and it happened so quickly that I didn't have time to be scared. So maybe this is the residual from the experience." We stared at each other in silence for several seconds. "How'd I do?"

He nodded. "That's pretty good."

"So am I cured?"

He laughed. "Just because you recognize it doesn't mean you're cured."

My problems weren't solved that day. I worked around different feelings. Religion played a part. I thought about my future donor, and came to understand that I wasn't responsible for his or her soul. But after the transplant, I would have to fully embrace every day as a gift. I likened it to the love of a spouse or, on a broader scope, the love of God. That type of love is unattainable through acts. None of us deserve it, but it exists just the same. Love is about serving others. Before therapy, I couldn't comprehend how that worked. I hadn't grasped that I was going to love someone that I had never met. The cost of getting new organs was that I would serve that love. It wasn't easy to wrap my head around, but that's the best way I can describe it.

After nine sessions, my psychiatrist dismissed me. I could return anytime, but he believed I would be okay going forward.

∞

In 2009, Woodland Hills lost our opener against a team from Ohio, but won every game after that. In November, on the night we played West Mifflin, I was walking into the stadium alongside George Novak and Rob Kozub. When my phone rang, I scanned the caller ID and recognized CORE. Recently, I had moved from number three to number two on the block transplant list.

Stepping off to the side, I answered the call. An organ procure-ment official told me there was a donor. I was given the age and a broad outline of the person, who was still alive but would pass away shortly. Organs would be recovered then. After being told to keep myself available, he asked my location. Could I travel to UPMC quickly if needed?

"I'm at a playoff game. I have to think the ambulance will get me there if I tell them I'm due for a transplant," I said. "Is it safe to say that by the end of the night, I'll either have new organs or be number one on the list?"

The man paused. "That's a good way of looking at it."

We were losing at halftime when CORE called again. The transplant was happening for another person, so I had moved to number one. The next available kidney and pancreas were going to me. I was ecstatic.

At that point, it got real. That might seem silly to say, but hypotheticals were a thing of the past. The situation required me to be ready any time. A friend wanted me to accompany him to Wheeling, West Virginia, on a day trip, but I said no. I didn't want to venture too far from Pittsburgh in case the call came. Every day, I woke up thinking that I was at the top of the list. I tried to stay busy, but the transplant was foremost in my mind. I even had my retina reattached, so it would be fixed before then.

Between Christmas and New Year's, I got the first call from CORE. A man east of Pittsburgh had died. I wasn't told specifics, but he had a history of drinking and it sounded like he swallowed pills to commit suicide. Doctors needed to open him up and exam-ine his pancreas to see if it was viable. Stay near the phone, I was told. This could be it.

I shared the update with my mom, then confessed that I didn't want to sit home and wait. She picked me up and drove me to

Dick's Sporting Goods, where I used Christmas gift cards to buy tennis shoes and new sweats. It was important to keep moving, knowing that I could be summoned to the hospital at any moment. Who wouldn't be nervous?

It turned out that the pancreas was not transplantable. There was an odd mix of relief and letdown. Not to speak ill of the dead, but selfishly, you want healthy organs. To learn that someone had a drinking problem, I had to consider that the organs might not be in the best shape. Thoughts like that kept me on an emotional roller coaster.

After that near-miss, I didn't hear of any potential donors through January. But on Saturday, February 13, 2010, my life changed.

It was a dreary winter day. I sat in my apartment in front of the computer when the phone rang. Caller ID revealed that it was CORE. I recognized the voice of the same organ procurement official with whom I had spoken before.

"There's been a car accident," he told me. "There is a 16-year-old boy whose organs are available." My heart dropped at the thought of such a young life lost. "Don't speed, but head to Montefiore and report to the fourth floor."

Dad picked me up and drove me downtown immediately. I phoned Mom and Tara as well. They promised to meet us. There wasn't much time to think, but I recognized the date, aware that thirteen was my lucky number. It had been my jersey at Woodland Hills. Dan Marino wore number thirteen. In midget football, my number was sixty-seven. The two digits added up to thirteen. The last four digits of my phone number were 1313.

En route to the hospital, I sent out a group text to close friends, updating them and requesting prayers for the young man's family. "No need to reply," I told everyone. "He carries me through."

It was mid-afternoon when we arrived at UPMC. I was admitted immediately, keeping on my shorts and tennis shoes while slipping into a hospital gown. Blood was drawn, and I was peppered with questions. Was I allergic to anything? When had I last eaten? I was instructed to keep my stomach empty, which meant the transplant could happen soon. We idled until after dinner, my sister taking photos of me lying in bed with a Curious George doll my father had brought along. As hours passed, my stomach growled. A nurse came in and told me the transplant would not occur until the next day.

"What's the holdup?" I asked.

"I can't tell you anything," she said.

I sensed the awful endgame for the boy's family, empathizing with their emotions. "They're keeping him alive because someone needs to say goodbye, right?"

"I can't tell you," she repeated, but nodded her head yes.

Mom and Dad and Tara left, planning to return in the morning. I prayed for the young man and his loved ones. I didn't know his name or any details about his life, but in years to come I would learn much about him. I would connect with his parents and sister, eternally grateful for the gift they gave me in their darkest hour. I didn't know then how much I would treasure their love.

When things quieted down and night fell, I read my phone. David Paul had returned my text, asking permission to call me. My mind was spinning from everything that had happened already, and I was nervous about the next day. I dialed David, whose words—as usual—provided wisdom and insight.

"I can't sleep," I lamented. "I'm just dozing for a few minutes then waking up again."

"Joe, you know the donor is in the same hospital with you. He's alive but he's already gone. Do you realize this is the only night when you and that young man are going to be on this earth together and know of each other? Think and pray about that and I'm confident you'll find peace."

I knew Sunday, February 14, was Valentine's Day. Ironically, it was also National Organ Donor Day. Come morning, there were more long hours of uncertainty and waiting. I began to worry whether the pancreas was transplantable. It took most of the day to get things ready; several plans needed to be modified. Amy Singh wasn't there because she was on vacation. Dr. Ron Shapiro was supposed to be my surgeon, but when everything stretched across the weekend, a different surgeon, Dr. Henkie Tan, swapped in. The sun was going down by the time they wheeled me into the surgery prep room.

The transplant was a go, and I was medicated to make me drowsy. My parents had been cautioned that the procedure would take between five and six hours, but in less than three hours, I had a new kidney and pancreas. The surgery went faster than normal because I didn't bleed much and wasn't overweight. In fact, the kidney worked while I was on the operating table. Amy later delivered the sobering news: that meant I peed during surgery.

The following day remains a blur. A few coaching buddies stopped by, and I woke briefly. By Tuesday I was transferred to another room. I spent several days with a catheter and IVs, and was moved to a liquid diet of clear broths, juices, and Jell-O. My Uncle Jim and Aunt Helen visited from Philadelphia. By Thursday, the catheter was removed and I could swallow soup, ice cream and pudding. Come Saturday, I was on a regular diet.

The professionals in the transplant wing are miracle workers. Within days, I was taking laps around the hall, feeling better than I had in a long time. On Monday, eight days after my transplant, I was released and sent home.

For the first month, I had to report to the transplant clinic daily. This was standard procedure. Blood was drawn, tests run, modifications made to the immunosuppressant drugs. My medications changed drastically. While taking dialysis, I had to be careful how much liquid I swallowed. Now I was told to drink as much as possible. Because my bladder had been underused, it needed to be stretched out. For a time I had to measure all the fluids going into my body against the urine coming out.

In the aftermath, I was given twenty-three prescriptions. The immunosuppressants were important so my body didn't reject the new organs. It made me susceptible to other ailments, but that was part of the deal. The first week out, I did so well that I was allowed to skip a visit to the clinic. I remained sore, however, and my mind was foggy.

The second Sunday after my transplant, I started to get sick, making hourly trips to the bathroom. Doctors had warned that if I experienced diarrhea, report immediately to the emergency room. I phoned the transplant team, and Tara drove me to the hospital. I did my best to hold it together, but worried about contracting C. diff.

C. diff is the abbreviation for Clostridium Difficile, a bacteria that infects humans or other animals. Symptoms include diarrhea or an inflamed colon. It is a post-surgery infection that could put my new organs in danger. In some cases, it can be fatal.

Blood was drawn so lab experts could grow a culture. This would take at least three days, so I remained in the hospital until results were available. Diarrhea stopped. Other than my incision scar, I felt great. I walked around the wing, begging the nurses to release me long enough to pace outside for fresh air. I was eager to reclaim my freedom.

On Wednesday, the good news arrived: C. diff was ruled out. The illness was a reaction to magnesium supplements, so I was given a different pill and released. I continued checking in at the clinic, and was soon downgraded from frequent visits to once a week.

By spring 2010, for the first time in a long time, I was free to face life with a new brand of hope.

Loving a "Christian Pit Bull"

—Rev. A. David Paul

DAVID PAUL HAS BEEN ALONGSIDE Joe during his myriad challenges. One of the most memorable was Joe's struggle for understanding before the transplant.

"You can get close enough to someone that it becomes a conflict of interest to serve as their counselor," admitted Paul. "Think of it this way: during your teen years, Mom or Dad can give you the best advice about everything. Eat your vegetables. Get enough sleep. Most teens will roll their eyes and mutter 'whatever.' But when a coach says the same thing, the kid will follow it to a T. My relationship with Joe had evolved to where he could finish my sentences. When we reached that point, I knew he needed to hear things with fresh ears and a fresh perspective."

Their relationship had begun several years earlier. Paul's friend John Stahl-Wert approached him about a new volunteer at the Pittsburgh Leadership Foundation who was unable to drive because of health problems. Could Paul pick him up and bring him to the office?

"You need to meet this guy," Stahl-Wert said. "His name is Joe Lafferty. I think you'll find him interesting."

Back in 2007, armed with an address, Paul drove to Joe's apartment in North Versailles, introduced himself, and the two men got in the car.

"I was doing what a person of faith is supposed to do," Paul said. "I took him under my wing as a wounded soldier who needed help, but my initial reaction wasn't very favorable. Joe can be rough around the edges. If people are quick to judge, or can't maneuver around that crusty exterior, the way he expresses himself can be pretty darn ugly."

Paul sensed right away that they were polar opposites. Yet he believes in service, and Joe was a valued volunteer who required transportation. Despite their varying opinions and Joe's aggressiveness, they spent two years regularly riding from dialysis appointments to the office and then home again.

"It was a 45-minute commute, twice a day," Paul noted. "Spend an hour and a half with someone on a consistent basis, and you get to know each other fairly well. When I picked him up from dialysis, the smell of iodine filled my car. It wasn't pleasant, but I never said anything. At the start, I was silent so he could let out all his feelings. I didn't share my thoughts, but often they included, 'are you fricking kidding me?'"

Paul learned that Joe is gifted at arguments and debate. Joe, he explained, would begin with an assumption. Even if the assumption was false, it was a ploy to suck him into verbal sparring.

"He's very intelligent," Paul said. "He makes declarative, definitive statements, and if you don't agree with him, you're wrong.

He's aggressive in his assertions, and that turns a lot of people off. He's usually right, but the way he presents himself can be offensive if someone doesn't know his story. He knew how to push my buttons. Sometimes I'd swallow the bait and sometimes I wouldn't. It took a while for me to learn that's Joe's method of saying he'd like to talk about a subject."

Gradually, Paul garnered respect for Joe.

"As I cracked his shell, I realized that at his core are the solid Judeo-Christian values of love. Joe doesn't do anything halfway. He always goes for gold, and I think that's because of everything he's survived.

"At age nine, he was an elite swimmer. People were saying he might be the next Mark Spitz. Suddenly, he's hospitalized with a horrible disease and has to fight for his life. In a functional family, that would be traumatic. But Joe didn't have a functional family. His parents, to their credit, put all their crap aside and came together for their son. They stood by him unquestionably."

Today, Paul lives in Omaha, Nebraska, where he shares the ministry of the First Congregational Church in Fremont and Arlington Community Church. He and his wife, Jen, married in 1997 and have three children: Josh, Anna, and Adelyn. They celebrated their twentieth wedding anniversary by making a medical mission to Kenya.

The affection is not one-sided.

"David has the biggest heart," Joe reflected. "He believes the best of every person. That's how we're supposed to love each other, according to Corinthians. He's rarely cynical. He wants to believe that he can serve people and in doing so, raise them up. I have an amazing admiration for him that powers me."

Both men recall the day they drove through downtown Pittsburgh and noticed a decorated bus.

"Isn't that John Madden's cruiser?" Paul wondered. The Steelers were playing a nationally televised game in a few days, so it was likely the former coach and fabled broadcaster was in town.

"Let's follow it!" Joe suggested.

The bus traveled to the South Side, pulling into team head-quarters. As Madden stepped off, Paul and Joe rushed over, introducing themselves in the parking lot, giving him a copy of John Stahl-Wert's book, "The Serving Leader." After a few minutes, Dan Rooney, the Steelers' owner, interrupted them, politely cutting short their conversation. It was another brush with fame in Joe's life.

Reflecting on their years of friendship, Paul described Joe as a "Christian pit bull." Joe wears the label proudly.

"A pit bull is known for having jaws stronger than a shark or alligator," Paul explained. "They crunch through things. If they're nurtured as loving, caring pets, they can be kind animals. But if they're raised to fight, a pit bull can be your worst nightmare. Joe is the same way. Underneath him is a beautiful, loving child of God. He's a man of impeccable character and integrity with a wonderful heart and soul. Over time, I came to love him as more than a best friend. It goes deeper, like he's my brother."

Paul's kids refer to "Uncle Joe." Despite the physical distance, Paul and Joe speak regularly, at least once a week, and still visit each other. Reflecting on the evolution of their friendship, Paul turns philosophical.

"John Stahl-Wert had an intuition that Joe and I needed one another, and it developed into a brotherhood," Paul said. "Joe has helped with my assertiveness. He was put into my life by God to show me how to have a backbone. I believe that by serving others, we are truly served. I've been wonderfully served by serving Joe."

CHAPTER 16

The Angel of My Life

TWO MONTHS AFTER THE TRANSPLANT, my Uncle Bob read an article from his hometown newspaper in Leechburg, northeast of Pittsburgh, about a sixteen-year-old boy who had been killed in a car crash. Nearly everything he learned matched what we had been told about my donor. The only discrepancy was the death date. It claimed the victim died on Friday, February 12, but I knew that my donor had stopped breathing on February 14.

Bob Hughes isn't related by blood, but I call him Uncle Bob. He's my godfather and has been my dad's best friend for many years.

Bob passed the newspaper onto my father. Dad didn't share the folded copy with me initially, but told me it was in his possession. He understood the emotions involved.

"It may be your donor, but we can't be sure," Dad said. "Do you want to read the article?"

"Let me think about it," I answered, chewing my lip. I needed time to process this information.

A few days passed before I finally summoned the courage to ask for the newspaper. For the first time, I learned about Justin Dale Boyer. I Googled him, and read blurbs from other news outlets. I even searched out the funeral home's website for his obituary. I discovered more about him, but there were no photos. Until then, all the information about my donor had been provided by CORE, yet no names had ever been exchanged; everything remained anonymous. Contact between the donor's family and recipient had to be made through official channels via CORE, and that had not happened. It was only a few months after the transplant, too early for everyone's emotions to have settled. I absorbed the news, thinking and praying for the young man who had passed away.

I thought often about the name I had. Justin Dale Boyer. I couldn't prove anything, but in my heart, I knew.

Part of Justin lived inside me.

With a new lease on life, there were two hurdles I faced as summer approached. One was that Woodland Hills planned a football showcase for eight teams, including squads from Florida and Ohio. It required in-depth planning, and I was put in charge of operations, preparing logistics for a marathon four games in one day. The other was my twentieth high school reunion, and for many reasons, I was apprehensive about that.

Although the football games were scheduled for the end of August, the sponsor hosted a press conference early in the month, just a few days before the reunion. The coach from Manatee High School in Bradenton, Florida was flown in, and the Ohio coach made the trip as well. I learned that the coach of Buchtel High School in Akron was Ricky Powers. He was the former Michigan running back who had been a blue-chip recruit. I recognized his name after my conversation with Steelers' running back Jerome Bettis. There are circular patterns in my life, and this was one of them.

After the media event, I walked up to Powers and introduced myself.

"I have to tell you this story," I said. "I have it on good authority that you're the reason Jerome Bettis went to Notre Dame instead of Michigan."

He began to laugh. "How do you know that?"

"Because I spoke to Jerome while he waited to be fitted for a free shirt." While I recounted what Bettis had said, Powers nodded.

"That story is absolutely true," he agreed. "You're one of the few people that knows it. But hey, I think Jerome got the last laugh. He won a Super Bowl, so he's doing a hell of a lot better than me."

The Woodland Hills class of 1990 produced people of great achievement. Thad Wilson, our class president, had attended Harvard and Northwestern business school and became a real estate titan in Chicago. Rich Smith, who had backed me up at quarterback, earned an engineering degree from Carnegie Mellon and went on to teach at MIT. Even though I had beaten the odds and fought to stay alive, twenty years out, I didn't feel like I had accomplished much. The duality of the reunion was that I looked forward to seeing everyone but felt reluctance as well.

We had lost seven classmates in the two decades that passed. I graduated with 535 people, so over time, people die. One that hit me hardest was Debbie Spahr, my first crush when we were eight years old. Although she lived in South Carolina as an adult, I had seen Debbie a few years earlier when she visited Pittsburgh. Lisa

Frentzos, a mutual friend who had lived across the street when we were kids, contacted and invited me to join them at lunch. I had just returned from dialysis that day, so I was exhausted and hadn't showered, but the window was limited, so I walked to a restaurant in North Versailles to meet them. She was Debbie Thamas by then, suffering from breast cancer. The disease had taken its toll, but she still retained that great smile. We talked about her sons; her husband and I spent time chatting because we were the only guys there.

Debbie asked about my health, and we laughed at the irony. As kids, we were both healthy and fit, known around town as swimmers. We were little athletes who embraced our youth. By high school, she was homecoming queen. I don't believe the cliché that youth is wasted on the young. We were ecstatic about life every day. Years later, it was difficult to see each other as sick adults and recognize that she was on the road to dying.

A few months after my transplant, Debbie passed away. I wasn't in a position to travel to her wake in South Carolina, but my old friend and teammate Tirrell Greene did go. He told me that she had refused home hospice care because she didn't want to die where her young sons lived. She worried about them having that daily reminder as they continued to occupy the house. I had never heard anyone act that thoughtfully before. It was such a selfless decision. Right up until the end, Debbie still possessed that kindness of spirit I had recognized in her when we were kids.

As part of the planning committee, I suggested to Thad that we dedicate time at the reunion to mention classmates we had lost. Ironically, Thad and Debbie had dated in high school.

"It's a great idea," he said. "Will you make a short speech?"

"Considering I've died and come back, I guess I'm qualified," I joked.

∞

The reunion was scheduled for Saturday, but the night before, a group gathered in the Wheelhouse Saloon of Rivers Casino to watch classmates who played in a band called Sho Nuff, named for the villain in the movie The Last Dragon. I was promised a ride down and back, and my old football buddy Chris Uram planned to be there with his girlfriend Holly, who was also a classmate.

Walking into the bar, I immediately ran into Amy Monheim. I hadn't seen her in years, but always enjoyed her company. She was up front and plain spoken, traits I admired.

"Lafferty," she said pleasantly.

I greeted her with a hug. Thanks to my new kidney, I was feeling great. I ordered a drink and mingled with former teammates and fellow classmates. When the band started to perform, I asked Amy if I could sit with her. Of course, she said, then nodded to her friend.

"Do you remember Jennifer Bruner?"

I smiled at a petite beauty with blonde highlights and the brightest, most beautiful blue eyes. She was a pixie; her gaze was like a tractor beam that reeled me in. I had known Jennifer in seventh and eighth grades, but remembered that she had not attended Woodland Hills.

"It's Jennifer Dimare now," she corrected. When I stared at her, she wondered, "Why are you looking at me like that?"

"You didn't graduate high school with us. You didn't even go to high school with us. I thought you went to a private school."

She explained that her family had moved to Florida around that time. She had attended high school in Melbourne.

"Wait," I interrupted. "That can't be right. Didn't I see you in the summer when we were teenagers?" I remember bumping into her around town, at the pool or at parties. She was not the type of girl I could miss.

Probably, she said. During high school, she spent a month in Pittsburgh every summer while living in Florida for the rest of the year.

"Oh," I said. "That makes sense. So why are you here?"

She pointed toward Amy, lips turned down. "Because these are my friends." She wasn't offended, but I could see she wasn't sure of my questions. Sarcastically, she said, "Am I allowed to be here?"

"Of course," I answered. "I'm just trying to piece it all together."

We talked off and on throughout the night. Jennifer and Amy thought it was interesting that I coached high school football at my alma mater. Jennifer's home was in Florida, where she was married with two boys, Brannon and Cameron. That weekend, she stayed at Amy's childhood home in Edgewood. Amy lived in Butler and had three kids of her own. I mingled around the room the rest of the night. Before leaving, I circled back to them.

"The team has a scrimmage tomorrow morning against Butler," I said. "Since you're here, you should come down to the field to watch."

They did. The next day, I looked up into the stands and saw them waving at me. I touched base briefly, saying I looked forward to seeing them later at the official reunion, then went back to coaching. It was a hot day, and my wool baseball cap trapped in the heat. As afternoon wore on, I suffered heatstroke, throwing up on the sidelines. The trainer had to give me fluids. I felt terrible toward evening, but I didn't want to miss the reunion.

When Chris picked me up that night, I wasn't doing well. I considered asking him to detour to the emergency room. Had I not been slated to speak about our fallen classmates, I would have gone to the hospital. I probably should have, but people were counting on me. At the reunion, I drank water and stayed seated, trying to hold it together. I wasn't the live wire I wanted to be. Give the speech, I told myself, then get out of there.

Everyone gathered on the top floor of Roland's Seafood Grill, a restaurant and bar in Pittsburgh's strip district. It was an old building, and the room was oddly shaped, with stairs on one side and a dining room on the other. The bar featured plenty of restored wood, like the interior of Cheers.

There was no stage, so when it came time to speak, Thad kicked things off. He talked over people because not everyone stopped their conversations. After a few words, he passed the microphone to me.

I don't remember details, but I spoke emotionally about the value of life. It wasn't the easiest subject, so I kept it short. One of my friends, John Poindexter, yelled out, "Tell it, Laff!" like he was shouting encouragement to a preacher. I locked my eyes on Tirrell Greene, who is a part-time pastor. I commanded attention from many, but with so much background noise, I reflected that some people weren't ready to hear a story about what life is really worth. Finishing, I passed the microphone to James Langer. He thanked me, then read the seven names of classmates who had passed away, pausing after each. One of the deceased, Sean Racine, had been a good friend of his.

Mission accomplished, I sat down and caught up with Jamal Webster, an old football friend. I hadn't seen him in a long time, although I coached his youngest brother five years earlier. That's when Jennifer wandered over. She had known Jamal in middle school, so the three of us talked. When she noticed that I wasn't feeling well, her motherly instincts kicked in.

"Have you eaten anything?" she asked.

She brought me water and bread from the buffet. It was a loving act. She spoke with Jamal about Florida and that her boys meant everything to her. She displayed a spark, and after the health challenges I had been through, I was pleased to see that a person could carry such a bright and cheery attitude.

Jennifer left a mark that night, but there wasn't some instant connection. The true takeaway was that I felt empowered from talking with people my age. I had a new lease on life, and my classmates inspired me. So many of them were happy with the life they created.

A life. I've got to get one of those, I thought. But I had no idea how.

Following the reunion, many of us stayed in touch. A year and a half later, in March 2012, Amy Monheim invited me to a surprise party in Pittsburgh for Jennifer's fortieth birthday. Chris was coming, she said, and I would know other people there.

Jennifer traveled by herself, and it was great to see her again. We talked at greater length, and she glowed when talking about her sons. I remained impressed with her energy.

Afterward, when I spoke with Chris, I confessed that I was ready to date someone again. I had consciously remained single through many of my health struggles, but now felt differently. I had a yearning to connect at a deep level. I had enjoyed talking with Jennifer, and that got me thinking about being a partner with someone. Chris understood because of his relationship with Holly. They knew each other fully, and that relationship was special. I wanted to open myself to the possibility of love.

Six months passed before Jennifer reached out to me, asking if I had time to talk. She admitted that she and her husband had drifted apart, and their marriage was over. They had been living together for the kids, but sleeping in separate rooms. We talked back and forth on the phone. The inspiration that I felt from her grew into a connection. When she visited Pittsburgh again, we met up. I traveled to Fort Lauderdale to spend time with friends, and she drove down to see me. Over time, our attraction strengthened. Her marriage ended and Jennifer grew into my true love.

I had prayed my entire life to know that love existed, that it was possible to feel complete alongside someone else. I read Billy Graham's book about angels, and believe that they're not chubby babies with wings; they're warriors. I've dealt with God on a very personal basis, and one of the true gifts he gave me was love with Jennifer.

Before her, I existed. I wasn't really living or loving life. I owe her all my happiness, because she saved me. I've had wonderful, diverse experiences with both ordinary and famous people, but finding love with her was the catalyst that brought everything together.

A few years passed. One day, as we sat quietly, I began laughing.

"What's so funny?" she wondered, resting her head against my shoulder.

My smile was wide. "I love my life," I said.

Christmas 2010 was my first with new organs. I thought about the donor family, who would spend the holidays without their sixteen-year-old son. I couldn't imagine their grief. I wanted to write them a letter, knowing it needed to remain anonymous. CORE would deliver it. Amy Singh had advised that I wait a year before reaching out. When I did, I should share the good news of my health. But that anniversary was two months away and by then the holidays would have passed.

I bounced the idea off my dad. He's always been a rock, and he talked me through the decision.

"I think it's a nice thing to do before Christmas," he said. "Try to put yourself in the family's position. What will their reaction be?

Your mother would tear open that letter. I'd need to think about it and get in the right frame of mind before reading something like that. Regardless of what you write, Joe, it's up to the family whether they want to read it."

I wrote the letter. I think I'm good with words, but how do you thank someone for such a gift? How do you express that gratitude on paper? Amy had suggested that I share what I do for a living. When I passed the letter along to CORE so they could screen it, they asked me to change one tiny detail. I had written that I coached football on the eastern side of Pittsburgh, but they wanted it to be more general, with fewer geographic clues. So the re-write said that I coached outside Pittsburgh.

Sending the holiday note left me satisfied, but the act wasn't ever about me.

I did not receive a response.

"The Richest Man I Know"

—Jennifer Dimare

WHEN JENNIFER BRUNER WAS IN seventh grade, she heard whispers about a new kid who was transferring from a private school to attend classes at Edgewood Middle School. The boy was a cancer survivor.

"Before I even met him, that was the story about Joe," she reflected. "It's horrible to think about now, but when we came in contact, I was puzzled. He didn't look like he had cancer."

Instead, Joe was a typical kid, with blonde hair, blue eyes, and braces. Bigger than many of his peers, Jennifer remembers him as cute, athletic and smart. A little cocky, even. He and his twin sister were inseparable.

"They were always connected, always hanging around together," Jennifer said. "They were a package deal."

Some time passed before Jennifer discovered that Joe and Tara were not twins, merely siblings. She was a year older. Jennifer was surprised. Many of her friends had brothers or sisters around their age, but few spent time together socially.

"Even today, Joe and Tara's personalities are so much alike," Jennifer said. "They fight hard, love hard, live hard, laugh hard, think hard, and work hard. They don't do anything halfway. Hearts are worn on their sleeves. They are all in, all the time. I'm the opposite of that. I can be a fence sitter. Maybe that's why Joe and I are attracted to each other."

In 1986, when she was fourteen, Jennifer's family moved to West Melbourne, Florida. Although she maintained contact with friends in Pittsburgh and visited during summer, gradually her connections to Edgewood lessened. After high school, Jennifer earned an education degree from Florida Atlantic University, lived in Fort Lauderdale, and eventually married. Her last name changed to Dimare, and she had two boys. Although she never attended Woodland Hills High School, many of her childhood friends had, and Jennifer was invited to the twenty-year reunion.

"It was fun to get reacquainted with people I hadn't seen," she said. "Someone asked if I remembered Joe Lafferty. The stories about him were that he lost one eye, had a pacemaker, and looked horrible. I had all these preconceived notions. Would I feel sorry for him? But when we met again, I had the same reaction as I did in middle school. He didn't look like a guy who had been through a double organ transplant."

After talking with Joe, she realized that he didn't dwell on his health issues or lament the difficult past. There was no negativity. Instead, Jennifer discovered a man who was curious, genuinely interested in the lives of others. He wanted to learn about everyone at the reunion.

"I thought my life was pretty benign," she reflected. "Most of us had husbands and wives and children and careers. Joe didn't have any of those things. I didn't learn until years later that he longed for that. He wanted an undisturbed, uninterrupted, normal life. That's when I realized that I had been privileged and taken so much for granted."

Joe's success was that he fought to remain alive. For anyone else that would be something to boast about. But sometimes, Jennifer realized, Joe grew depressed, believing that he should have achieved more.

"His obstructed vision does not get in the way of seeing things," Jennifer observed. "He's an amazing man. He has such discernment when it comes to dealing with people. With only one eye, he doesn't sit around and wonder why. Instead, he appreciates that he can see. When I met him again, something about him lit me up. I don't mean romantically, not at first. I mean that I was drawn to that positivity. I needed more of that in my life."

During the next few years, Jennifer's marriage ended. Amid the changes, she was attracted to Joe's spirit. As they grew closer, he turned inward and reflective, frightened by the future, worried about the things he lacked.

"I can't speak from a man's point of view," Jennifer said. "But I know the role men take, providing for their partner, whether it's physical safety or security or money. One day, with a bowed head, Joe conceded that he had none of those things to offer me. He was so afraid. He loved me, but admitted that he couldn't give me anything like that."

Jennifer cradled Joe's cheeks in both her hands, staring at him intensely.

"You're the richest man I know," she declared, then hesitated, voice pausing. "I meant it. I meant it. It was a life changing moment in our relationship. We needed no more words, because he understood exactly."

CHAPTER 17

My New Family

IF THE DONOR FAMILY EVER planned to contact me, I expected it would coincide with the first anniversary of my transplant. But I didn't hear anything, despite having just sent them a letter in December. Two months passed, but I didn't reach out again for fear of crowding them. They must be struggling, I reasoned. There was a real possibility that they might never seek me out, and I would have to accept that, despite wanting to learn more. Many organ recipients never choose to connect with their donor families. Likewise, some donor families don't want to be reminded of the pain of a loved one's death. Each response is legitimate and valid. There is no right or wrong with such a sensitive subject. Whatever was to happen, I quietly continued to pray for the family's peace.

I began volunteering for CORE, traveling to high schools and colleges to speak about organ donation. Across the country, there are fifty-eight organ procurement organizations, abbreviated OPOs, which are privately funded yet federally regulated. There is no competition, no financial issues. The biggest challenge is educating the public to increase the pool of donors.

During my early speaking engagements, CORE sent along Colleen Sullivan to coordinate the presentation, showing a PowerPoint then introducing me as a recipient. Soon I asked Colleen and her staff to teach me how to run the slide show so I could go solo. I'm a sales guy; having one person instead of two seemed more logical. We revamped the process so that I simply walked in, introduced myself as a representative from CORE, then presented information and ran the PowerPoint. The kicker came at the end, when I discussed my kidney and pancreas, revealing that I was a transplant survivor.

While this was going on, in February 2012, I watched the New England Patriots lose to the New York Giants in Super Bowl XLVI. Two kids I had coached played in that game, both for New England. Rob Gronkowski gutted it out with a sprained ankle; Lousaka Polite was a fullback who had signed with the Patriots in December after bouncing around with a few other teams. I had known Lou since he was nine years old, and was bummed that my guys lost. Despite being hobbled, Gronk was in position to catch Tom Brady's Hail Mary pass on the last play, but the ball bounced the opposite way.

Those thoughts were on my mind the following morning when my phone rang. I recognized the caller ID from CORE, and expected them to go over plans for my next presentation. But the news was completely unexpected. It had been almost two years since the transplant, and my donor's family finally requested a meeting. I was over the moon with excitement.

After signing paperwork to authorize everything, initial contact was coordinated by CORE. It took several weeks to receive confirmation about what we suspected all along: Justin Boyer was in fact my donor. Originally from Dayton, Pennsylvania, his family moved to Mount Joy, near Harrisburg, after his passing. His mother Rhonda, sister Courtney, and stepfather Scott Bussard would attend our face to face. While plans were organized, I grew excited about the meeting, which was scheduled for May on the Friday before Mother's Day.

Accompanying me to the CORE office in Pittsburgh was my mom, dad, stepmother Mary, and Tara. Dad had remarried, and everyone in the family, especially Mom, recognizes that Mary treats us the way she treats her own blood. We waited in a spacious conference room filled with tables and chairs. I wore a sport coat and nice pair of pants, feeling nervous. I've never been overly concerned with how strangers perceive me. Perhaps it's because I've been through so many health challenges. Having lain naked in a hospital bed with several strangers in the room, there is little that phases me. Shame or fear are foreign concepts. Maybe that's just my personality. But this felt different. I was anxious, unfamiliar with the emotions involved.

"I want this family to like me," I confided to my sister.

"Joe, relax," Tara said, dragging out the command like a drill sergeant. "You're a good person."

"I think I am," I agreed. "But I want them to think it too."

I sat near the door on the edge of my chair so that when the family entered, I could jump up and be the first to greet them. Rhonda came in first and my heart pounded. She was tall, wearing a dark dress. We seemed about the same age—I've since learned she's only a few years older than me. Tears wet her cheeks. Beside her, Scott was even taller, six-foot-two and 230 pounds. He was like a bear, and when he spoke, his voice was deep. Justin's sister, Courtney, was a fifteen-year-old blonde. I extended my hand, but

Rhonda wasn't going to settle for a handshake. She wrapped her arms around me and clenched longer than normal.

"We're huggers," was the first thing she said. "Get used to it."

My mom shrieked. "We're huggers too!" and she embraced these strangers who had given me the gift of life.

All my apprehension released when Rhonda grabbed onto me. It was cathartic. In that long moment, I knew we were connected at a level beyond words and that everything would be okay. The guilt I had experienced melted away. I was put at ease by Justin's family.

Over the next two and a half hours, the Laffertys and Bussards got to know each other. I introduced myself and shared details about my past and what I did. They told me about Justin. We traded questions. Gradually, as we talked, Justin's story came into focus.

On Friday, February 12, 2010, Justin was off from school for a snow day. He and some friends were hanging out at another house, where the younger sister of one of the boys asked if someone could drop off her thirteen-year-old friend. Six teenagers, including Justin, piled into the van. Despite snow on the ground, roads were cleared and dry. The sun was bright. There was no excessive speed as they traveled along a country road between Spring Church and Elderton. When it came time to make a left turn, the driver put on his signal and stopped because a car approached in the opposite lane. A tractor trailer followed the minivan, and the trucker later admitted that he reached for his lunch, fumbled it, and closed the distance. He hit the brakes before rear-ending the minivan.

Justin sat there, in the row closest to the back, next to the girl. When police questioned her, she said they both wore seat belts, but the van was old and did not have shoulder straps. She remembered Justin yelling, then lying across her lap. They assume Justin leaned over to protect her, but no one will ever know for sure

The girl broke her jaw and ribs, probably from crashing into Justin. The other boys had to get staples and stitches and one was secured with a neck brace. Justin, however, took the brunt of impact. Later, no bruises or scratches were discovered on his body, but he suffered a double sideways whiplash. Once medics arrived on the scene, his prospects looked bleak. As Justin was airlifted to the hospital, his life was saved, but tests later that day revealed that there was no brain activity. During these awful hours, in the depths of grief, his family elected to donate Justin's organs.

Justin's older brother, Ron, served in the Army, stationed at Fort Huachuca in Arizona. Informed of the accident, he immediately made plans to fly home, but it was too late to catch a flight east when he received the news on Friday. The Bussards said prayers in Justin's hospital room Friday night, then left after midnight, assuming his organs would be recovered at once.

After picking up Ron at the Pittsburgh airport on Saturday afternoon, Rhonda received a call from the transplant coordinator at CORE. The woman said she checked on Justin frequently throughout the day.

"Checked on him?" Rhonda asked. "He's still there?"

Justin was being kept alive as the hospital waited for another organ recipient to arrive. That wasn't me, because I was already there. The Bussards did not realize that Justin was still breathing, or they would have stayed by his side.

"Can you keep him there a little longer?" Rhonda wondered. This gave Ron the opportunity to say goodbye in person. I recalled the confusion on our end. The transplants were supposed to happen Saturday but were delayed a day until Sunday. I had suspected then that someone close to the young man needed extra time to say goodbye, but I didn't know the full story.

The Bussards gave me a framed school portrait of Justin, so I saw him for the first time. He had dark hair, long in the style that teens wear, and a great smile with bright eyes. The frame had the inscription "Live, love, laugh, smile." He liked to play guitar. The Bussards told me stories about how their son would act goofy, pretending to stumble and fall, just to make someone chuckle. He wanted people around him to be happy. His personality came into focus, and it was clear that Justin owned a kind soul.

Justin's sister and stepdad were polite but reserved. I've since come to know that Courtney and Scott are beautiful people, but quiet until you know them. Courtney wore a look on her face that seemed familiar. It was the expression my own sister used to display when we were kids and the conversation revolved exclusively around sick little Joey. I didn't want her to feel ignored, so I kept pivoting to Courtney and asking her questions, hoping to draw her out. I had shared that I coached football, and told them how two of my former players had lost the previous Super Bowl. I didn't mention names, but Courtney began whispering to Scott. I asked if they were talking about me.

"Go ahead," Scott prodded. "Ask him."

"Do you know Rob Gronkowski?" Courtney wondered sheepishly.

I took out my phone, pulled up a photo of us together, and slid it across the table. Courtney's eyes grew wide.

"He's my favorite," she said.

"Favorite player?"

"No, favorite person on earth," Scott said

I laughed. "Everyone loves Gronk. We'll have to get you two together some day."

Rhonda talked about savoring that afternoon because she wasn't sure if we would ever see one another again. I cut her off.

"No, no, no," I told her. "We'll see each other again. We're family now."

When I said that, she recounted a story from Justin's funeral. Most of those days were a blur, she confessed, but one memory lingered. At the wake, people took turns sharing memories of Justin. Two teenage girls took the floor. Through tears they explained how they had grown up as best friends. Sometime before he passed, Justin moved to Virginia to live with his father for six months. When he returned to Pennsylvania, he ran into one of the girls, surprised to discover her walking alone.

"Where's your best friend?" he asked.

They had had a fight, the young lady admitted, and hadn't spoken in the months since Justin moved away.

"What?" Justin said. "You two were inseparable the last time I saw you."

Not anymore, the girl told him. The friendship was done.

"I'm going to put you two back together," Justin declared. And by the end of the week, he did just that. In his own way, he reconciled the girls and they were best friends again.

Rhonda never heard that story until her son's funeral, but it was a great memory for a mother to have. It showed me so much about the person that Justin was. Even today, telling it gives me goosebumps.

"I'm going to ask a favor," Rhonda said. "After we leave here, I want you to do something fun tonight. A few hours from now, Justin would be attending his senior prom."

"When I get home, I'll put on music and dance," I promised.

My relationship with the Bussards didn't end there. A few weeks later, they invited me to the graduation ceremony for Justin's senior class. West Shamokin, northeast of Pittsburgh, is a small school; in 2012 they graduated fifty-three students. Because they no longer lived in the area, they made a trip back especially for the occasion. Three rows of graduates lined the stage. Near the front, a chair was vacant, cap and gown folded neatly on the empty seat to honor Justin. The ceremony celebrated the students, but part of the night was about remembering their lost classmate.

The Bussard family and I had agreed to speak, so Rhonda thanked everyone for the love and support during the difficult times they had endured more than two years earlier. She turned the microphone over to her stepson, Aaron Bussard, who was twenty-two. He used a line Courtney had suggested. It was one of the best introductions I'd ever heard.

"I'd like to thank you for how you treated our family," Aaron told the audience. "Although Justin couldn't be with us tonight, we brought a part of him along. I'd like to introduce Joe Lafferty."

Through tears I stood up and moved to the podium. I told the graduates and their families that I hoped they embraced the importance of living every day. It was a message they could learn from my experience. I asked them to serve others as Justin and his family had served me.

The night was a beautiful, moving tribute to Justin's memory. Afterward, as we walked to our cars, Rhonda and my mom were deep in conversation. Scott and I strolled a few steps behind.

"You have no idea how much you're helping my wife," he said softly. "She's just starting to smile again."

I was helping them? With my new kidney and pancreas, I was the one who had been helped. In the most awful moment, they had given me the gift of life.

"Scott, there's no end to this. We'll continue because we're family now."

∞

That summer, I was invited to Courtney's sweet sixteen party. I knew exactly what gift I wanted to bring. I dashed off a quick note to Rob Gronkowski. In the years since he left Woodland Hills, he had moved to the University of Arizona for three years before becoming the premiere tight end on one of the best teams in the NFL. We had stayed in touch, so he knew about my health problems and how I had gotten better. I explained the situation, asking if he could send along an autographed picture with a personal note to Courtney. He messaged me back the same day, promising it was on the way.

But he didn't send a photo. Instead, he went above and beyond, signing a New England Patriots jersey with his number 87, personalizing it to Courtney. When she opened the gift, her eyes dilated and she went crazy. She and her friend held the jersey, and her friend cautioned Courtney not to wash it.

"I'll never wash it," Courtney said earnestly, "because Rob Gronkowski touched this!"

Today, the Bussards and I speak every week. When they come through Pittsburgh, we make it a point to get together. They attend Lafferty family events, and I attend theirs. Rhonda asked me to call her "mom," so I'm honored to do that. I'm incredibly blessed by their love and generosity. Knowing me is bittersweet for them. I'm a reminder of the pain of losing Justin. Going forward, I want to continue honoring his memory.

On the day Justin would have turned twenty-one—June 23, 2014—his family, my mother, and I gathered at the cemetery. Tears were shed, but we wanted to have a celebration, so everyone drank a shot in his honor.

On his birthday in 2017, I sent out this text:

"Justin Dale Boyer would be 24 years young today had he and five young people in a minivan not been struck from behind in a very unfortunate car accident. The others walked away. No one was drinking, it was mid-morning on a clear cold February day in 2010. Justin taught himself to play guitar, stuck his nose in the middle of friends when they fought to help resolve to lead them to love, and like the mission of a clown, he'd embarrass himself to make sad people smile. Happy birthday, kid. I owe my life to you. I'll see you in heaven."

Carrying Justin's Memory
—Rhonda and Scott Bussard

THE 2010 HOLIDAY SEASON WAS hard. Rhonda Bussard had lost her younger son, Justin Boyer, the previous February. He would have been seventeen by now, and his absence left a hole in everyone's life.

On Christmas Eve, Rhonda retrieved the mail and opened an envelope from CORE, the Center for Organ Recovery and Education. A cover letter explained that one of the recipients of Justin's organs was requesting to meet the family. Included was a four-page typed letter from a man named Joe. Everything remained anonymous, so no last names were included, but Joe explained how the kidney and pancreas he received had offered him a second chance at life.

Many of Justin's organs had been donated: both kidneys, his corneas, and his skin, which was used to aid military burn victims. Justin's heart was too damaged to be donated. (In retrospect,

Rhonda finds comfort in that, believing it too big to ever be used by another.) None of the recipients, however, had contacted the Bussards—until now.

Rhonda scanned a few words of Joe's letter and immediately began to cry.

"You're going to have to read this out loud," she told her husband, Scott.

The family gathered around, including daughter Courtney and Rhonda's son, Ron Jr., who spent the holiday on leave from the Army. As Joe's words were shared, everyone's reaction was different.

"My first thought was, how dare you?" Rhonda recalled. "I was very angry with Joe. I thought, I don't want to meet him because he'll never be good enough. What if he's a terrible person? I knew that Justin's organs had given life to others, but to have one of those people contact you on Christmas Eve was a very strange feeling."

In the letter, Joe explained what he had been through, thanked the family, and told how much it would mean to meet them. Rhonda and Courtney cried. Ron Jr. seethed. It was only later that they realized Joe had no control over the timing. He had written the letter in early December. CORE had mailed it on his behalf.

"Maybe receiving that on Christmas Eve was a blessing," Rhonda reflected. "But on that day, I was angry."

"She was grieving," Scott explained, "and going through the anger stage."

"I was angry about a lot of things," Rhonda agreed. "I was angry with God for taking my son. It's a pain no mother should ever go through and a pain you don't ever get over. You live with it. I'm not angry anymore, but I still don't understand. There are days when I see something, or hear a phrase or song and I just lose it and start crying."

They harbored no ill will toward the truck driver who crashed into the minivan where Justin rode with five friends. The Bussards come from a family of truck drivers. Scott drove a truck before becoming an electrician. They offered immediate forgiveness, understanding it was truly an accident.

"He reached for a sandwich on the passenger's seat," Rhonda shrugged. "We've all done that. I would have felt differently if it was a drunk driver, but I never held blame or hatred. I wanted him to know that."

From the police report, the Bussards read the driver's name. They learned through a family member that the man was devastated by Justin's death. He had two children of his own. He had wanted to apologize, they heard, but his company advised him against making contact. Rhonda sent word through a relative about forgiveness. She is unsure if the message was ever delivered.

"I hope he got himself together," Rhonda reflected. "I lost a son. His children don't need to lose their father too."

While reflecting on the Christmas Eve letter, Rhonda's feelings toward Joe gradually softened over time. Two years after Justin's death, she suggested to her husband that they should meet Joe. On May 11, 2012, Rhonda, Scott, and Courtney carried a framed photo of Justin to the CORE office in Pittsburgh.

"We were very nervous," Scott admitted. "We had no idea how we would react. Would this be good or bad?"

"When I hugged Joe, I knew it was going to be okay," Rhonda explained. "I felt it right away. We had just met, but it wasn't a quick hug. It lasted a long time."

The families blended immediately, and a fast friendship grew. As they learned about one another, Joe vowed to honor Justin's memory. When Joe discovered that Courtney was smitten with Rob Gronkowski, he traveled with the Bussards to Foxboro,

Massachusetts, in 2013 to watch the New England Patriots defeat the Pittsburgh Steelers. Gronkowski met with them in the team hotel the night before kickoff to give them tickets.

"Courtney was sixteen at the time, so you can imagine her reaction," Rhonda recalled. "When Rob walked into the lobby, she quit breathing. Her neck turned red and she was nervous and afraid to talk."

Joe, however, is rarely at a loss for words. He introduced the family. Gronkowski noticed that Courtney's phone case was decorated with a photo of him, so he found a marker and signed it. He invited Joe and the Bussards to his house following the game. There, in a crowded setting, Courtney spent time casually talking to her favorite player.

"Courtney had been hammered by sadness," her mother explained. A grandfather had passed away the year before Justin did, then after her brother died, Ron Jr. deployed for a year. Kids at school had stopped seeing her as an individual. Instead, she was the girl whose brother was killed.

"Courtney had given up hope in life," Rhonda said. "Rob gave something back to my daughter. I don't think he realizes what he did. He made Courtney believe in dreams again. He gave us tickets because Joe asked. But Rob could have easily said no and no one would have held it against him. Then he took time to talk with Courtney and let her see him as a friend. I'll never be able to thank Joe enough for making that happen."

Two years later, when Courtney was eighteen, they took another trip to New England. This time, Courtney met Gronkowski's father and oldest brother on the infamous "party bus."

Meeting Gronkowski was a thrill, but Courtney confessed to her parents she would trade all those memories to have Justin back.

Today, Rhonda wears a necklace to honor her son. During Justin's wake, she learned that funeral directors are able to make a thumbprint. A company then creates a medallion with the image. Scott, Courtney and Ron Jr. each have keychains, but Rhonda's thumbprint hangs around her neck. She never removes it.

"Joe has made us laugh," Scott reflected. "We also cried along the way. Meeting him was a difficult process, but it helped our healing. In my mind, Justin is still here. He's still with us through Joe. Even though Justin passed, something good came from a tragedy. It wasn't just a senseless accident."

Although he was sixteen, Justin did not have a driver's license, so his father and the Bussards made the decision to donate his organs. They are confident that's what Justin would have wanted.

"I carry in my heart that Justin helped people continue their lives," Rhonda said. "It's an honor to know that my son did that."

"Joe has been given his life back," Scott said. "We're grateful that he hasn't forgotten Justin along the way."

Love Will Find a Way
If You Want It Too

SHORTLY AFTER MY TRANSPLANT, I worked at a Woodland Hills basketball tournament, posted at a door with Keelan Rozier, a good friend and fellow football coach. During a break, as we sat, I took out my medications and lined them up. I was swallowing fourteen different pills then.

"I don't know how you can take all those pills," Keelan said.

"I stuck a needle in my body every day for almost twenty-three years," I told him. "This is easy."

The number of pills I take now has whittled to eight different medications. There is a blood thinner, a baby aspirin, a magnesium supplement. I'll probably be on these pills for the rest of my life. Today, I carry around a little plastic container that opens like a change purse. I take differing amounts of the same drug every other day. It begins when I wake up, then two hours later. Then at twelve o'clock, then between three and four p.m., right before dinner, near eight o'clock and again before I go to bed. The immunosuppressants are a cocktail. One pill lasts four hours a day; another is twelve hours. But the pill I take four times a day can't be swallowed within two hours of the twelve-hour pill. I've figured out ways to get into a groove. You might think it's a chore, but it's far easier than pricking your finger and using a needle.

My challenges are unique and I embrace them. My late grandfather Jim Lafferty once asked me to imagine walking into a hospital carrying a bag filled with all my medical issues. Envision everyone else there doing the same thing. If the sacks were tossed in the middle of a room, Grandpa said, you would fight like hell to get your bag back. No one wants anyone else's problems, but can figure out a way to deal with their own. My life isn't that bad. Whatever I'm going through, I can make it.

My dad read this manuscript, and told me I didn't praise Mom enough. I love her completely, and believe that is clear. She's always been there, and from her I learned to be a fighter. I needed that. Dad, on the other hand, was a rock. He was steady, his mood always the same. Truth is, that mix was necessary, because you can't be fighting all the time. I'm a perfect example of the balance between nature and nurture. I was given bad cells genetically, but was also nurtured in the proper way at the right time by good people. That allowed me to be successful and navigate through so many tough days.

Initially, I wanted this book to center around my opinions about our troubled world. My friend Mike Campolo informed me that no one would care. "It's not about you," he scolded. Instead, he suggested, I should chronicle my life because it was inspiring. This may sound like false modesty, but I don't see my story as inspirational. I never did. My thirties were stolen from me because of health issues. But that's okay. What else could I do but keep going? I've tried to savor the steps along the way, no matter how unpleasant they were. My medical challenges have been the true blessing of my life. They've allowed me to experience things that no one else has.

There's an expression "God only gives us as much as we can handle." I read a meme that added this line: "He must think I'm a badass." I laughed, because if those sentiments are true, God must think I'm a world-class-operator warrior badass, better than the commanding officer of Seal Team Six.

I believe that good can emerge from the worst things. God allowed his son to be nailed to a cross. That was awful but necessary. Today we reflect on the good that came out of it. I've tried to take the best experiences from the worst moments. I've always kept God first.

Sometimes people find me difficult to deal with. I am a prideful and proud loudmouth. I've been criticized for being argumentative, for taking ordinary debate and discussion to the extreme to make my point. Maybe that's a result of my past. You don't fight for your life without developing a few bad habits when it comes to conflict resolution. I'm a flawed man, but those flaws have kept me alive.

Because of my experiences, I know that whenever challenges come to me, I can make it through. I've tried to live life the right way, remaining positive and accepting all people. Color, money, and status don't matter to me. Many days were about surviving. I've tried to serve others. If this book inspires someone, well, I'm glad to help.

But I have work to do. Eighteen people die every day waiting for an organ transplant. I'd love for that number to drop to zero.

Hopefully this story has knocked away barriers to organ donation. There are many famous people who have had organ transplants and then gone on to do amazing things. Basketball star Alonzo Mourning received a kidney in 2003 and made a comeback, winning a championship with the Miami Heat in 2006. Snowboarder Chris Klug received a liver transplant in 2000 and won a bronze medal in the 2002 Winter Olympics in Salt Lake City. The list of celebrities who had organ transplants is long: Steve Jobs, Tracy Morgan, Gary Coleman, Natalie Cole, George Lopez, former vice-president Dick Cheney, and late in life, Mickey Mantle.

Let's tear down the myths. It's not against any religion. You won't be required to have a closed casket if an organ is removed. *Law and Order* is one of my favorite TV shows, but they air episodes with dark plotlines about malevolent doctors who kill people for their organs. There are movies like this too. It might make for dramatic storytelling, but the reality doesn't work that way. Doctors are good people who take an oath to do everything they can to save their patient. No one will hasten the end of life if you sign up to be an organ donor. If we can educate and break down the barriers, generosity of people like Justin's family can help save patients who suffer. Truth is, one life can offer a second chance to eight other people. When someone dies, useful organs go to waste.

Looking back, I recognize that so many good things happened just in time. Eight-year-old kids shouldn't get cancer and pancreatitis and later, diabetes. But doctors caught these maladies and implemented a treatment plan that worked. It was awful to lose my eye, but had we waited longer, the infection could have spread to my brain and killed me. Armed with that knowledge, I'm happy I can still see. Organs failed in the prime of my life, but because of medical professionals and generosity of strangers, I was able to pull through and take advantage of a second chance.

I'm filled with gratitude for everyone who helped me. I can't adequately express my thanks in words, and I haven't mentioned everyone who has touched and influenced me to be better. If I tried, the book would read like pages of roll call. I'll never be able to repay the kindness.

I've found there is a difference between life and a normal life. I have a normal life now and I've never been happier. Because of God and everyone's blessings, I'm eager to live it on Justin Time.

This is Justin

LIVE ~ LOVE ~ LAUGH ~ SMILE

Acknowledgements

THERE IS NO BOOK WITHOUT Justin Dale Boyer; there is no book without Jeff Schober. There is no book without me, and there is no Joe Lafferty without so many people. For everyone, there is no life without so many people. If you had to write a thank you page for everyone in your life it would likely be a book. If I had to thank all the people who helped me, I'd need another book.

I attempted to thank everyone who touched my life. There were dozens and dozens of names and then I spoke to Rhonda Bussard. I suggested she draft a thank you page for Justin but being the beautiful mother and person that she is, she said not even she could speak for Justin. In wanting to thank hundreds of people, I spilled out the following words. Thank you God for giving me these words.

I want to thank so many people because no one lives a life alone and God doesn't want us to ever be alone. I want people to know that they should live a life of Justin Time. A life where you act responsibly, love others, and savor every day because no one is guaranteed tomorrow. I know God, in his infinite and ongoing wisdom, put Justin into my life. Justin Time is not a clever title or a cute turn of phrase, it's providence. God knows my mind and how it works and how I would turn that name into inspiration. It wasn't an accident that brought Justin and I together and although we will never understand it until we stand before Him we have faith that all things work towards good. At some point in my life so many people gave me a smile, a pat on the back, a prayer, a hug, a much needed kick in the ass, and that all spells love. There are a few people I will thank but by no means is this anywhere close to the list I made when I started this process. Because this is a book and not a reference of each day I've lived, there are significant people who have touched me and supported me whose names don't appear here. Those people know who they are and they know that I love them and would not be alive and happywithout every one of them.

Scott, Rhonda, Courtney, Brittany, Ron and Aaron, I owe you all so much. Every day for the rest of my life I live to represent your family in the best way possible.

Jeff, I wanted to write a book and found a brother. That's God. Thanks to Teri, Matty, and Nicky for allowing me to have your time. Maybe we should have titled it "Dog Biscuits."

Jim, Tara, Adam and Reilly, your family unit and closeness taught me that I wanted what you four have. The way you love is amazing.

Dad and Mary, your generosity and steady support can't be described. Mary, you changed my Dad and it made me realize his lessons are the framework that have held me upright my whole life. Dad, I owe my ability to stand up to anything from the lesson you taught me when I was eight. You saved my life that afternoon in July. I'm sorry it took so long to figure out that you were always right.

Mom, you are the fighter in me. No one has ever asked "How did you become so tough?" But if they do, I simply will say, "I was raised by a fighter." I would not be alive without you.

Jennifer, you are my heart and my angel. I prayed for years for God to show me that love existed. I didn't pray and ask for Him to bring me someone to love, just that love was out there. And again He blessed me in a way I could not have imagined. I only survived every day before you. I only breathed shallow breaths. I didn't feel the sunshine and I only knew to fight before you loved me. Thank you for turning on my heart. Heaven can wait.

—Joe Lafferty

∞

AS ALWAYS, I'D LIKE TO thank my family: Teri, Matty, and Nicky, for their love and generosity and for sharing me during the time it took to write this book. My dad, Tom, has always been my biggest cheerleader. He read early drafts and provided feedback. My late mother, Mary Jo, would have loved this book.

Thanks to Gordy Gronkowski for introducing me to Joe.

Thanks to Joe's family and friends for their time and honesty about his virtues and vices. It is clear Joe has surrounded himself with exemplary people. As part of this book, I was thrilled to sit with Dan Marino, a childhood hero.

The Bussards, Rhonda and Scott, welcomed me to their home. I'm certain it was difficult to discuss Justin with a stranger, but they did so willingly and with grace. Justin was a kind-hearted young man, and like so many others, I felt his loss.

Joe Lafferty and I didn't know each other at the outset, but during our regular conversations, we recognized one another as kindred spirits. We each gained a brother. I'm humbled that he trusted me to tell his inspiring story. Yes, Joe, you are inspiring. Thanks for a great ride... and it's not over yet.

—Jeff Schober

Made in the USA
Middletown, DE
27 January 2019